A BOOK OF
GREY OWL

Pages from the Writings of

WA-SHA-QUON-ASIN

Edited by E. E. REYNOLDS

With Preface by LOVAT DICKSON

MACMILLAN OF CANADA
TORONTO

FIRST PUBLISHED 1938
SECOND EDITION (RESET) 1941
REPRINTED 1942
REPRINTED 1946
REPRINTED 1949
REPRINTED 1951
REPRINTED 1951
REPRINTED 1960
REPRINTED 1971

PRINTED IN CANADA BY
T. H. BEST PRINTING COMPANY LIMITED

CONTENTS

With the exception of the sketches
by Grey Owl on pages 28, 36, 64
and 68, all the illustrations to this
edition appear between
pages 144–145

PREFACE

A Book of Grey Owl contains selections from all Grey Owl's written work so far published. The four books left behind by Grey Owl form the most vivid record we have in literature of that vast, silent and remote land called the Wilderness, which stretches across the whole of the North American Continent. Though it is called the Wilderness, it is not waste or barren land. In these tremendous forests, broken by innumerable lakes, there is both animal and human life which lives much as it did centuries ago. Civilisation, like ripples from a restless lake, has lapped against its fringes, altering these but not changing its essential character. Like a great tapestry of grey and green, the Wilderness hangs there, back of civilisation, its mystery known only to those who have penetrated it, who have known the thrill of the danger it offers and the joy of having conquered its difficulties.

As a youth of seventeen, Grey Owl came for the first time to the Wilderness, a slender, dreamy youth with a passionate desire to learn the ways of woodsmen and the secrets of the forest. He gave his name as Archie Belaney, and said that his father had been an Indian scout in the South-western States, and his mother a member of the Jacarilla band of the Apache Indians. There were many half-breeds in the North, and the presence of yet another in this quiet, strange boy attracted no particular attention. He worked as a packer and a canoeman, and showed an increasing aptitude for the arduous work. Unlike many of half-breed parentage, he preferred the company of Indians to that of white men. He quickly learned the language of the Ojibway tribe who inhabited the district, and was soon living amongst them on an island in Lake

Temagami. Before long they adopted him into the tribe, naming him Wa-Sha-Quon-Asin, meaning: 'He who walks by night', translated into English as Grey Owl.

His reputation as a woodsman and trapper spread throughout the Northland. He became known, in a country in which it was not an uncommon quality, for a reckless disregard of danger, and he undertook feats of endurance in the age-old Indian custom, never yielding when pain or discomfort or privation followed. In the years between 1907 and 1914 he lived in the fastness of that giant Northern Ontario forest, and the slender boy of seventeen became a tall, broad-shouldered, hardy man.

When the War came he joined the Canadian army, and for three years fought in France as a sniper. He was wounded and suffered the effects of gas, and at the end of 1917 was returned to Canada, and discharged unfit for further service. Weakened by his wounds, and sad in spirit, he made his way North to the woods again. For a time he did no work, but travelled the old trails by himself, happy to be free but lame from his wound, and depressed by the thought that never again could he follow with his old companions of the trail the wild, carefree life he had known before the War.

But into his weary and battered frame strength gradually flowed back, and in a year he had become a trapper again. Yet something had altered. Was it the memory of the blood that he had seen shed so wantonly on the fields of Flanders, or was it the effect of the sufferings he himself had borne? No one can say, and of these things Grey Owl himself did not speak. But the cruelty of his trade frequently now presented itself to him. 'I killed that lynx to-day', he wrote at this time to the English nurse who had looked after him in hospital, 'and somehow I wish that I hadn't. His skin is worth only ten dollars, and he didn't act cross, and the way he looked at me I can't get out of my mind. I don't think I will sell that skin.'

The stirrings of conscience more and more troubled him, and at the same time a deep love for the vast North began to fill his mind, and to find expression in the letters he wrote. 'I would like to show you this country,' he wrote to this same correspondent, 'with its big waters and black forests and little lonely lakes with a wall of trees all around them, that lie so quiet and never move, but just look on and on. You know as you go by them that those trees were there ahead of you and will be there after you are dead. It makes a person feel small, only with us, it is our life to be amongst these things.'

The years passed after the War, and still Grey Owl with snowshoes or canoe followed the trails his people had followed for centuries. As distaste for his bloody occupation grew, he became more solitary and his way branched from the well-worn trails into wilder country farther North in the Hudson Bay District. As a trapper he was successful, as a woodsman there were few in the North who were his equal, but he had no pleasure in achievements that seemed to him an offence against Nature and the living but inarticulate world of creatures that surrounded him. Though he did not realise it, a humanitarian spirit was being born in Grey Owl.

The final surrender came suddenly. He had set a trap for beavers. A mother beaver had been caught in it and had drowned at the bottom of the lake. When he was raising the trap he heard the pathetic whimper of the two kittens left in the beaver-house. His first instinct was to kill them for the sake of their skins. But the inner voice that had been murmuring protests for so long at this point spoke with authority. 'Save them,' it said quite clearly, 'save them from a death they don't deserve.' So Grey Owl took the two little beavers to his cabin, and he and his companion nursed the wet, bedraggled and lonely little beasts back to life. They were like mischievous children, subject to moods and little bursts of temper and affection that before long won the hearts of their captors. Soon it was not a question of humans indulging their sympathies over two little creatures of the wild; and the little community, living in a rough hut they had constructed themselves in a clearing in that Northern forest, faced what fate had in store for them.

Fate did not present a benign appearance. Winter was upon them. They had to keep warm and live, and they had to do it on Grey Owl's pension as a wounded soldier. For he had suddenly but resolutely forsworn the trappers' trade. With the thought of these two small furry bodies at home, with the memory of their affectionate cries, the trust they put in him when their small hands clutched his fingers, he could not set another trap. The humanitarian spirit that had been sown in the War, and had germinated in these long arduous years in the Northern forest, reached its fulfilment in the winter they faced together in 1926.

The rest of Grey Owl's story can be briefly summarised, for he has written of it himself in *Pilgrims of the Wild*, and noble extracts from that story are reprinted in this book. When he had touched the depths of destitution, and he and his little companions faced what seemed a future without hope, a representative of the Canadian Government found him. From that moment actual want was removed, but the hardest part of Grey Owl's task commenced.

He set himself, with the support of an enlightened Canadian Government, to awaken the world's conscience to the injustice it so often metes out to animals. He did this not by preaching, but by example. He did not inveigh against man's cruelty to dumb animals. Instead, he showed how responsive, intelligent and affectionate animals could be once their fear of danger was removed, and how constructive and useful the plan of their lives was unless man disturbed its routine or design.

Grey Owl was not a highly educated man, but he had an intense sincerity of purpose and a deep and passionate love for the little creatures of the wild that began to come and live about him. His books were begun as diary observations of what he saw around him in the forest. He saw that animals had a sense of humour; that tragedy, when it came into their lives, brought its burden of grief and intolerable suffering just as it did amongst mankind. He saw that animals became attached to one another in the way that human-kind do, that they made homes for their young, and planned for the future with a sense of responsibility that many a man might envy. He noticed that the animals accepted him as readily as they did one another, and he noticed that their attitude towards him did not suggest that they regarded him with awe as a superior or god-like being. Noting down these things, and giving them names and little endearments the way one does with the things one loves, he began to write, in the solitude of those Northern woods, something that, not-withstanding his own background, was literature.

When his work for animals was almost done, and he had undertaken another task, that of rehabilitating his fellow Indians, Grey Owl's life came to a sudden and tragic end. He had returned weary from one of the tours he had agreed to make in the last few years of his life. For six months he had had to live in the civilisation that to one of his blood and upbringing was a constant threat to his health. He had reached Prince Albert, the town where the railroad is left behind, and he had travelled by sleigh and snowshoe the one hundred miles of rough country that separates Prince Albert from Ajawaan. At last, on a winter's afternoon, he reached the cabin that was his home, beneath the floor of which his beaver family were still locked in their winter sleep.

There, as evening came on, he became ill. Alone in the woods, he crawled to the nearest Park telephone and asked for help. They came the next day and took him back over the trail to Prince Albert. Within forty-eight hours his brave spirit had fled. Once again, the party made the difficult journey to Lake Ajawaan, and on another afternoon when the sun tipped with its light the waving tops of the pine trees about the lake, they buried him in a simple grave on a high mound near his cabin.

Grey Owl was fifty when he died. Thirty-three years before, he had come to the Wilderness as a boy. Nearly all those years had been spent in adversity. The Wilderness had exacted continual toll of his strength, had made daily demands on his courage and spirit; and had offered him in return only hardship and a precarious existence. But he loved it as a living, animate thing, and the books that he wrote, with such sincerity and without artifice, were love songs for the Wilderness. In his prose there is the beat and cadence of a Northern tempest, or the quiet sighing of the wind in trees that reach for unnumbered leagues towards the shores of the Arctic sea. In his descriptions of the land he loved, and of the characters that peopled it, there is the very essence of great writing, which is perfect simplicity. And there seems to me, who know his work and who knew the man himself so well, a record in these pages of all that he suffered and rejoiced over in the days when the Empty Cabin was inhabited, the far-off days of long ago.

LOVAT DICKSON

The full story of Grey Owl is told by Lovat Dickson in his biography, *Half-Breed*, and in his tribute to Grey Owl's memory entitled *The Green Leaf*.

GLOSSARY

Abitibi. This river flows from a lake of the same name, northwards into Hudson Bay from eastern Ontario.

Ajawaan. The lake where Grey Owl had his cabin. It is situated in the Prince Albert National Park, about one hundred miles north of the town of Prince Albert in central Saskatchewan.

babiche. *See* below, 'Snowshoe.'

bannock. A form of bread made with flour, water and baking-powder, baked in the ashes or in a fry-pan. Eaten fresh, and dipped in hot lard or pork-grease. (See also page 120).

bridle. *See* below, 'Snowshoe.'

brigade. Consists of four canoes or more, but loosely applied to parties of any size.

buckskin. A soft leather made of deer or other skin. Caribou or reindeer skin does not stretch when wet. The buckskin jacket or hunting shirt keeps out the wind, remains soft, will not catch on thorns, and wears for ever. The fringes are not purely ornamental, as in rain the water drips off them and the shirt dries better. (*See* illustration, p. 49.)

caribou. North-American reindeer.

Cartier, Jacques (1494–1557). The great French explorer, who, discovered the St. Lawrence in 1534, and so opened up Canada to the white man.

Cree. A tribe of North-American Indians of Algonquin stock, like the Ojibways. The Crees occupied the region round Lake Winnipeg and the Saskatchewan River. Their chief enemies were the Blackfoot tribe.

crik. Creek.

Fall. Autumn; the season when the leaves fall. The term is chiefly used now in North America, but it is also an old English word.

Fire Rangers. These men are employed by the Canadian Government to patrol the vast forest areas to fight the menace of fire. Incalculable damage has been done, and is still done, by forest fires, which may devastate thousands of square miles of country. A vivid account of fire-fighting is given in pp. 163–7 of this book. For a fuller description of the fire-service, the chapter entitled 'The Altar of Mammon' in *The Men of the Last Frontier* should be read. Aeroplanes are now used for patrol work, as well as an elaborate system of outlook towers, etc.

Hudson's Bay Company, generally known as 'The Company.' The history of Canada is bound up with that of the H.B.C. The company was founded in 1670 by Prince Rupert to promote the fur trade round the shores of Hudson Bay, in an area vaguely defined as Prince Rupert's Land. Gradually the Company extended its interests and its traders pushed westwards to the Rockies, and much early exploration was due to them. The trading posts were important links in the spread of the white man's influence. The story of the H.B.C. is a romance in itself.

Hudson Bay blanket. Originally made for the servants of 'The Company,' this blanket soon became an article of trade on account of its excellent qualities; to say 'Hudson Bay blanket' is equivalent to saying 'Rolls-Royce.'

husky. The Eskimo sledge-dog; is a semi-wild animal of mixed breed, but of great endurance. A charming account of these dogs may be read in *Husky*, by F. and K. Conibear.

Indian. Grey Owl rightly objected to the term 'Red Indian.' He said it was 'too suggestive of the dime novel and blood-and-thunder literature.' The correct term is 'North-American Indian.' Grey Owl had a high opinion of the knowledge of Indian life and customs shown in Longfellow's *Hiawatha*, and he recognized that Fenimore Cooper 'must have done some travelling with Indians.' The North-American Indians, before the white man came, lived in tribes; each tribe had a hunting area large enough to allow for wandering in search of game. They were nomadic and lived in wigwams, or teepees, which could be moved easily. This life made the men experts in woodcraft and backwoodsmanship, and they have never had their equals. With the coming of the white man, the numbers of Indians decreased through the introduction of new diseases, the sale of spirits, etc. To-day there are probably not more than 100,000 pure-bred Indians in the whole of North America. Some of the deterioration has been arrested by the formation of Indian Reservations, areas where the Indians can live their own lives and maintain their native customs. It is interesting to note that Indian blood—and there has been much inter-marrying—is not regarded with the same distaste as black (slave blood); indeed, many notable men in the United States and in Canada have Indian blood. Grey Owl claimed to be a half-breed, and took pride in his ancestry.

Indian Summer. A period of fine, mild weather during late autumn.

Janitor. Doorkeeper, porter.

Keewaydin. An Indian word meaning land of the north-west wind, applied to the northlands generally. It is also the name of a kind of rock.

larrigan. An oil-tanned moccasin of heavy leather, sometimes having a hard sole.

loon. The great northern diver, a bird with a peculiar cry likened to the howl of a wolf.

Mississauga. A river running from the north into the North Channel of Lake Huron. Its mouth is about seventy miles east of Sault Ste. Marie.

moccasins. Soft shoes made of moose-hide or inferior skin. There is no hard sole, and consequently they are ideal for woods travel, as the wearer can feel the ground under his feet and so avoid making alarming noises, such as treading on sticks, etc.

moose. The elk of North America and some parts of Northern Europe and Asia. Distinguished by its overhanging upper lip, and, in the male, by the wide-spread palmated antlers. (*See* illustration, p. 193.)

Mounted Police. The North-West Mounted Police is a famous body of men who police the vast North-West Territory of Canada.

muskeg. Swampy ground.

Nevada. An almost rainless state on the east of California.

Ojibway. An Indian tribe of Algonquin stock, and sometimes known by that name. They formerly hunted over lands on the north of Lakes Huron and Superior. Grey Owl was adopted by the Ojibways, who gave him his name Wa-Sha-Quon-Asin, 'he who walks by night.' He wrote: 'Half-breed trapper I am, and far more closely identified with the Ojibway Indians than any other people. I want the Ojibways to get their share of any credit that may accrue. I am their man. They taught me much.'

pan. The fan-shaped spread of the moose-antler.

peltry. Fur.

Pontiac. Chief of the Ottawa Indians. He fought with the French against the English, and after the French left Canada he carried on a campaign of bitter ferocity against the English. He was murdered by a Kaskaskia Indian in 1769. His story is told in Parkman's *Conspiracy of Pontiac.*

portage. A part of the trail where it is impossible to go by water; all gear must be carried overland to the next navigable stretch. Portages are divided into sections called 'stages,' about six or eight minutes apart, that being the length of time experience shows a man can carry a big load without fatigue. He recuperates on the way back for the next load. This is an Indian system, and it has proved better to work in this fashion than by taking smaller loads right through. (*See* illustration, p. 112.)

Prince Albert. A town of some 12,000 inhabitants on the Saskatchewan River. To the north of it lies the Prince Albert National Park, where Grey Owl had his beaver lodge. There are a number of these National Parks in Canada; each is of considerable size, and remains a natural preservation of forest and lake; the public can use them for holidays, but not for hunting.

reservation, or reserve. *See* above, 'Indian.'

runway. A slope made for greater ease down to the shores of a lake, etc.

Saskatchewan. The central province of the prairie region of Canada.

shingle. A wooden roof-tile.

snowshoe. The Canadian snowshoe is so designed that its broad surface prevents the foot sinking into the snow. It is 3 to 5 ft. long, and 1 to 2 ft. wide. The largest are used by the man who goes ahead to break the trail. The snowshoe is roughly pear-shaped. The frame is made of tough wood, and a network of raw-hide thongs (*babiche*) is interlaced between, rather like a tennis racket. There are two loops (*bridles*) into which the toes fit, while the heels are left free. The snowshoe lifts in front only and so crunches down the snow.

squaw. Indian woman.

Temagami. A lake in the Temagami Forest Reserve of Ontario; the Ottawa River is near by.

teepee. Conical-shaped tent of skins or birch bark supported by poles.

tump-line. Two 10-ft. leather thongs attached to a broad band, which goes over the forehead; the thongs are fastened round the load, and the weight is thus partly taken by the head-band; especially useful in going uphill. (*See* illustration, p. 129.)

voyageur. A man employed by traders to carry goods from place to place. Used generally of Canadian canoe-men. A reminder of the days when Canada was French.

whiskey-jack. Common grey jay of Canada; also known as the camp-bird. (*See* illustration, p. 225.)

wigwam. General term for any Indian lodge, cabin or shelter.

Wolfe, James (1727–1759). He captured Quebec from the French in 1759 and died in the hour of victory.

I

SAJO AND SHAPIAN

CONTENTS

CHAPTER ONE

BIG SMALL AND LITTLE SMALL

The Indian, Gitchie Meegwon, Big Feather, lived with his motherless boy and girl, Shapian and Sajo, in a log cabin by the shores of a lake in the wild lands of Northern Canada. The place was called O-pee-pee-soway, which means, The Place of Talking Waters.

One day he went out hunting, and found two baby, or kitten beavers, who had been swept downstream far from their home. Big Feather knew that they would soon die as they were so helpless. So he decided to try to save them. He made a basket of birch bark, and in the bottom he put some bedding of grass, and some green food-stuffs such as beavers love. The kittens soon settled down after a good feed.

Then Big Feather put the basket in his canoe and set off back to his log cabin; he knew that his little girl, Sajo, would be happy at getting such pets, and the boy, Shapian, who was three years older, would also enjoy looking after the kitten-beavers.

The kittens quickly took a liking to their new way of living, and although no human beings could ever quite take the place of their own parents, everything possible was done to make them feel at ease.

Shapian partitioned off the under part of his bunk with sheets of birch bark, leaving one end open; and this was their house, in which they at once made themselves very much at home. Gitchie Meegwon cut a hole in the floor and fitted down into it a wash-tub, for a pond, and they spent nearly half their time in it, and would lie on top of the water eating their twigs and leaves. Whenever they left the tub, they always squatted their plump little persons upright beside it, and scrubbed their coats, first squeezing the hair in bunches with their little fists to get the water out. That done, the whole coat was carefully combed with a double claw that all beavers are provided with, one on each hind foot, for this purpose. All this took quite a while, and they were so business-like and serious about it that Sajo would become as interested as they were, and would sometimes help them, rubbing their fur this way and that with the tips of her fingers, and then they would scrub away so much the harder.

They often sat up in this manner while eating the bark off small sticks, and as one or other of them held a stick crossways in his hands, rolling it round and round whilst the busy teeth whittled off the bark, he looked for all the world like some little old man playing on a flute. Sometimes they varied the show, and when the sticks were very slim they ate the whole business, putting one end in their mouths and pushing it in with their hands, while the sharp front teeth, working very fast, chopped it into tiny pieces. The rattle of their cutting machinery sounded much the same as would a couple of sewing-machines running a little wild, and as they held up their heads and shoved the sticks, to all appearances, slowly down their throats, they looked a good deal like a pair of sword-swallowers.

They had to have milk for the first two weeks or so, and Sajo borrowed a baby's bottle from a neighbour in the village, and fed them with it turn about. But while one would be getting his meal (both hands squeezed tight around the neck of the bottle!), the other would scramble around and make a loud outcry and a hubbub, and try to get hold of the bottle, and there would be a squabbling and a great confusion, and the can of milk was sometimes upset and spilled all over; so that at last there had to be another bottle, and Shapian fed one while Sajo fed the other. Later on they were fed with bannock and milk, which made things a little easier, as each had his own small dish which the children held for him. The beavers would pick up the mixture with one hand, shoving it into their mouths at a great rate; and I am afraid their table manners were not very nice, as there was a good deal of rather loud smacking of lips and hard breathing to be heard, and they often talked with their mouths full. But they had one excellent point; they liked to put away their dishes when they had finished, pushing them along the floor into a corner or under the stove; of course if there was a certain amount of milk-soaked bannock left in them, that was quite all right, so far as the beavers were concerned, and by the time the dishes had arrived at their destinations these remains had been well squashed and trampled on the line of march, and the floor would be nicely marked up with small, sticky beavers' tracks, having sometimes to be partly scrubbed.

The larger one of the two was called Chilawee, or Big Small, and the not-so-large one was called Chikanee, or Little Small. Unfortunately they did not grow evenly; that is, one would grow a little faster than the other for a while, and then he would slack down and the other would catch up, and get ahead of him. First one was bigger than the other, then the other was bigger than the one! And it would be discovered that Little Small had been Big Small for quite some time, whilst Big Small had been going around disguised as Little Small.

It was all very confusing, and Sajo had just about decided to give them one name between them and call them just 'The Smalls', when Chilawee settled matters after a manner all his own. He had a habit of falling asleep in the warm cave under the stove, between the stones, and one day there was a great smell of burning hair, and no one could imagine where it came from. The stove was opened and examined, and swept off, and the stove-pipes were tapped, and rapped, but the smell of burning hair was getting stronger all the time; until someone thought of looking *under* the stove, to discover Chilawee sleeping there unconcernedly while the hair on his back scorched to a crisp, and he was routed out of there with a large patch of his coat badly singed. This made a very good brand, something like those that cattle are marked with on a ranch, and it stayed there all Summer, making it very easy to tell who was who; and by calling one of them (the burnt one) *Chila*wee, and the other Chik*anee*, so as to be a little different, they got to know each their name, and everything was straightened out at last.

They were a great pair of little talkers, Chilawee and Chikanee, and were always jabbering together, and sometimes made the strangest sounds. And whenever either of the children spoke to them, which was often, they nearly always answered in a chorus of little bleats and squeals. When there was any work going on, such as the carrying in of water, or wood, or the floor was being swept, or if the people laughed and talked more than usual, or there were any visitors, the two of them would come bouncing out to see what it was all about and try to join in, and they would cut all kinds of capers, and get pretty generally in the way. It had been found that if given any titbits from the table, they always took them into their house to eat or store them. So when they, like bad children, got to be something of a nuisance to the visitors, they had to be bribed with bits of bannock to make them go back in again; but before long, out they would come for some more bannock, and take that in with them, and out again, and so on. And very soon they got to know that visiting time was bannock time as well, and when meal-times came around they knew all about that too, and would be right there, pulling and tugging at the people's clothes and crying out for bannock, and trying to climb up people's legs to get it. And of course they always got what they wanted, and would run off with it to their cabin under the bunk, shaking their heads and hopping along in great style.

They followed the children around continuously, trotting patiently along behind them; and their legs were so very short and they ran so low to the floor on them, that their feet could hardly be seen, so that they looked like two little clockwork animals out of a toy-shop, that went on wheels and had been wound up and never *would* stop. Anything they found on the floor, such as moccasins, kindling wood and so forth, they dragged from place to place, and later, when they got bigger and stronger, they even stole sticks of firewood from the wood-box and took them away to their private chamber, where they sliced them up into shavings with their keen-edged teeth and made their beds with them; and nice, clean-looking beds they were too. Any small articles of clothing that might happen to fall to the floor, if not picked up at once, quickly disappeared into the beaver house. The broom would be pulled down and hauled around, and this broom and the firewood seemed to be their favourite playthings; chiefly, I suspect, on account of the noise they could make with them, which they seemed very much to enjoy.

But their greatest amusement was wrestling. Standing up on their hind legs, they would put their short arms around each other as far as they would go, and with their heads on each other's shoulders, they would try to put each other down. Now, this was hard to do, as the wide tails and the big, webbed hind feet made a very solid support, and they would strain, and push, and grunt, and blow until one of them, feeling himself slipping, would begin to go backwards in order to keep his balance, with the other coming along pushing all he could. Sometimes the loser would recover sufficiently to begin pushing the other way, and then the walk would commence to go in the opposite direction; and so, back and forth, round and round, for minutes at a time, they would carry on this strange game of theirs, which looked as much like two people waltzing as it did anything else. All the while it was going on there would be, between the grunts and gasps, loud squeals and cries from whoever was getting pushed, and much stamping of feet and flopping of tails, trying to hold their owners up, until one of them, on the backward march, would allow his tail to double under him, and fall on his back, when they would immediately quit and scamper around like two madcaps.

But they were not always so lively. There came times when they were very quiet, when they would sit solemnly down together, with their hands held tight to their chests and their tails before them, watching whatever was going on, still as two mice, looking, listening without a word, as though they were trying to make out what everything was all about. And sometimes, as they squatted there one beside the other, like two chocolate-coloured kew-pies or little manikins, Sajo would kneel in front of them and tell them a story, marking time to the words with her finger before their noses, as though she were conducting an orchestra. And they would sit there and listen, and watch her finger very closely, and soon they would commence to shake their heads up and down and from side to side, as beavers always do when they are pleased, and at last they would shake their whole bodies and their heads so hard that they would topple over and roll on the floor, exactly as if they had understood every word and just couldn't help laughing themselves to pieces over the story. And Shapian would stand by taking it all in, and finding it rather ridiculous; but at the same time he wished—very privately of course—that he was not quite such a man, so he could join in this story-telling business himself.

Sometimes the little fellows were lonely, and would whimper together with small voices in their dark little chamber, and Sajo, who had never forgotten her own mother and knew why they were lonesome, would take them in her arms and croon softly to them, and try to comfort them. And they would snuggle up close to her, holding tight to each other's fur all the while as though afraid to lose one another, and would bury their wee noses in the warm, soft spot in her neck where they so loved to be; and after a while the whimpering would cease and they would perhaps forget, for this time, and they would give big, long sighs and little moans of happiness, and fall asleep.

And especially Chikanee loved Sajo. Chikanee was not as strong as Chilawee, was quieter and more gentle. Chilawee had a rather jolly way about him, and was more of a roisterer, one of those 'all for fun and fun for all' kind of lads to whom life is just one big joke; but Chikanee often had lonesome spells by himself, in corners, and had to be picked up, and petted, and made much of. Often he came out in the night and cried beside Sajo's bed to be taken up and allowed to sleep there beside her—while Chilawee lay on his back in the hut, snoring away like a good fellow. When Chikanee was in some small trouble, such as bumping his nose on the stove, or getting the worst of a wrestling match, he came to Sajo for comfort. And Sajo, always ready to sympathise with him because he was the weaker of the two, would kneel down beside him on the floor; and then Chikanee would climb on to her lap and lie there, happy and contented. Chilawee, when his badness was all done for the day, and he was feeling perhaps a little left out of things, would come over to get *his* share of the petting, squeezing in tight beside

Chikanee, where he would settle down after giving a few deep sighs, vastly pleased, no doubt, with his day's work. And Sajo, not wishing to disturb them, would stay there until they were ready to go.

It was very easy to tell them apart by now, as they had become quiet different in their ways. Chilawee was stronger, bolder and more adventurous than his chum, a kind of a comical fellow who seemed to enjoy bumping his head on the table-legs, or dropping things on his toes, or falling into the wood-box. He was as inquisitive as a parrot and wanted to be into everything, which he generally was, if he could reach it. Once he climbed up on to the edge of a pail of water that someone had left on the floor for a moment, and perhaps mistaking it for a plunge-hole, dived right into it. The pail, of course, upset with a bang, splashing the water in all directions. He was most surprised; and so was everybody else. But in spite of all this wilful behaviour, he was just as affectionate as Chikanee, and dogged Shapian's footsteps (when not otherwise engaged!) nearly as much as the other one did Sajo's. And he could not bear to be away from Chikanee very long. Everywhere they went they were together, trotting along one behind the other, or side by side, and if they should become parted on their wanderings in the camp, they would start out to look for each other, and call to one another. And when they met they would sit quite still for a little time, with their heads together, holding each other by the fur—though this wistful mood soon passed off, and it was not long before it all ended up in one of those queer wrestling matches, which seemed to be their way of celebrating.

*   *   *   *

And then there came a time when Big Feather said that the kittens should be allowed their freedom. They were now quite a good size, and very active and strong, and the children were a little afraid that they would wander off and be forever lost. But their father told them how little beavers will not leave their home, if kindly treated, but would always return to the cabin as if it were a beaver house. He said they got lonely very quickly and would only stay away an hour or two.

So, one great, glorious and very exciting day, the barricade that had been kept across the bottom of the doorway was taken away, and out they went. Not all at once, though, for they did a lot of peeping and spying around corners, and sniffed and listened to a whole host of smells and sounds that were not really there at all, and they made two or three attempts before they finally ventured down to the lake, with Sajo and Shapian on either side for a bodyguard. They started off at a very slow and careful walk, sitting up every so often to look around for wolves and bears; of course there weren't any, but it was lots of fun pretending, and as they came closer to the lake the walk became faster, and broke into a trot, which soon became a gallop and into the water they rushed—and then dashed out again, hardly knowing what to make of so large a wash-tub as this. However, they soon went in again, and before very long were swimming, and diving, and screeching, and splashing their tails and having a glorious time, 'Just like real beavers', said Sajo.

It wasn't long before they commenced to chew down small poplar saplings. These they cut into short lengths, and peeled the bark off them in great enjoyment, while they sat amongst the tall grass and the rushes at the water's edge. They played and wrestled, and ran up and down the shore, and romped with their young human friends, and tore in and out of the water in a great state of mind. They stuck their inquisitive noses into every open-ing they saw, and found in the bank an empty musk-rat hole. They being just about the same size as the late owner of the hole, this suited them exactly, and they started to dig there. The opening was under water, and as they worked away there the mud began to come out in thick clouds, so that nothing in the water could be seen.

They spent hours at a time digging out the burrow they had found, and when it was far enough back to be safe, as they considered, it was turned upwards and made to come out on top of the ground, and so become a plunge-hole, and over it, to the intense delight of Sajo and Shapian, they built a funny little beavers' house! So now they had a real lodge, with a small chamber in it and an under-water entrance, a tunnel and a plunge-hole, all complete. The lodge was a little shaky about the walls, and was not very well plastered, but it was really quite a serviceable piece of work, considering.

Then they collected a quantity of saplings, and poplar and willow shoots, and made a tiny feed-raft with them in front of their water-doorway, the same as grown-up beavers do, although it was ever so much smaller. They had a warm bed of their own up in the cabin, same as the big folk had, and there was always plenty of bannock, and, on certain occasions, even a taste or two of preserves, and each had his own little dish to eat it out of, so that, counting everything, they owned a considerable amount of property for the size of them and were really quite well-to-do. So they didn't need either the crazy-looking lodge or the feed-raft, but it was great fun fixing things up, 'n'everything—and cutting little trees, and digging, and playing with mud, and doing all those things that beavers like so much to do, and cannot live contentedly without.

Shapian built a play-house by the water-side, and they were often all in there together, while they rested in the shade of it; and this was Chikanee's favourite spot, and he often went there to look for Sajo, and would always come there when she called him. But Chilawee, the adventurer, who was more of a rover, and something of a pirate, I'm inclined to think, could not stay still anywhere very long and would soon ramble away, and was continually getting lost. Of course *he* knew he wasn't lost, but the others thought he was, which amounted to the same thing so far as they were concerned; and then, of course, there would be a hunt. And he would turn up in the most unexpected places, and would be found in the play-house when it was supposed to be empty, or in the cabin when he was supposed to be in the play-house, or hidden away in the beaver wigwam, or under the canoe, where he would be asleep as likely as not. And when found, he would sit upright with his tail out in front of him, and would teeter-totter and wiggle his body and shake his head, as if he were either dancing or laughing at the trick he had played on the rest of them.

Nor was Chikanee quite the saint you may begin to think he was; he had as much fun as any of them. But there were times when he would break off quite suddenly, as though some thought had come into his little head, perhaps some dim memory of his home-pond that was so far away among the Hills. And then, if Sajo were not there to comfort him, he would waddle on his squat little legs, up to the play-house to look for her. If he found her there, he would sit beside her and do his careful toilet; and after he was all tidied up, he would nestle close to this so well-loved companion, and with his head on her knee, try to talk to her in his queer beaver language and tell her what the trouble was; or else lie there with his eyes half-closed and dreamy, making small sounds of happiness, or perhaps of lonesomeness, or love—we cannot know. Very, very good friends indeed were these two, and where one was, there would be the other, before very long.

And what with all the lively antics, and the skylarking

and the work (not too much of it, of course), and all the play, it would be hard for me to tell you just who were the happiest among these youngsters of the Wild, those with four legs, or those with two. But this I *do* know, that they were a very merry crew, in those happy, happy days at O-pee-pee-soway, The Place of Talking Waters.

* * * *

The titbits of bannock had been getting smaller and smaller lately. Big Feather had been away some days now to get more provisions, and had not yet returned, and now there was hardly any flour. Nobody, children or beavers, had very much to eat, until one day the four playfellows arrived back at the cabin to find Gitchie Meegwon there.

He looked very grave and troubled about something. But the provisions were there; a bag of flour and some other goods lay on the floor, and beside them stood a white man, a stranger. This man had with him a large box. Big Feather spoke kindly to his children, but he never smiled as he generally did, and they wondered why. The white man, too, stood there without speaking. Somehow things didn't look right. Even the little beavers seemed to feel that there was something amiss, for animals are often quick to feel such things, and they too, stood there quietly, watching.

And Shapian, who had been to Mission School and understood English fairly well, heard his father say to the man:

'There they are; which one are you going to take?'

What was that! What could he mean? With a sudden sick feeling Shapian looked at his sister; but of course she had not understood.

'Wait till I have a look at them,' said the stranger, answering Big Feather's question. 'Let them move around a bit.' He was a stout, red-faced man with hard blue eyes

—like glass, or ice, thought Shapian. But Big Feather's eyes were sad, as he looked at his boy and girl. He asked the white man to wait a moment, while he spoke to his children.

'Sajo, Shapian; my daughter, my son,' he said in Indian, 'I have something to tell you.'

Sajo knew then that some trouble had come to them. She came close to Shapian, and looked timidly at the stranger—why! oh why, was he looking so hard at the beavers!

'Children,' continued their father, 'this is the new trader, from the fur-post at Rabbit Portage; the old one, our good friend, has gone. A new Company has taken over the post, and they ask me to pay my debt. It is a big debt, and cannot be paid until we make our hunt, next Winter. We now have no provisions, as you know, and this Company will give me nothing until the debt is paid. So I must go on a long journey for them, with the other men of the village, moving supplies to the new post at Meadow Lake, which is far from here. My work will pay the debt, and more, but I will receive no money until I return. In the meantime, you, my children, must live. I cannot see you go hungry. This trader will give us these provisions.' Here he pointed at the bags and parcels laying on the floor. 'And in exchange he wants—he wants one of the beavers.' He stopped, and no one so much as moved, not even the beavers, and he continued, 'Live beavers are very valuable, and whichever one he takes will not be killed. But my heart is heavy for you, my children, and'——he looked at Chilawee and Chikanee, 'and for the little beaver that must go.'

Shapian stood very still and straight, his black eyes looking hard at the trader, while Sajo, hardly believing, whispered, 'It isn't true; oh, it isn't true!'

But Shapian never spoke, only put his arm around his

sister's shoulder, and stared hard at this man, this stranger who had come to spoil their happiness. He thought of his loaded gun, so close behind him in the corner; but his father must be obeyed, and he never moved. And he looked so fiercely at the trader that, although he was only a fourteen-year-old boy, the man began to feel a little uneasy; so he opened his box, and reaching out for one of the beavers, picked the little fellow up, put him in it and shut down the lid. He nodded to Gitchie Meegwon:

'Well, I'll be seeing you down at the post in a couple of days', he said, and walked out with the box under his arm, shutting the door behind him.

Just like that.

And then Sajo, without a sound, fell to her knees beside her brother and buried her face in his sleeve.

The trader had chosen Chikanee.

And Chilawee, not knowing what to think, suddenly afraid, went into his little cabin, alone.

CHAPTER TWO

THROUGH FIRE AND WATER

Big Feather went off next day on his journey, and Sajo, Shapian and Chilawee were left alone. They were very unhappy, and little Chilawee spent hours searching for his companion, until Sajo thought her heart would break. She and her brother tried hard to be brave about the loss of Chikanee, but as the days went by, they missed him more and more.

Then one drowsy afternoon, Sajo took Chilawee with her up to the waterfall, and there she went to sleep with him in her lap, and she had a dream. It seemed as if the Waterfall said to her:

> *Sajo, Sajo,*
> *You must go.*
> *To the city,*
> *You must go.*

When she awoke, she hurried back to the cabin and told Shapian of her dream, and said that they must go off to the Big City and fetch back Chikanee. Her brother shook his head: the City was a long way off; they had never been so far away from their lake, and they had no money. But Sajo would not hear of any difficulties: they must *go—the Waterfall had told her. So at last Shapian agreed.*

Late the same night everything was in readiness for the journey. It would take them nearly a week to get to the trading post at Rabbit Portage, the first step of their long journey to the city; and they had no idea what lay beyond the post. So they took plenty of everything that was needed for a long trip. Sajo had made several large bannocks, and filled different sized canvas bags with flour,

c

tea and salt, and she made up a parcel of dried deer meat and set aside a small pail of lard, and put matches in a tight-topped can where they would remain dry; while Shapian rolled up a tent and blankets, fixed up a fish-line, sharpened belt-axe and his hunting-knife, whittled a thin edge on the blades of the paddles, and boxed up whatever pots and dishes and other small items of cookery they would have need of.

The sun had not yet arisen on the following morning when breakfast was over and the full outfit was loaded in the canoe, along with Shapian's rifle; for much as he prized this gun, he intended to sell it if he could, hoping that it would bring at least enough to pay their way to the city. What was to happen after that he didn't dare even to think about. Chilawee went in the same birch-bark basket in which he and Chikanee had first come to O-pee-pee-soway, and in the cookery-box Sajo had put *both* the little beaver dishes, as this helped her to feel more certain that they were going to bring back Chikanee and Chilawee together.

'We will need them both,' she said aloud, 'for'—and here her voice dropped a little—'we *are* going to get him, I think,' and then louder, as she nodded her head and pursed her lips, 'I just *know* we are.'

The village was some distance away from their cabin, and they had told no one about their plans, for fear the older people might try to stop them. The old Chief, especially, might forbid them. So they slipped away into the mists of early morning without anyone being the wiser. And as they floated out from the landing, Sajo shook her paddle above her head, as she had seen the men do when they started on a journey, shouting the name of the place they were bound for; and so she held her paddle up and cried out 'Chik-a-*nee!* Chik-a-*nee!*' You could hardly call Chikanee a place, but, she thought, wherever he is, that's where we are going. But Shapian did not wave his paddle, nor did he shout; for he was not so sure about where they would end up.

And so they left the Place of Talking Waters, and started out on what was to be, for all three of them, their Great Adventure.

They stopped occasionally in order to put Chilawee over the side to have a drink and swim around for a minute or two so as to get cool, for the weather was very hot; and that evening they put up their tent in the woods along the shore, and spent the night there. The next morning at daybreak they were away again, and paddled steadily till dark, stopping only to eat and to exercise their furry chum. Each morning they were on their way before the sun rose, and every evening they made camp in some sheltered spot beside the water, where Chilawee swam around all night, always returning to the tent at daylight to fall asleep in his basket, where he remained quietly all day. Both children worked on the portages, of which there were a number, each carrying a share of the load. There were two trips apiece, including the canoe, which Shapian carried alone.

And so day after day they forged ahead, onward, onward, ever onward; and two small backs bent and swayed like clockwork and two paddles swished and dipped all the long day, as regularly and evenly as the step of marching soldiers, while the burning sun rose on one side of them, passed overhead, and sank again like a great red ball behind the dark wall of the forest. Day after day the faithful bark canoe carried them staunchly and steadily forward, outward bound on the long search for the absent Chikanee.

One morning they awoke to find a faint smell of wood-smoke in the air, a smell of burning moss and scorching brush and leaves, and they knew that somewhere, seemingly far away, there was a forest fire. But it was closer than they had at first supposed, for as soon as they were well out on the lake and were able to look about them, they could see an immense pillar of smoke billowing up from behind the distant hills; and they did not paddle very far before they found that their route would bring them more and more in its direction. The lake was getting very narrow, and farther on it ended and became a river, across which the fire could easily jump, and Shapian determined to get through this narrow place as quickly as possible to a large lake that lay beyond, where they would be safe. So they hurried on, and as they went the smoke spread higher and wider, so that it was no longer a pillar, but a white wall that seemed to reach the sky, and rolled outwards and down in all directions, becoming thicker and thicker until the sun was hidden, and the air became heavy and stifling, and very still. The whole country to the eastward seemed to be on fire, and although the blaze itself was hidden by the hills, even at that distance there could be heard a low moaning sound that never ceased and was, minute by minute, becoming closer, and heading straight towards them—they were right in the path of the fire. The big lake was some distance away, across a portage, and there was no time to be lost if they were to cross over to it before the fire rushed down upon them; for, while some forest fires move slowly, others have been known to travel as fast as thirty miles an hour.

As the hot smoke cooled off, it began to come down, settling in a dark, blue haze over all the land, making far-off points invisible and near ones look dim, so that soon nothing could be seen but the row of trees nearest the shore-line, and the children were only able to keep their right direction by watching this, and by the sound of the rapids that lay ahead of them. Very soon they arrived at the head of this steep place in the river, where the water rushed and foamed wildly between, and over, dark jagged rocks for several hundred yards. It was a dangerous place, but Shapian dared not take time, with the double trip they had, to cross the portage that went round it, and he decided to take the quicker route and run the rapids. For the fire was now not far away, and the sharp turn that he knew to be at the end of the swift water would head them straight for it. The roar of the fire was now so loud as almost to drown the sound of the noisy rapids, and Shapian soon saw that it was to be a hard race, and a swift one, to gain the lake—and then there was the portage, and it was a long one.

The smoke was now so thick that when they neared the rapids they could not see fifty feet ahead of them, and Shapian had all he could do to find the place to enter it. Standing up in the canoe to get a better view, he at length found the starting point; and then with a swift rush they were into the dashing, boiling white water. Although he was hardly able to see through the smoke, Shapian skilfully picked his way down the crooked, difficult channel between the rocks. Great curling, hissing waves lashed out at the frail canoe, throwing it violently from one white-cap to another; dark, oily-looking swells gripped its under side like evil monsters seeking to pour in over the sides and sink it. Spinning eddies snatched wickedly at the paddles as the little craft leaped like a madly charging horse between the black, savage-looking rocks that lay in wait to rip and tear the light canoe to pieces.

And above the thunderous roar of the tumbling waters there came the duller, deeper, and terribly frightening sound of the oncoming fire. Smoke poured across the river in dense, whirling clouds, and through it sped the leaping canoe with its crew of three. And the sleeping passenger in the basket woke up, and excited by all the noise, and quite aware that something unusual was happening, began to take a part in the proceedings, and added his little thin voice to the uproar, though it could hardly be heard, and he rocked and shook his house of bark so violently that a moment had to be spared to lay a heavy bundle on it to keep it right side up.

Shapian strained and fought with his paddle and all of his young strength, against the mighty power of the racing torrent, turning the canoe cleverly this way and that, swinging, sidling, and slipping from one piece of clear water to the next, checking the canoe in the quieter places while he stood up to get a better view of what lay ahead— and then away into the white water again. Meanwhile Sajo pulled and pushed and pryed on her paddle with might and main, as Shapian shouted to her above the rattle and the din 'Gyuk-anik, to the right hand,' or 'Mashk-anik, to the left hand,' or 'Wee-betch, hurry,' and sometimes 'Pae-ketch, easy there.' Sheets of spray flew from the sides of the canoe as it heaved and bounced and jerked, and some of it came in, and Sajo, who was in front, soon became soaked. Except that the smoke made the safe channel so hard to find, they were in no real danger from the rapids itself, for Shapian, like all his people, both young and old, was very skilful in a canoe and understood, even at his age, a great deal about the movements of water; and he had often run these rapids with his father. Sajo, trusting in him completely, laughed and cried out in her excitement, for this was like a show to her, and she let out little yelps as she had heard her father and the other Indians do, with their louder whoops and yells as they ran a dangerous piece of water—though she had always been left safely on the shore to watch. But Shapian, who knew how serious things really were, never made a sound besides his loud commands as captain of their little ship, and when he could spare an eye from the turmoil of madly boiling water all about him, gave anxious glances to the side from which the fire was coming. And coming it was—with the speed of a train, it seemed—rushing down the hills towards them like a crimson sea, with great roaring streamers of flame flying high above the burning forest. Once he looked back, to find that the fire had crossed the narrow lake behind them; now there was only one way to go—forward, though he said never a word to Sajo about it. The air, that had been thick with heavy rolls and banks of smoke, now commenced to turn darker and darker, and the light was dimmed till it appeared almost as though twilight had fallen, so early in the day, and hardly anything could be seen around them; and nothing seemed real any more, and they moved like people in a dream.

Desperately Shapian drove the canoe ahead, for well he knew that if they were caught in this place they would be either burnt alive or suffocated. By now the portage was not very far, and beyond it lay the lake that they must get to—and get to fast!

They shot out from the foot of the rapids into a deep, still pool, and here they found themselves surrounded by strange moving shapes, dimly seen through the smoke-clouds, as on all sides all manner of animals were passing, tearing along the shore, or swimming through the pool, or splashing noisily along the shallows, by ones and twos, separately or in small groups, all headed for the big lake, the same one our own travellers were aiming for, each and every one making for the safety that he knew he would find there. Animals that seldom wetted their feet were swimming in the pool—squirrels, rabbits, woodchucks, and even porcupines. Deer leaped through or over the underbrush, their white tails flashing, eyes wide with terror. A bear lumbered by at a swift, clumsy gallop, and a pair of wolves ran, easily and gracefully, beside a deer—their natural prey; but they never even looked at him. For none were enemies now; no one was hungry, or fierce, or afraid of another. And all the people of the woods, those that went on two legs and others that had four, and those with wings and some that swam, animals and birds and creeping things, creatures, some of them, that dared not meet at any other time, were now fleeing, side by side, from that most merciless of all their foes, dangerous and deadly alike to every one of them from the smallest to the greatest—The Red Enemy of the Wilderness, a forest fire.

Sajo, now realising what all this meant, became terror-stricken, and Shapian, almost in despair himself, yet knowing that their lives depended on him, kept his courage up and soothed her as best he could, and she paddled bravely on. But the forest that had always been their home, and had always seemed so friendly, had suddenly become a very terrible place to be in. It would have been so to any grown-up; yet these two children, one of them eleven and the other fourteen years of age, remember, kept their heads and fought like good soldiers for their lives, and for Chilawee's. And this same Chilawee was no great help, as you can well believe; on the contrary, he showed every sign of causing trouble and delay. Sensing real danger, as all animals do, and scared out of his wits by the sounds and scent of the other creatures that passed on every side, he was screeching at the top of his lungs and pounding and tearing at the lid of his prison, as it must now have seemed to him, and if some way were not found to quiet him, would soon be out of it; and once in the water he could never again be found in all this hurry and confusion.

A few short minutes and they were at the portage. The trail was nearly hidden by the blinding smoke, and down the slopes of the near-by ridge the hoarse roar of the fire was coming swiftly. The darkness that had fallen as the smoke poured over the forest was now lighted up by a terrible red glow, and the heat from it could be plainly felt. Quickly they threw their stuff ashore. Chilawee was now in such a state that he could never be carried in any other way except as a separate load. This landing being safe for the minute, and not knowing what shape things were in at the other end, they at once decided to leave him here, and it was but the work of a moment to turn the canoe over on top of the basket, so as to hold down the lid (like all his kind when very frightened, Chilawee forgot to use his teeth), and taking each a load the children started across, running at a dog-trot. On all sides thick moving coils of black and yellow smoke wound and billowed around them as they ran, and took strange shapes and forms and seemed to reach out with pale waving hands to hold them back, and through the whirling smoke-clouds the trees beside the trail loomed indistinct like tall, dark, silent ghosts; while here and there red eyes of flame glowed at them through the haze.

But they kept right on at their steady trot. At the far side there was a breeze from off the lake, and the end of the portage was clear. Gulping a few breaths of fresh air, they left their loads beside the water's edge and raced back for Chilawee and the canoe—I say 'raced,' but the race was often little but a scramble as, gasping and half blinded, they staggered down the trail, half the time with their eyes closed to relieve the pain in them, and to shut out the stinging, burning smoke, while they groped their way along, their hearts filled with a fear such as they had never before known. By the time they were back at the canoe, sparks and burning brands were falling everywhere, and the angry glow had deepened so that everything—trees, smoke, and water—was red with it. And now, close at hand, could be heard a dreadful low, rushing sound.

The fire was almost upon them.

And at the same time Chilawee, having made up his mind to save his own little life as best he could, was gnawing steadily away at the thin bark sides of his box; in no time at all he would be through. If only it would hold together for just five more minutes!

In a moment Shapian tore off his sister's head shawl, and quickly soaking it in water, with swift movements wrapped it about her head and face, leaving only her eyes and nose showing. Then splashing water over her clothes he said:

'Do not wait. I will come quickly. Go!'

And hugging Chilawee's basket tight to her body with both arms, Sajo disappeared into that awful, glowing tunnel of a trail.

*   *   *   *

After he had seen his sister pass from sight, Shapian was delayed perhaps a full minute while he wetted his own clothes and slipped the paddles into the carrying-thongs. How he wished now for his father's guiding hand! He was doing the best he knew, with his small experience, to save the lives of all three of them, and he hoped he had chosen aright. And now Sajo was in there ahead of him, alone; he must hurry!

Throwing the canoe up, and over, with his head inside between the paddles, which formed a kind of yoke, he was quickly on his way. But in that short minute that he had been detained, the fire had gained on him, and while he ran as swiftly as a boy of fourteen could well do with a twelve-foot canoe on his shoulders, he saw, not far away to one side, a solid, crackling wall of flame. Trees fell crashing in the midst of it, and others burst with loud reports like gun-fire. Onward he tore through what had now become a cave of crimson smoke, half-choked, his eyes stinging, his head throbbing with the heat. But he clenched his teeth and kept on, while close beside him the blazing forest crackled, and thundered, and roared.

Whole tree-tops caught fire with a rush and a horrible screeching, tearing sound, and flames leaped from tree to tree like fiery banners, ever nearer and nearer to the trail.

Beneath the canoe some clear air remained, which helped him a little, but the heat was all he could stand. Once a burning spruce tree came crashing down so near the portage that its flaming top fell across the trail ahead of him in a flurry of sparks and licking tongues of flame, and he was obliged to wait precious moments while the first fury of the burning brush died down; and then he jumped, with the canoe still on his shoulders, over the glowing trunk. The hot breath of it fanned his body and nearly choked him, and he stumbled to his knees as he landed. Righting himself, he cleared the canoe before the fire had harmed it.

On the upturned canoe fell large flakes of burning bark and red-hot ashes, that lay there and smoked and smouldered, so that to anyone who might have followed him, it must have seemed to be already burning, which, in very truth, it was not far from doing. And now he should have caught up to his sister; she would be slower than he, for the basket was an awkward affair to run with, whereas a bark canoe, though very much heavier, was a steady, well-balanced load, even for a boy. And he suddenly became terrified lest Chilawee had cut open his box and escaped on the way, and Sajo having delayed somewhere to capture him, that he had passed them. But just ahead the smoke was clearing, and he felt the wind from the lake. And then, sick and dizzy, his sight blurred by the water that streamed from his eyes, he stumbled again, and this time fell heavily, canoe and all, over something soft that lay in the pathway—there, face down across the trail, lay Sajo! And clutched tightly in one of her hands was the basket—empty. Chilawee had at last cut his way out, and was gone!

Hardly knowing what he was doing, Shapian crawled

Carrying a canoe through a forest fire (*Drawn by Grey Owl*)

from under the canoe, lifted Sajo across his knees and scrambled, somehow, to his feet, and then, his breath coming in choking sobs, his knees bending under him and a great ringing in his ears he staggered with her in his arms to the lake shore.

Here he laid her down and threw water over her face, and rubbed her hands, and cried out: 'Sajo, Sajo, speak to me, speak!' And she opened her eyes and said faintly: 'Chilawee.' And he dared not tell her there was no Chilawee any more, only an empty basket.

And now the smoke was rolling out over them even here; the whole portage was aflame, and waiting only to wet Sajo's shawl and throw it over her face, Shapian went back for the canoe. Fortunately it was not far, as, unable to lift it any more, he seized it by one end and dragged it to the water, stern out and bow inshore so as to load the quicker. Quickly he threw in the bundles, and lifted Sajo into the bow, while she held tightly to the basket and cried weakly: 'Chilawee, Chilawee, Chilawee,' and moaned, and kept repeating: 'Chilawee.'

All this took but a short time, and running lightly over the load to the other end, Shapian commenced to back the canoe out stern first, as fast as he was able; and a big sob came in his throat as he thought of their little furry friend who was now past all help, left behind. Yet surely, he thought, the little creature, gifted to find water easily, might have reached the lake, and even if lost might still be living—when behind him, from out on the lake, came the sound of a smart slap, and a splash upon the water, and there was the lost Chilawee, alive and quite well, thank you, giving out, by means of his tail, his private and personal opinion of this Red Enemy that he had so narrowly escaped. And Shapian shouted out in a great voice: 'Sajo! Sajo! Chilawee is safe, Chilawee is out on the lake—look!'

And at that Sajo, lying there in the bow of the canoe, burst into tears and sobbed as if her heart would break; she would not cry before, when she believed her little friend was dead, but now he was known to be safe she was free to cry all she wanted, to cry as loud and as long as she liked—with joy!

Chilawee was quite far out, and in no danger, but a canoe does not start very quickly when paddled backwards, and being still in shallow water, was too close to shore for safety; and at the edge of the forest, leaning out over the water, was a huge pine tree that was hollow, and had been burning fiercely all this time. Shapian was still struggling to get the canoe backed away far enough to turn it (and it did not take nearly as long for all this to happen as it does to tell about it), when the bark of the pine, dried out by the intense heat, cracked wide open, and the hurrying tongue of fire rushed up this channel as if it had been a stove-pipe, to the top of it. The great fan-shaped head of the towering tree, that had looked proudly out over the wilderness for many a hundred years, burst into a mass of flame that leaped into the air above it, the height again of the tree itself. And then the burnt-out butt, unable to stand against the force of the soaring flames, gave way, and the mighty trunk tottered and began to fall, outwards towards the lake, swayed a little sideways, and then started on its fiery path, straight for the canoe. Slowly at first, then faster and faster the hundred-foot giant overbalanced, and the terrible fan of flame rushed downwards. Real terror, for the first time, seized on Shapian, and with desperate strength he stopped the canoe and drove it smashing into the shore, while just behind him the burning tree plunged into the lake with a deafening crash, and a hissing and a screeching that could have been heard for a mile or more as the fire and water met. Smoke and steam poured up and smothered everything as the flames went out, so that Shapian could see nothing, and the waves from this terrific splash rocked the canoe violently, and Sajo, beside herself with fright, jumped to her feet in the dangerously rolling canoe and screamed, and screamed, and Shapian sprang over the side and ran through the water to her, and held her in his arms, and comforted her, and told her that there was nothing more to fear.

And out on the lake Master Chilawee slapped his little tail in small defiance. In a few short moments the canoe was away, this time without any accident, and the little beaver, seeming mighty glad that he was found again, gave himself up quite cheerfully, and was lifted by this so-impudent tail of his and dropped aboard, where he clambered around on the load, and smelled at the children, and ran about, and altogether showed signs of the greatest pleasure and excitement. He did not seem to have lost one single hair, no doubt because he ran so low to the ground on his short legs, so that everything passed over him; and so now he was celebrating, and they all had quite a reunion out there on the lake.

Before they had gone very far, Sajo began to feel better, and soon was well enough to sit up. Shapian would not let her paddle, and made her sit facing him, while she told her story, and related how, choked by the hot, burning smoke, and not being able to see, she had been unable to catch Chilawee when he fell from the basket, and had become confused and fallen, where, she did not know, and had then been unable to get up again. And that was all she knew about it until she found Shapian pouring water over her face. She did not remember calling Chilawee, though she knew he had run away, having seen him, as though in a dream, disappear into the clouds of smoke. And when she had finished her story, she began to look hard at her brother's face, and then commenced to laugh!

And the more she looked the louder she laughed, and Shapian was a little frightened, and began to wonder if the dangers she had been through had touched her mind, until she exclaimed:

'Shapian!—your face—you should see it, why—you have no eyebrows!' And then suddenly she stopped laughing and felt for her own eyebrows, and asked anxiously. 'How are mine, are they all right?' and looked over the side of the canoe at the water to see the reflection of her face. But the canoe was moving, and ruffling the water, and she could, of course, see nothing, and now very alarmed she cried:

'Oh, stop the canoe so I can see—tell me, are my eyebrows there?'

And she got into a great way about it, and Shapian laughed at her, in his turn, and would not say; until at last he told her they were there all right, yes, both of them; which indeed they were, as her face had been covered most of the time. But it was just like a girl, said Shapian to himself, to worry about a little thing like eyebrows when they had all so nearly lost their lives.

That afternoon they made an early camp, in a good safe place, on an island far out on the lake, and here they looked over the damage. Shapian could not very well repair his eyebrows, which would grow out later of their own accord, but he had plenty to do with the canoe.

The hard smash the bow had got against the shore when they had dodged the falling tree had torn off a good-sized strip of bark; the spruce gum at the seams had melted, and the burning embers that had fallen on it had smouldered long enough to scorch a number of pretty thin places in the sides and bottom. Also their tent and blankets had a few holes burnt in them by flying sparks. But the loss was quite small considering, and they could easily have fared a great deal worse. The top was gone off Chilawee's box, and it had a hole the size of a quart measure in the side of it (Chilawee's part in the battle!). But there were plenty of birch trees around, and Shapian cut sheets of bark from them, and sewed a patch on the hole and made another lid that fitted nearly as well as the old one, and he fixed up the canoe with a few patches and some fresh gum. Sajo, meanwhile, busied herself with needle and thread which no Indian girl or woman will travel very far without, and soon had the tent and blankets serviceable again, and by the time darkness fell, everything was in readiness for a new start in the morning.

CHAPTER THREE

THE LITTLE PRISONER

And meanwhile what of Chikanee!

We must go back to the day the trader walked out of Gitchie Meegwon's camp with him, right out of the lives of his friends, it seemed, for ever.

During the four or five days it took the trader, with his Ojibway canoe-men, to make the journey back to Rabbit Portage, Chikanee did not fare so badly, as one of the Indians took good care of him, keeping him well supplied with food and water. But he could not understand why Chilawee was not with him, and wondered where Sajo and Shapian had disappeared to. And he began to be lonesome for them all, and often cried out for Sajo to come to him, as she had always done when she heard the little beaver calling. But no one came except the stranger Indian, and then only to change his water and to give him food. This man, by the trader's orders, accompanied Chikanee on the steamboat to see that he arrived safely at the railroad, and there left him; the money for him was paid over to the Indian, and what happened to him now did not greatly matter.

Having now come to a stop, and thinking that he must be home again, he wailed loudly for liberty and recognition, expecting his playmates to come and take him out of this stuffy and uncomfortable box. But none came. So he started to chew at the box, and strange, harsh voices spoke angrily to him. He next tried to climb the walls of his prison, but they were too high, and these strangers shouted at him, and pounded on the box to keep him

34

quiet and now, thoroughly frightened, he lay still, whimpering and lonely.

A little later he was loaded on to a train that thundered and roared its way for many hours. When the train first started the noise drove him nearly crazy, and in his terror he tried to dive to freedom through his tiny dish of water, and upset it; so that besides his other misery he soon began to suffer from thirst. He had been snatched away from home too hurriedly for Sajo to have time to drop a bannock in the box, which would have lasted him several days, and no one now thought of providing him with anything to eat. And so sick, hungry, lonesome, and wild with fear, he started desperately to cut his way out of the crate. In this he would have quickly succeeded, but striking a nail he broke one of his four cutting teeth, which made gnawing too painful to continue. His bedding, what little there was of it, became dirty, and the motion of the train thumped and bumped him against the hard sides of the box, so that he became bruised and sore. He tried hard to stay in the centre, away from the walls of his prison, but never could. One of the trainmen, intending to be kind, threw to him some crusts of bread from his own lunch, but he thought that the little beaver's frantic clutchings at his hands was a sign of ill-temper, and from then on they were afraid of him—so small a little creature to be afraid of!—and no one attempted to give him any more bedding or food, and his water-dish remained empty for the same reason.

And he raised his voice in cries of misery and called and called for his small companions, who now could never hear him, wailed in his childlike voice for them to come and take away this great trouble that had befallen him. But no one paid any attention, if they ever even heard him, drowned as was his feeble outcry by the roar of the train.

At length, after many stops and starts, each of which

Chikanee in captivity (*Drawn by Grey Owl*)

jolted and slammed him from one hard side of his prison to the other, and a last, and cruelly rough ride in a delivery van, there came a sudden quietness. The cleats were taken from across the top of the box with a frightful screeching as the nails were drawn, and he was lifted out by a hand that held him very firmly by the tail; a large, strong hand, yet somehow a very gentle one. Then the other hand came up and was held against his chest as he hung head down, bringing him right end up, and a finger rubbed gently on one hot, tired little paw, and a deep voice spoke soothing words; so that suddenly he felt rather comfortable. For this man was a keeper of animals, and attendant in the Park where Chikanee was to stay, and he knew his business very well. And when he examined his small captive, and saw how miserable, and bedraggled, and covered with dirt the little creature was—he who had been so proud and careful of his coat!—the keeper said angrily to the delivery man (who, poor fellow, was not to blame at all):

'No water, nothing to eat, dry feet, dry tail, dry nose, teeth all broken up; if that isn't a shame, nothing ever was. Some way to ship a beaver, I'll say! But we'll soon fix you up, old-timer.' For the man had been expecting his little guest, having had a letter about him, and had everything ready to receive him, and Chikanee soon found himself in an enclosure built of something like stone, but not nearly as friendly as stone, and surrounded by a rail of iron bars.

And in this gaol of iron and concrete Chikanee, for no crime at all, was to spend the rest of his days.

Chikanee, gentle, lovable Chikanee, was now supposed to be a wild and probably dangerous beast!

It was not a very large place, a mere hutch after the freedom of the big lake beside which he had spent most of his short life, but that did not matter for the moment—he smelled water! And then he saw, right in front of him, a deep, clear pool; not a very big one, to be sure, but at least it was water. Into this he immediately threw himself and drank thirstily, floating on the surface, while the cracked and dried-out tail and feet soaked up the life-giving moisture, and the cakes of dirt loosened and washed from off him as he swam slowly back and forth. This seemed like the beaver's heaven itself, after more than three days of noise, starvation, dirt, and utter misery, and the hot, fevered little body cooled off and all the bumps and bruises ceased to throb, as the cool water slowly got in its good work on him.

And now, he thought, this must be just the plunge-hole. Down there, somewhere, lay the entrance, and through this he would set out and would, no doubt, come to his home-lake, there to find his playmates on the shore; and then Chilawee would run to welcome him and roll on his woolly back with joy, and Sajo would come and pick him up, and hug him, and make much of him, and whisper in his ear, and tickle him in that funny place under his chin, and all these hard times would be forgotten.

So, with a great splurge he dived straight down—to strike his head on the hard bottom of the pool, almost stunning himself. Again he tried, with the same result. He scratched and bit at the concrete, thinking to tear his way through it to the tunnel that must, somewhere, lead out of it. But he only cracked and split his claws and took more chips out of his remaining teeth. Then he scrambled out of the pool and over to the bars, and tried to squeeze through them; but they were too close together. He tried to gnaw at them, but his broken teeth never even scratched them. So he ran round and round inside the enclosure, stopping here and there to dig, but to no purpose. For a long time he worked, running back to the pool and out again to the bars, trying to gnaw, trying to dig; but it was useless. And then at last he realised that there was no opening anywhere, no plunge-hole, no escape; and weary, wretched and hopeless, he lay flat on the hard, hot floor of the pen and moaned, moaned as he had done when Sajo had nursed him to sleep whenever he had been lonesome— only then he had moaned with joy, and now it was from misery.

The attendant stood by for a long time, and watched and shook his head, and said: 'Too bad, little fellow, too bad.' This was his job, taming these wild creatures that were sent to him from time to time; yet, liking animals as he did, he sometimes hated the work. And he pitied the little beaver that was struggling so helplessly to be free, for this was not the first one that had come under his care, and he knew their gentle nature. And stepping in through the gate of the pen, he picked up Chikanee carefully and cleverly, so that, as in the first place, he was not scared or excited, but was actually comfortable in his hands—they were so much more friendly than the concrete!

The keeper carried Chikanee to his cottage, which was close by, inside the Park. He had three young children, and when they saw their father bringing in a little beaver, they crowded round to see, and they shouted and clapped their hands with glee, so that Chikanee was afraid again, and tried to burrow into the man's coat; for already he had begun to trust him. And their father quieted the young ones and set the little creature on the floor, where, finding himself once more in a house, he felt a little more at home than in the cage. They all stood watching to see what he would do, and the keeper's wife said:

'The wee mite! Look how thin he is—Joey,' to one of the youngsters, 'go get an apple; those other beavers we used to have were just crazy for apples.'

So this Joey fellow went and got one right away, and put it down on the floor in front of Chikanee. He had never seen an apple before, but he sniffed at it, and oh! what a wonderful smell came from it! And so he cut into it as best he could with his poor wee broken teeth and then, what a taste!—the most delicious taste in all the world! And seizing hold of this wonderful titbit with both hands, he demolished nearly the half of it. At this the keeper was very pleased, for some of his prisoners refused all food, and died, but now he knew that this one would recover; somehow he had been none too sure about it. And the delighted children laughed to see him sitting up there like a little man while he ate, and the keeper's wife exclaimed: 'There, didn't I tell you? He'll be all right in no time.'

Then the man brought in the sprays of fresh, juicy poplar leaves he had placed in the pen for him, but which he had not touched. But now he ate them, and the children wondered to see him holding the leaves in little bunches in his hands while he put them in his mouth. Feeling a good deal better by now, he made small sounds of pleasure while he ate, and at that the young ones marvelled even more, and one, a little girl with golden hair and a round, rosy face, said:

'Listen, listen to him talk, just like a little, wee baby. O daddy, do let's keep him in the kitchen!' And their mother spoke up too: 'Yes, Alec, let's keep him here for a spell; there's no one in the Park—it's almost like putting a child in prison.' And Alec answered:

'Perhaps you're right. We'll fix him a place in here for to-night.'

So they made a place for our Chikanee in the kitchen, and Alec the keeper fastened a low, wide pan of water to the floor, and set a large box down on its side, with plenty of clean straw in it for a bed for him. And there the little beaver spent the night, not happily perhaps, but very comfortably.

The next morning Alec returned him to the pen, so that any of the public who came to the Park could see him; but when evening came round again and the grounds were empty, the keeper brought him back to the cottage. And from then on he did this every day, and Chikanee spent all the hours when he was not 'working' in the keeper's house, and in the kitchen had his bed, and his big pan of water, and ate his leaves and twigs there. And each day he had a nice, juicy apple, which quite made up for a lot of his troubles, though not for all of them. Every morning there was a considerable mess to clean up, of peeled sticks, and cut branches, and left-over leaves, and the floor was all slopped up with water, but the children willingly turned to and cleaned up, after he was carried away to his daily task of being stared at in the cage. Nobody seemed to mind the little trouble he was. He got along famously with the family and, in his own small way, soon became quite a part of the household.

As time went on he got to know them all, and he would romp clumsily with the youngsters; and to them he was a kind of tumbling, good-natured toy, a good deal like one of those roguish wool puppies to be found on Christmas trees. But to Chikanee, it could never be the same as it had been at O-pee-pee-soway, and often he didn't want to play, but lay quietly in his box, his little heart filled with a great empty longing for his old playmates.

Before very long his teeth had grown in, and he spent a lot of time sharpening them against one another, grinding and rattling them together at a great rate. His coat, which he had sadly neglected for a time, so that it had become all tangled and awry, now got its daily scrubbing and combing, and his small frame, that had for a while been little more than a bag of bones, soon filled out, and he began to look like the old Chikanee again. And in a way he was happy; but never quite.

While in the cage he was really miserable, and the keeper knew this, and always felt badly when he put the little fellow in there each morning, and looked back at this pitiful little creature that gazed after him so wistfully as he walked away, sitting there alone on the bare cement floor, surrounded by bars that would have held a grizzly bear. He remembered that a beaver may live more than twenty years—twenty years in that prison of iron and concrete! In twenty years his own family would be grown up and away from there; he himself might be gone. The town would have become a great city (it was not really a very big place); people would come and go—free people, happy people—and through it all, this unhappy little beast, who had done no harm to anyone, and seemed only to want someone to be kind to him, would, for twenty long and lonely years, look out through the bars of that wretched pen as though he had been some violent criminal; waiting for the freedom that would never be his, waiting only to die at last. And, thought the keeper, for no good reason at all, except that a few thoughtless people, who never really cared if they ever saw a beaver, might stare for a minute or two at the disconsolate little prisoner, and then go away and forget they had ever seen him. Somehow it did not seem fair, to this kind-hearted man, and when he watched the little creature rollicking with the children in his funny, clumsy way, he wished very much that there was something that he could do about it, and decided to make his small prisoner as happy as he could, and give him the freedom of the cottage as long as it was at all possible.

CHAPTER FOUR

THE PRISONER RELEASED

Two days' more travelling brought Sajo and Shapian to Rabbit Portage, the trading station. They made camp nearby, and then Shapian set off to see the trader who had bought Chikanee. But the trader would not help: the beaver had been bought for fifty dollars for a Zoo in the Big City many miles away. Poor Shapian had never heard of so much money, but he bravely offered to sell his gun, and to work ever so hard to earn enough to buy back Chikanee. It was no good; the trader was very firm; it was a business affair, and had been settled once and for all.

Shapian did not know how to break the news to his sister, but in his despair a friend came to his help. A missionary wondered who the two Indian children were, and as he was so friendly to them, they told him all their story, and, of course, Chilawee came along too to play his part.

The missionary was poor so he could not give them the money needed, but he had a good idea. He called a meeting of all the folk at Rabbit Portage, and told them the story of the children and their beavers. Everyone wanted to help, so a collection was made, and this proved enough for the railway journey with a little over. The missionary bought the tickets, and gave Shapian the few dollars left; these the boy put into a little bag which he hung by a cord round his neck for safety.

Then the missionary wrote a letter to some friends in the Big City who would look after the children. He wrote the address on the envelope and told Shapian to ask a policeman to show them the way to the house. The Indian boy had never seen a policeman, but he kept saying 'poliss-man' to himself so that he should not forget the name.

The next morning everyone came along to see Sajo, Shapian and

Chilawee off; there was much waving of handkerchiefs and many cries of good wishes as the train puffed out of the station.

When the train on which Sajo, Shapian, and their small fellow-traveller Chilawee, were riding, made the last of its many stops and came to a standstill in the city station, the children were almost too scared to get off. The guard, who had had his eye on them all the way, helped them out, spoke a few words of encouragement, and left them to attend to his other duties.

They found themselves in a world of noise. The hurrying throngs of people, the hiss of escaping steam, the clang of engine bells, the shriek of whistles and the thunderous bellowing of starting and stopping locomotives, deafened and terrified them, and they stood hand in hand on the platform, not knowing which way to turn and not daring to move. Before, behind, and on every side of them was a terrific confusion and a ceaseless din. Lorries piled high with baggage of every kind rumbled by, and one of these came straight for them, and Shapian pulled his sister aside only just in time to escape being run over by it. The station was, to them, a vast, echoing cave filled with terrifying sights and sounds, and never before had they felt so small and defenceless. They felt more alone here, in the midst of all these people, than they had ever done in the forest, with its silence and its quiet, peaceful trees. People looked at them curiously as they passed, but everyone seemed to be too busy rushing this way and that to pay much attention to them.

So there they stood, in all that deafening uproar, two little people from the Silent Places, as scared and bewildered, and nearly as helpless, as the two tiny kitten beavers had been when Gitchie Meegwon found them. Yet Sajo, with all her fear, had only one thought— Chikanee had come through all this *alone!* While Shapian

began to wish himself back in the forest fire again, amongst
the friendly animals, Chilawee, for his part, closed his ears
as tight as two tiny black purses and lay perfectly still,
jammed tight into a corner of his basket.

They had been standing there for what seemed to them
an hour (though it had really been only a few moments),
and Shapian was thinking of making *some* kind of move
towards a huge door through which crowds of people were
flowing like a swift, rushing river, when there stopped in
front of them a young boy. He was about Shapian's own
age, and was dressed in a neat, red uniform with bright
buttons all down the front of his short, tightly fitting coat,
and on the side of his head there was a little hat that
looked more like a very small, round box than anything
else.

'Hullo, you kids,' he said cheerfully. 'Are you lost?
Who are you looking for?'

Poor Shapian, confronted by this self-possessed and
magnificent-looking personage, never before having seen a
page boy, found that he had completely forgotten any
English he ever knew, and could remember only one word;
so he said it.

'Poliss-man,' he stammered nervously.

'You want a policeman, eh?' said the page, who was a
smart lad and got to the point at once. 'O.K. Come along
with me.' And beckoning to them he set off at a great
pace, his shiny boot-heels tapping sharply on the hard
platform. The little Indians, silent-footed in their
moccasins, slipped softly along behind him, though they
almost had to trot to keep up, Shapian carrying Chilawee's
basket in one hand and holding tightly on to his sister with
the other. It must have been a queer-looking procession.
Their guide steered them through the crowds, over to the
entrance and down a great hall filled with more people
(nearly all the people in the world, thought Shapian), and

brought them over to a big, stout man who stood beside a door at the far end. He also had a number of bright buttons on his coat.

'Hey, Pat,' the page called to him. 'Here's a couple of kids want to see a policeman,' and pushed them forward, continuing—rather disrespectfully, I fear: 'You shouldn't be hard to see, you're big enough. Look like Indians to me—better watch your scalp!' And with an impudent grin at the police officer and a wink at the children, he dodged into the crowd and disappeared.

'Oho,' exclaimed the policeman loudly, looking down on the two youngsters, with his hands behind his back. 'Oho, so it's scalps, is it?' said he, looking very fiercely at them, as though he were about to take them prisoner— though his eyes had an odd twinkle about them and were pleasantly crinkled at the corners. ' 'Tis young Injuns yez are, eh? The little craytures! Well, 'tis a mighty poor scalp ye'll get from me, that's been bald as an egg this twenty years; and well did the little imp know it that brought ye here!'

Although he talked so fiercely, his face was round and jolly, and he wore his helmet a little to one side of his head in rather a jaunty sort of fashion, as though being a policeman was the most entertaining business imaginable. But seeing that the 'little craytures' were becoming alarmed, he asked, in what he considered to be a lower voice:

'And what can I be doin' for ye?'

'You—poliss-man?' asked Shapian timidly.

'Yes, me lad,' answered the constable, putting his helmet just a trifle more to one side, 'I'm a policeman, and a good one—and where would ye be wantin' to go?'

Shapian, along with his English, had quite forgotten the letter the missionary had given him, but now remembering one, he thought of the other, and pulling it out gave it to the officer, who read the address on the envelope and said:

'I see. I'm on dooty and cannot leave; but set ye down and wait, and I'll take ye there. And it's Patrick O'Reilly himself will see that no harrm comes to yez.'

And so our two young wanderers, feeling a good deal more at their ease, sat on the end of a long row of seats and waited. And the big policeman, who seemed to be in such continual good humour over nothing at all, asked them a number of questions, and Shapian, having got his English into pretty fair working order by now, told him most of the story. And the jolly Irishman became quite depressed about it, and said that he—Patrick O'Reilly himself, mind you—would take them to the people who owned the Park.

* * * *

And the friendly 'poliss-man' was as good as his word, for when he came off duty, he took them along to a restaurant and gave them a good meal. It was all very strange to Sajo and Shapian, and they were really rather frightened, but the thought that they were near Chikanee gave them courage. After the meal—and Chilawee had his share too—the policeman took them off to the address which the missionary had written on the envelope. There they were to stop the night, and their new friend said he would call for them in the morning. They were much too excited to sleep.

* * * *

Early the following day, Patrick O'Reilly called for his charges, as he had promised. But they did not go right away to the animal Park as they had expected, but to a large building in the city, where the Park owners had an office.

Afraid that at the last moment some accident might happen to the money, Shapian often felt at the lump under his shirt, where the little bag was; they were going to need it very soon now, and he was getting nervous. In the other hand he carried Chilawee in his basket, and beside him, never more than three feet away, Sajo walked with short, little-girl steps, her shawl wrapped about her head and shoulders.

There was a swift ride in an elevator, which they far from enjoyed, and then they found themselves, with the Irishman beside them, standing before a desk behind which sat a man.

And this was the man in whose hands was the fate of their little lost friend.

Sajo, who up till now had had such faith in her dream, became suddenly fearful and anxious, and trembled like a leaf. She had no idea what they were going to do if their offer was refused; and now that the moment had arrived she wanted to scream and run away. But she stood her ground bravely, determined to see it through, no matter what happened.

The man behind the desk was a youngish man with a pale, narrow face and a weak-looking chin. He had a cigarette in the corner of his mouth, burnt almost down to his lips, and one of his eyes was screwed up unpleasantly, to keep the smoke out of it, while he looked around with the other, so that at times he appeared cross-eyed. He spoke without removing the cigarette, squinting sharply at them with the eye that was in working order; and a very colourless, unfriendly looking eye it was.

'Well, what do you want?' he asked shortly.

There was a moment's silence, a very heavy, thick kind of a silence. I think that Sajo and Shapian had even stopped breathing. Then:

'Sorr,' commenced Pat the policeman, 'I telephoned Mr. H—— last night concerning me young friends there, and we were all to meet him here, to talk over a small matter of business, belike——'

'You can do your business with me,' broke in the young man, in no very civil tone. 'Mr. H—— is busy at present.' And he glanced towards a door that led into another room, which stood slightly open.

'You see, 'tis this way,' began Pat once more, when the young man looked at his wrist watch and interrupted again:

'Make it snappy, constable; I'm busy this morning.'

Pat got a little red in the face, and again started his speech, this time successfully. It was a speech that he had carefully rehearsed the night before, the story that, as he had said at the railroad station, was going to 'bring tears to the eyes of a heart of stone.' Evidently the young man did not have a heart of stone, however, for there were no tears; in fact, while Pat was talking, this impatient personage looked several times at his wrist watch, and lit a fresh cigarette from the stump in his mouth. Far from having a heart of stone, it began to look very much as though he had no heart at all. And the honest policeman became a little discouraged towards the last, and finished his tale rather lamely.

' . . . so the young people wants to buy the little baste back from ye: and I'll be so bold as to say that I think ye'll be doin' the Lord's own wurrk if ye let them have it.' And having done his best he stood there, nervously wiping his face with the big red handkerchief. The man straightened some papers on the desk and leaned back in his chair.

'Are you quite done?' he enquired coldly.

'Yes,' answered Pat, none too happily, for he began to fear, and with good reason, that he had lost the battle already.

'Oh,' said the clerk, 'thank you. Well, let me tell you'— his words fell like chips of ice on a plate of glass—'that beaver was bought in a fair and perfectly business-like way, and not from these ragamuffins at all, but from a reputable trader. We paid fifty dollars for him, which was a great deal more than the little brute was worth, and we have no intention of selling him back—unless we can get a good profit on the deal, and'—here he looked at the two little Indians—'I don't think your red-skinned *friends*, as you call them, are very well off judging by their looks.'

Pat turned redder than ever, but shrewdly suspecting that money alone could talk to this hard-headed fellow, he pushed Shapian forward.

'Money,' he whispered hoarsely, 'that money. Money, give it now!' And Shapian, sick with fear, for he had understood nearly everything, stepped forward, fumbled for a moment in the pouch, and dropped his little wad of money on the desk.

The clerk took it, counted it. He sniffed:

'There's only fourteen dollars here.' He handed it back. 'Nothing doing,' he said, and to make sure that everybody understood he added, for good measure: 'All washed up; no sale; no good; no! Get me?'

They got him; every one of them.

Nobody spoke, nobody moved; but to Shapian it was the end of the world—but no—was this true? And then the silence seemed suddenly to be choking him; the white face of the man behind the desk was getting bigger and bigger, was rushing towards him—the floor seemed to be going from under his feet—was he going to fall like a woman, faint, like a weak girl! He closed his eyes to shut out the sight of that pale, weak face with its one eye that leered at him so mockingly; he gritted his teeth, clenched his fists, and stiffened his young body upright in his old, proud way; and the dizzy feeling passed, leaving him cold and trembling.

And Sajo? She had been watching every move with painful eagerness, her eyes flitting from face to face like two frightened birds in a cage; and she had seen. No one needed to tell her.

They had failed. In just two minutes they had failed. She came softly over beside Shapian. 'I know, my brother,' she said very quietly, in such a strange little voice that Shapian looked at her quickly, and put his arm about her, while she stood close, looking up at him, 'I know now. He is not going to give us Chikanee. I was wrong—about my dream. We have come to the city not to get Chikanee, after all. I think—perhaps—it was—to bring Chilawee to him. That must be what the Waterfall meant; so they could be together—so they won't be lonesome any more. That must be it. So——'

And her childish voice fell to a whisper, and the little dark head drooped. 'Tell this man—I—give him—Chilawee—too.'

And she set Chilawee's basket upon the desk and stepped back, her face like a sheet of paper, her lips pale, and her eyes wide and dry, staring at the basket.

'What's this?' exclaimed the clerk, becoming angry. And Shapian told him:

' 'Nother beaver, Chilawee. His brother, that Chikanee, very lonesome. You keep him Chilawee too; not be lonesome then. Those are words of my sister. Me——' His voice stuck in his throat, and he couldn't say any more.

'Well, now,' said the clerk, smiling for the first time, though the smile improved his features very little. 'That's a horse of a different colour! We'll fix that up very quickly,' and he reached for his pen——

'NO!!' suddenly shouted the policeman in a terrific voice, bringing his fist down on the desk with a crash, so that everybody jumped, and the ink-bottles and paper-weights and the pens and the pencils all jumped, and even the pale young man jumped, and turned a shade paler and his cigarette jumped from his lips to the floor.

'No, you don't,' bellowed Pat in a tremendous voice.

'No son of an O'Reilly will stand by and see a couple of helpless kids bullyragged and put upon by ye, nor the likes o' ye. Ye're a black-hearted scoundrel,' he roared. 'An' I'm an officer of the law, an' I'll arrest ye for conspiracy, an' fraud, an' misdemeanour, an' highway robbery, an' assault, an'——' Here he ran out of the more attractive-sounding crimes, and growing fiercely started round the desk towards the now badly scared young man, who was backing away as hastily as possible in the direction of the other room, while Sajo and Shapian stood by with eyes as big as saucers. Just what this rather violent son of the O'Reillys intended to do, never became known, for at that moment the other door opened, and the fleeing young man found his line of retreat cut off, as he stumbled backwards into yet another guest to the party, and a voice, a very quiet, low voice said, 'Pardon me,' as there appeared just inside the room a slim, grey-haired old gentleman, who stood peering over his spectacles as this astonishing scene.

He gave a slight cough, and said again: 'Pardon me, if I appear to intrude,' and then, very politely, 'Won't you sit down?'

Pat still snorted angrily and glared at his intended prisoner, who was not at all sure if he *hadn't* committed some crime or another, so that his hands trembled a little as he fumbled with a new cigarette.

'Pray sit down, gentlemen,' again invited the grey-haired man.

They sat down; somehow you felt that you must do as this mild-mannered old gentleman asked you. And he it was that owned the Park; it was Mr. H—— himself.

'Now, let us talk matters over,' he suggested, looking from the policeman to the clerk, then to the children and back to the policeman again. 'Now, constable, on the telephone last night I promised to hear these children's story, and to consider what should be done. I have heard everything—from the other room, far better than if I had been here; for then certain things *did* happen, that would not otherwise have done so. I had already learned from you how far they have come, and what hardships and dangers they have been through to try and regain their pet. But I had to be careful; I had to know that it was not a fraud, and as I cannot understand their language, I wanted to see what they would do, before I could even consider the matter. Now I know the *whole* story, and I see that matters are going to be very difficult—for me.'

At this, the clerk looked around with a pleased expression, as if to say: 'There now, didn't I tell you?' Mr. H—— looked around too, tapping his spectacles on his knee:

'Everyone is listening, I hope?' he continued. 'Very good. Now, I heard these Indian children offer to give up their other pet, so the two little animals could be together, which proves to me their truthfulness. But, there is my side to be thought of. As George, here, says, it was a perfectly proper piece of business, and it cost me quite a sum of money. I cannot decide all at once. Moreover, it is not good for people, especially young people, for them to have everything they ask for—not, that is, unless they have worked for it.' And he looked at them a trifle severely through his glasses.

'But what are ye goin' to do about it, Sorr?' asked Pat, nearly exploding with impatience.

'Do?' queried this exasperating old man. 'Do? Oh, yes; I think I have decided what to do—just this!' And taking Chilawee's basket he beckoned the children over. 'There,' he said gently, 'there is your small friend. Now'— and becoming all at once very brisk and business-like, he wrote something on a card and handed it to Pat—'and now, go down to the Park with Mr. O'Reilly, *and get the other one.* He is yours; you most certainly have earned him.'

Shapian stared, his mouth open—did he hear aright? Or was this another one of Sajo's dreams in which he had become entangled? Or perhaps it was one of his own!

*   *   *   *   *

I greatly doubt if either Sajo or Shapian remembered very much about that trip to the amusement park, up to the time that Pat pointed out the entrance that could now be seen not far ahead of them. Then Sajo started to run. She was not pale now, and her eyes, that had been so dry and staring, were all aglow. Her shawl fell back unheeded, and her braids flew out and bobbed up and down on her shoulders, as her little moccasined feet pattered on the pavement. Behind her came Shapian, unable to keep up with her on account of carrying the basket, inside which Chilawee, tired of being cooped up for so long, was making a great uproar. Next came the stalwart Mr. O'Reilly, very red in the face, his helmet off, dabbing with his large red handkerchief at the head that had been 'bald as an egg for twenty years,' puffing and blowing like a tug-boat that had a light touch of asthma.

Once he bellowed, 'Hey! What is this, a race?' But the youngsters kept going right on, and it is very doubtful if they ever heard him; so he fell to grumbling, 'The little haythens, they'll be the death of me yet, so they will.' But he kept valiantly on.

Several passers-by stopped to look at the young Indians in their forest clothes, racing along the street with the policeman apparently chasing them. They heard, too, the shrill cries and wails coming out of the basket, as Chilawee objected loudly to the shaking up he was getting in all this hurry; so a few of them turned and joined this strange parade, and followed this small, running, black-haired girl.

And behind them all—far, far behind—there came another person: a tall, brown-skinned man who strode along so softly, yet so swiftly through the city streets. And he looked so dark and stern that people were glad to step aside and let him pass, and stared after him and said to one another: 'Who is that? What kind of a man is that?' But he never so much as glanced at any one of them.

There was some delay at the entrance, as the Park was not yet open for the day, but O'Reilly soon caught up, and showed his card, and they were let in. Quite a respectable crowd had gathered, and pushed in with them as soon as the gates were opened. The attendant, who was none other than our friend Alec the keeper, already knew what to do, as Mr. H—— had decided, at the last moment, to come too, and had given his orders and now stood in the crowd. At a nod from Mr. H——, the keeper led Sajo quickly over towards the beavers' pen. And all at once she was pale as a ghost again. She seemed to be running in a great empty space at the end of which, miles away, was a dark, ugly-looking row of iron bars, and now, now—she could see through them, and there—yes, there was a brown, furry little animal sitting up in the centre of them, and—— Oh! was it?—could it be?—yes, it was—Chikanee!

And Sajo, no longer shy, forgot the watching people, forgot the noisy city, forgot everything but the small furry body that was now so close, and rushing to the iron fence she threw herself on her knees in the gravel, thrust her two arms through the bars, and screamed 'Chikanee! Chikanee!! CHIKANEE!!!'

The little beaver, not believing, sat without a move, looking.

'It's me, Sajo. Oh, Chikanee!' The cry was almost a wail. Oh, had he forgotten?

For a moment longer the little creature stood there,

stock still, his chubby brown head cocked to one side, listening, as Sajo cried out again:

'*Chik*-a-*nee-e-e-e!!!*'—and then he knew. And with a funny little noise in his throat, he scrambled, as fast as his short legs would carry him, to the bars.

At that a little cheer broke out amongst the crowd, and there was a small commotion. And Alec the keeper now came forward and opened a small iron gate, and said, 'This way, Miss—a—Mam'selle—a—Senorita——' for he didn't quite know how he should address her, and was rather excited himself. And she rushed in, and kneeling down gathered the so-long-lost Chikanee up on her lap and bent over him; and they both were very still. And the gay head-shawl hid everything; and neither you, nor I, nor anyone else will ever know just what passed between those two on that fateful, that glorious, that never-to-be-forgotten morning.

And the grey-haired Mr. H—— took his handkerchief from his pocket and blew his nose rather loudly; and Alec the keeper had suddenly become troubled with a cough. 'Humph,' he said, 'hurrumph.'

'You bet,' exclaimed Pat the policeman in a hearty voice, although the keeper hadn't really said anything at all.

And now was to come the biggest thrill of all. Chilawee and Chikanee were to have *their* party now. They were only ten feet apart, and didn't know it! What a thrill was there!

So it was with wildly beating heart that Sajo and Shapian carried the basket in (one of them alone could never have handled this affair; it took the two of them to pull off the lid, they were in such a state); and they lifted Chilawee out, and set him down facing Chikanee, a short distance away. Then they stood and watched, breathlessly. For a second or two neither of the kittens moved, just stared at each other. Then, the truth slowly dawning in the little twilight minds, they crept towards one another, eyes almost starting out of their heads, ears wide open, listening, sniffing, creeping slowly forward until the creep became a walk, and the walk became a little shuffling trot, and now, sure at last that they had found each other, the trot broke suddenly into a gallop, and with a rush they met, head-on. And so violent was the collision, in a mild way of speaking, that, not being able to go any farther ahead, they went straight up on end, and with loud shrill cries they grasped each other tightly, and there, in front of all those people, began to wrestle!

The ceaseless, hopeless searching, the daily disappointments, all the misery and longing, the dreary empty nights of lonesomeness were over.

Big Small and Little Small were together again.

Before long they were disporting themselves all over the enclosure, and what had been a grim and ugly prison had now become a playground, the best use that it had ever yet been put to, I'll guarantee! And the children clapped their hands, and shouted, and laughed and hallooed at them excitedly, while the wrestlers, or dancers, or whatever you have a mind to call them, stepped around in high feather, enjoying to the utmost what must have been to them the greatest moment in all their lives, up to that time and perhaps for ever after. Never before had they given quite such a brilliant performance; and the people cheered them on, and laughed, and the grey-haired Mr. H—— waved his handkerchief quite furiously in the air, and I am not at all sure that he didn't shout a little himself.

Mr. O'Reilly, just about dying to take a part in this happy occasion which he had helped so much to bring about, and very proud to think that he was the only one present who knew the whole story, appointed himself Master of Ceremonies, and while he performed his duties as a policeman and kept back the crowd, he also played the part of a modern radio announcer, and explained to them what it was all about, and cracked jokes, and beamed around on everybody in the most amiable fashion, and otherwise enjoyed himself immensely. And he ended up by declaring for all to hear:

'Well, I'm seein' it, but, bejapers, I'll never believe it.'

And then, having been there, watching, for quite some time—for he had not wished to interrupt this little celebration—there now came out from behind the people another figure—a tall dark man in moccasins. He was the same man who, a short time before, had been seen striding so swiftly through the city streets in this direction. A quietness fell upon the wondering crowd as he stepped forward. But Sajo and Shapian, busy with their playfellows, never noticed him until a voice, *the* voice, the one they knew so very well, said softly there behind them, in the quiet, musical language of the Ojibways:

'O-way, the clouds have indeed gone from off the face of the sun. Now my sorrow has gone too, melted away like the mists of early morning. These people have done much—very much—for us, my children. Let us now thank them.

'My son, my daughter, take up your Nitchiekeewense, your Little Brothers.

'O-pee-pee-soway is waiting.'

Big Feather had come to take them, all four of them, back to The Place of Talking Waters, to the Land of the North-West Wind.

And Sajo's dream had, after all, come true.

The full story is told in 'The Adventures of Sajo and her Beaver People', by Grey Owl.

II

THE BEAVER PEOPLE

CONTENTS

CHAPTER ONE

THE HOME OF THE BEAVER PEOPLE

Right across the front of a small, deep pond, and blocking the bed of the stream that came out of it, was a thick, high wall of sticks and brush. It was all very tightly woven, and the chinks were filled with moss and the whole business well cemented with mud. Along the top of it a number of heavy stones had been placed to keep it solid. It was nearly one hundred feet long and more than four feet high, and the water flowed over the top of it through a narrow trough of sticks, so that the stream was wearing away at it in only this one spot, where it could be easily controlled. So well had it been made that it looked exactly as if a gang of men had been working at it—but it was animals, not men, that had built it.

This wall, which was really a dam, seemed as if it were holding the lake in place: which is really what it was doing, for without it there would have been no lake at all, only the stream running through.

The pond was bright with sunshine; very silent and peaceful it was, and so calm, that the few ducks dozing quietly upon its waters seemed almost to be floating on air, and the slim white poplar trees that stood upon its banks were reflected so plainly on its smooth surface, that it was hard to tell where the water stopped and the trees began. It was very beautiful, like a fairy-land, with its silver poplars and May flowers and blue water. And it was very still, for nothing moved there, and it seemed quite lifeless except for the sleeping ducks. Yet, had you watched patiently for a little while, being careful not to move or talk, or even whisper, you would have seen, before very long, a ripple on the water near the shore as a dark brown head, with round ears that showed very plainly, peered cautiously out from the rushes at the water's edge, and watched and listened and sniffed. The head was followed by a furry body, as its owner now came out in full sight and swam rapidly, but without a sound, to another place on the far shore, there to disappear among the reeds. The tall reeds swayed and shook for a minute as he worked there, and then he reappeared, this time holding before him a large bundle of grass, and swam over towards an enormous black mound of earth that we had been wondering about all this time, and dived, bundle and all, right in front of it. He had scarcely disappeared before another head, with another bundle, could be seen swimming from a different direction when—somebody moved, and with no warning at all, a huge flat tail came down on the water with a heavy smack, and with a mighty splash and a plunge the head and its bundle were gone. The great mound, taller than any of us, before which the swimmers had dived, was a beavers' house, and the dark brown, furry heads were those of the Beaver People themselves. And they had been very busy.

The lodge had been built up to more than six feet in height, and was a good ten feet across. It had lately been well plastered with wet mud, and heavy billets of wood had been laid on the slopes of it to hold everything firmly in place. It all looked very strong and safe-looking, like a fortress, and even a moose could have walked around on top of it without doing it a bit of harm. Up the side of it there was a wide pathway, on which the building materials were carried, and had you been more patient or careful awhile ago, or perhaps had the wind not played a trick on you and given you away to those keen noses, you might have seen old father beaver dig out a load of earth from the shore, go with it to the house, swimming slowly and carefully so as not to lose any, and then, standing upright like a man, walk to the top of the roof with the load in his arms and there dump it, pushing it into nooks and crannies with his hands, and shoving a good-sized stick in after it to keep it there.

And all this work had been done with a purpose. It was a very important time, this Month of Flowers, May, for inside that queer-looking home, hidden away from the eyes of all the world, were four tiny little kitten beavers. Woolly little fellows they were, perfectly formed, with bright black eyes, big webbed hind feet, little hand-like fore-paws and tiny, flat, rubbery-looking tails. They had marvellous appetites, and their lungs must have been very good too, for they were the noisiest little creatures imaginable, and cried continuously in long, loud wails that were very much like the cries of small human babies; and like any other babies, they needed a great deal of attention—and you may be sure that they were getting a lot of it too.

The living-room, or chamber, inside the lodge, was large enough for a man to have curled up in it with ease, and was very clean and sweet smelling, with its floor of willow bark and bed of scented grasses. The entrance was through a short, slanting tunnel, one end of which, called the plunge-hole, was in the floor, and the other end came out below, near the bottom of the lake. The dam held the pond up to a level nearly even with the floor, keeping the plunge-hole always full, so that the tiny kittens, who were a little wobbly on their legs as yet, could drink there without falling into it; or if they did (which happened rather regularly), they could climb out again quite easily. The whole tunnel and the outer doorway were under water, so that no land animals could enter, or even see it, unless they were first-class divers, which most of them are not. But if the dam should break and

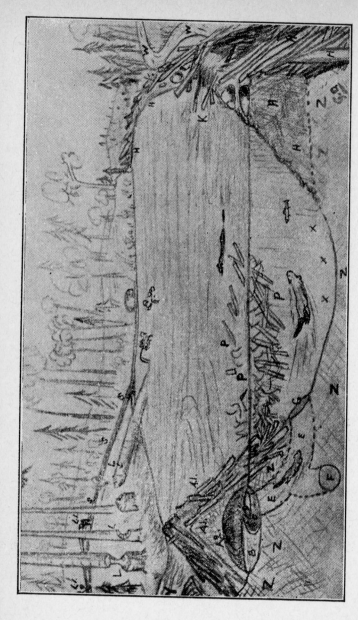

Plan of a beaver pond (*Drawn by Grey Owl*)

KEY TO DIAGRAM OF BEAVERS' WORKS ON PAGE 64

A.1, A.1.	Beavers' house.
A.2.	Interior of beavers' house. The living-room, or chamber.
B.	Sleeping platform.
C.	Lower level for drying off, draining into plunge-hole, at D.
D.	Plunge-hole.
E, E.	Tunnel leading out into deep water.
F.	Side, or emergency entrance, also used in discarding old bedding and used sticks.
G.	Main entrance.
H, H.	The dam.
K.	Spillway, for regulating overflow, and maintaining correct water level.
L, L, and L.1.	Trees felled, and partly felled by beavers.
P, P.	Feed-raft. Greatest portion under water, below the reach of ice.
S, S.	Beavers' runway, or hauling trail, used for removing required portions of tree, cut down by beavers, and marked L.1.
W, W.	Original stream resuming its course.
X, X.	Bottom of pond has been dug out below the feed-raft and in front of the dam, so as to obtain a greater depth of water. The materials thus obtained are used in the construction of the dam and house.
Y.	Stream running into pond, passing out at K.
Z, Z.	Former dry land, now under water on account of dam. Without the dam there would be no pond, only the stream.

Remarks.

(i) The house may be built close to the dam, but is often a considerable distance from it.

(ii) Note that the water level is exactly even with the plunge-hole.

(iii) Note that the swimming beavers have their front paws tucked up against their chests. The hind feet only are used in swimming, the front paws being used as hands, for working and picking up objects, or as feet for walking. Beavers do a considerable amount of walking on their hind feet, marching along slowly but very steadily; all loads consisting of earth, mud, or other loose materials, are carried in the arms, the beavers walking upright, like a man. The heavier sticks are drawn by means of the teeth, on all fours.

(iv) Beavers never use their tails for working in any way, except as a support in walking erect, or as a balancing-pole when clambering amongst fallen trees. In the water the tail is used as a rudder, sometimes as an oar, and for signalling by splashing on the water. This slapping sound is varied slightly, according to whether it is intended for an alarm signal, or as an indication of the owner's whereabouts. The kittens sometimes take a ride on their parents' tails.

F

let the saved-up water out, the beavers would be in grave danger, as not only could their enemies, such as wolves and foxes, find their way into the house, but the beavers would be unable to protect or hide themselves by diving suddenly out of sight, as you saw them do a little while ago.

If you look at the sketch you can see how it was all arranged, and will be able to realise how very important this dam was, and why the father spent so much of his time watching it and fixing any small leaks that appeared. He had, too, a pretty steady job keeping the trough, which you might call a regulator, clear of rubbish, so that the water could flow freely and not become too high, and so flood the house, but was always at exactly the right level. Between whiles, both he and the mother attended to their babies' every want, changing their bedding every so often, bringing in small sprays of tender leaves for them to eat, combing and brushing their wool (you could hardly call it fur), while they made queer, soft sounds of affection and talked to them in that strange beaver language that, at a little distance, sounds almost as though human people were speaking together in low voices. And the shrill wailing cries of the little ones, and their chattering, and their little squawks and squeals, could be heard even through the thick walls of the lodge, so noisy were they when they were hungry, or pleased or in some small trouble, which, one way and another, was pretty nearly all the time. And when either their father or their mother returned (they were never away together; one or the other was always on guard) from a trip to the so-important dam, or brought in new bedding of sweet-grass, he or she would give a low, crooning sound of greeting, to be immediately answered by a very bedlam of loud shouts of welcome from the youngsters, that went on long after it was at all necessary. They were never still unless they were asleep, and were continually scrambling around, and tussling together, and clambering over everything, and by the noise they made, seemed to be enjoying themselves immensely. And altogether they were pretty much like any other family, and were very snug and happy in their home.

The little ones were now old enough to try their hand at swimming in the plunge-hole, though at present this exercise consisted mostly in lying on top of the water, not always right side up, and going round and round in circles, screeching with excitement. And being so very light, and their fluffy coats containing so much air, they could not seem to sink deep enough for their webbed hind feet to get a grip on the water both at the same time, so they swam with first one foot and then the other, rolling from side to side and bobbing up and down, squirming and squealing and wriggling, while their parents passed anxiously around amongst them, giving them encouragement, or perhaps advice, in their deep, strong voices. From what I have seen of such goings on, it must have been rather a trouble-some time for the old folks, this business of learning to swim, but the youngsters seemed to be having a good time, which, as you will agree, is, after all, something to be considered.

But they would soon become tired, and climbing out on to the drying-off place (a little lower than the rest of the floor, so the water would soak away and not run all over the beds), every little beaver carefully squeezed, rubbed and scrubbed the water from his coat on the front, sides, back, every place he could reach, sitting upright and working very industriously, puffing and blowing like most of us do after a swim. Then, when this was all over and everybody was dry, or thought he was (some of them would topple over once in a while and made rather a poor job of it), the call for lunch would go up in a loud chorus,

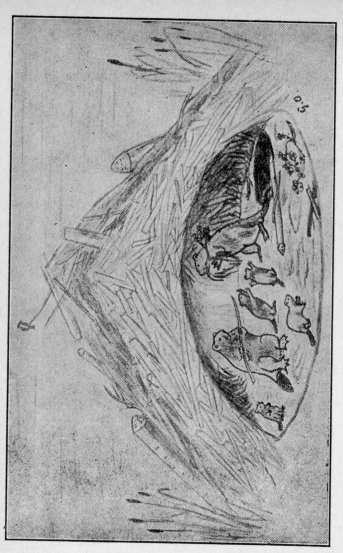

A beaver family at home (*Drawn by Grey Owl*)

and the new green leaflets and water plants that had been provided ahead of time (with the idea, no doubt, of putting a stop to the uproar as soon as possible), would be divided up, and pretty soon all the busy little jaws would be munching away, and the piercing cries died down to mumbles and little mutterings of contentment. And soon the little voices became quiet and the small black eyes closed, while they lay cuddled together on their sweet-smelling, grassy bed, with their tiny fore-paws, so much like hands, clutched tightly in each other's fur.

This would be their daily programme until, after perhaps three weeks, would come that glorious day when they would venture down the long, dim tunnel out into the brightness of the great unknown world that was all about them, but which they had never seen. And while they slept the old ones stood watch and guard, turn about, and took turns to inspect the defences of their castle and the dam on which their very lives depended, and kept a weather eye out for enemies, and collected food and bedding for when the babies should awaken, and carried on at the hundred and one jobs that make father and mother beaver a very busy pair of people during the latter part of May, the Month of Flowers.

From *The Adventures of Sajo and her Beaver People.*

CHAPTER TWO

McGINTY AND McGINNIS

A loud thud, a crash, the tinkle of broken glass, then silence. A sound as of a hand-saw being run at great speed by an expert, a bumping, dragging noise and a vicious rattling; then another crash; more silence.

'And what,' asked my guest as we neared the camp, 'is that; an earthquake?'

'That', I answered, with some misgiving, 'is the beavers, the ones you are coming to see!'

We entered the cabin, and the scene within was something to be remembered, the devastation resembling that left in the wake of a whirlwind. The table was down, and the utensils it had held had disappeared; a four-foot stick of wood protruded through a shattered window, and below the one that remained a quantity of wood had been piled. The washstand had been dissected and neatly piled in the bunk from which the blankets had been removed, these being included in a miscellany of articles such as dishes, moccasins, and so forth, with which the stove was barricaded. With hurried apologies to my visitor I assessed the damage, but beyond the disarrangements just mentioned, there was no serious harm done; that is, so far, no lives had been lost. I had been away two days, being delayed by soft weather, which, with its exhilarating effect on these animals, accounted for the attack on my humble fixtures.

There was no sign of the raiders, they having retreated to their house at the presence of a stranger but later they appeared and were introduced, and again retired, hopping and capering like little round gnomes, taking with them the peace offerings of chocolate and apples which they accepted from my companion.

McGinty and McGinnis, having put their house in order, were receiving from five to half-past, the guest providing the luncheon.

*　　　*　　　*　　　*　　　*

After open water on until early in June, the Spring hunt is in full swing on the frontier, and towards the end of that period the young beavers are born. The mother, who lives at this time in a separate lodge built and tended by the male or buck beaver, being generally larger than the rest of the family is much sought after. She is easily caught close to the house, and drowns at the entrance, whilst the kittens within listen in terror to her frantic struggles to escape. Crying continuously in child-like wails, they wait in vain for the big kindly brown body that is supporting their feeble existence, till the thin little voices are stilled, and two pitifully small bundles of fur cease to move, and lie in the house to rot.

A neighbouring hunter once came to me and asked if I would come and remove a live beaver from a trap from which the drowning-stone had come loose. After several hours' travelling we arrived at the spot, when my companion refused to go to the trap, saying he could not bring himself to inflict any further torture on the suffering creature.

'Wait till you see,' he told me.

I went to the place he described, and this is what I saw.

The beaver, a large female, moaning with pain, was shaking the trap that was firmly clamped on one front foot, and with the other she held close to her breast, nursing it, a small kitten beaver, who, poor little fellow, little knew how close he was to having his last meal.

I liberated her as gently as possible, and she made no effort to bite me.

With a sharp blow of my axe I severed the crushed and useless paw, when, parched with thirst, she immediately commenced to drink the blood which flowed from the wound as though it had been water. She then made slowly and painfully for the lake, only to return for the young one, who had become intensely interested in my footwear and was with difficulty prevailed on to enter the water. My companion approved of my action, although he had lost a valuable hide; he had seen the young one there, he said, and his heart had turned to water. This experience gave me some food for thought, and had its effect in hastening a decision I later arrived at, to give up the beaver hunt altogether.

Since that occurrence I have been the means of saving several pairs of small lives by following the carcase-strewn trails of the spring hunters, keeping the little fellows for about a year, after which period they get too reckless with the furniture to be any further entertained as guests.

Only those who have had the opportunity of studying living specimens over an extended period can obtain any idea of the almost human mentality of these likeable little creatures. Destructive they are, and their activities have much the same effect on the camp that two small animated sawmills running loose would have. They resemble somewhat an army tank, being built on much the same lines, and progressing in a similar manner, over or through anything that is in the way. After the first six months they can sink themselves through a six-inch log at a remarkable speed, biting lengthways with the grain of the wood for three or four inches, cutting the cross-section at each end and pulling out the chip.

They roam around the camp, and, with no evil intent but apparently from just sheer joy of living, take large slices out of table-legs, and chairs, and nice long splinters out of the walls, and their progress is marked by little piles and strings of chips. This is in the forepart of the evening. After 'lights out' the more serious work commences, such as the removal of deerskin rugs, the transferring of fire-wood from behind the stove into the middle of the floor, or the improvement of some waterproof footwear by the addition of a little open-work on the soles. They will gnaw a hole in a box of groceries to investigate, and are very fond of toilet soap, one brand in particular preferred, owing, no doubt, to the flavour incident to its school-girl complexion-giving qualities.

In Winter they will not leave the camp and I sink a small bath-tub in the floor for them, as they need water constantly. They make a practice of lying in the tub eating their sticks and birch-tops, later climbing into the bunk to dry themselves. To accomplish this they sit upright and squeeze and scrub the entire body. The water never penetrates beyond the guard hairs into the fur, but I suppose half a pint is no exaggeration of the amount of water one of them will squeeze out of his coat.

Tiring of this performance, I once removed the bench by which they climbed into the bunk and prepared for a good night's rest at last. I had got so used to the con-tinuous racket they created all night, between the drying-off periods, that, like the sailor who hired a man to throw pails of water against the walls of his house all night while on shore, I could not sleep so well without the familiar sounds, and during the night I awoke to an ominous silence. With a premonition of evil I lit the lamp and on taking stock saw one of my much-prized Hudson Bay blankets hanging over the edge of the bunk, and cut into an assortment of fantastic patterns, the result of their efforts to climb into the bed. The regularity of the designs startled me, and I began to wonder if I had gone suddenly insane, as nothing short of human agency, it seemed, could have cut those loops and triangles so symmetrically. Closer examination showed that the effect had been produced by their gathering the blanket in bunches with their forepaws, and cutting out a few pieces from the pucker, with more or less pleasing results.

Apparently realising, by the tone of certain carelessly worded remarks which I allowed to escape me, that they had gone a little too far this time, the guilty parties had tactfully retired to their trench under the wall, awaiting developments. This excavation they had made themselves. In building the camp I had made an aperture in the bottom log, and constructed outside it, at great trouble, what was, I considered, a pretty good imitation of a beavers' house. The first night in they had inspected my work, found it unsuitable, and proceeded to block up the entrance with sacking. They then commenced operations under the bunk, cutting a hole in the floor for the purpose, and digging out the soil. This dirt they trundled up from the depths, pushing it ahead of them, walking with the hind feet only, the fore-paws and chin being used to hold the mass together. Whilst thus engaged they rather resembled automatic wheelbarrows. They brought up, on each journey, perhaps the full of a two-quart measure apiece of earth, which was painstakingly spread on the floor as it accumulated; as the tunnel was dug out for about six feet beyond the wall, there was quite an amount of dirt brought into the shack, and there were times when I, also, was quite busy with a shovel. They took my interference in good part, hopping and capering about my feet in their clumsy way, much as I imagine elephants would gambol. They eventually got pretty well organised, one sleeping and the other working in shifts of two or three hours each.

After about a week of this a large mound of earth was

eventually patted down smooth and solid near the water supply, and operations apparently brought to a satisfactory conclusion; so I considered that we should all now take a good rest. But the beaver is not a restful animal. Doubtless they had been warned by those advertisements that remind us that 'those soft foods are ruining our teeth', for anything that offered resistance enough was bitten, the harder the better. Anything that gave good tooth-holds was hauled, and everything that could be pushed was pushed high, west, and sideways. Quantities of birch bark were carried into the bunk and shredded, this contribution to the sleeping accommodation supposedly entitling them to a share of the blankets. They apparently took notice that I put wood into the stove at intervals, and in a spirit, no doubt, of co-operation, at times they piled various articles against the stove. Once when I had been out for a short time, I returned to find the camp full of smoke, and a pillow, a deer-skin rug, and a map of some value to me, piled around the stove, and all badly scorched. Eventually I was obliged to erect a wire screen for safety.

It is remarkable that in spite of the orgy of destruction that went on for the first two weeks in camp, the door, an easy target, was not molested, and nothing was cut that would occasion an air leak into the camp. It is their nature to bank up against the intrusion of cold, and any loose materials that they could gather would be piled along the foot of the door, where there was a certain amount of draught. They barred the door so effectually on one occasion that I had to remove a window to enter the cabin.

Some mornings, at daylight, I would awaken to find one on each side of me sleeping, lying on their backs snoring like any human. At intervals during sleep they sharpen their teeth in readiness for the next onslaught.

When working, if the teeth do not seem to be in good shape, they pause for half a minute or so and sharpen them, repeating this until they are suited. The skull is fitted with a longitudinal slot which allows for the necessary motion of the jaws, and the resultant grinding is much like the whetting of an axe. The sound of an axe or knife being filed struck them with terror, and they would drop everything and run to me for protection, evidently thinking the noise came from some large animal whetting its teeth.

Beavers are the most persevering creatures I know of, man not excepted, and any job which they undertake is never abandoned until completed or proved impossible. They conduct their operations with all the serious intentness and economy of movement of trained artisans, and at the conclusion of each stage, small adjustments are made, and little pats and pushes given, either expressing satisfaction with the work or testing its solidity, I know not which.

These queer little people are also good housekeepers. Branches brought in for their feed are immediately seized on and piled to one side of the entrance to their abode. After feeding on pancakes or bread pudding, which they dearly love, the dish is pushed away into some far corner, along with the peeled sticks and other used portions of feed. Their beds, consisting of sacks, which they tear to shreds, mixed with shredded birch-bark and long, very fine shavings cut from the floor, after being used for a period, are brought out and scattered on the floor, apparently to dry, and taken in again after a couple of days. They spend long periods on their toilet. One of the toes of the webbed hind feet is jointed so as to bend in any direction, and is fitted with a kind of double claw; with this they comb their entire coat.

They seem capable of great affection, which they show

by grasping my clothing with their strong forepaws, very hands in function, pushing their heads into some corner of my somewhat angular person, bleating and whimpering. At times they clamour for attention, and if taken notice of they shake their heads from side to side, rolling on their backs with squeals of joy. If left alone for as long as twenty-four hours, on my return they are very subdued until I talk to them, when they at once commence their uncouth gambols and their queer wrestling.

They conduct these wrestling matches—for they can be called nothing else—by rising on their hind feet, supported by the tail, while the forepaws are locked in neck and under-arm holds, looking like dancers. In this position they strain and push, each striving to overcome the other, until one begins to give way, walking backwards, still erect, pushed by his adversary. Then, perhaps by the judicious use of his tail, he recovers, prevails, and the walk commences in the opposite direction. They go at this for all they are worth, and the changes in the expression of their voices, according to the luck they are having, are remarkably plain. This performance resembles a violently aggressive fox-trot about as closely as it does anything else, and is continued until one or the other allows his tail to double under him and is bowled over, protesting loudly.

One peculiarity they have is that, when hungry, they do not fawn as most domestic animals do, but complain loudly, standing on their hind legs and grasping at the dish. If the food is withheld they scold shrilly, beating the air with their forepaws. Also, if in their work they fail in some object such as the placing of a stick, they jerk the limbs and head violently and show every sign of irritation, resuming the attempt with an impetuous violence that either makes or breaks. But as a rule they are very tractable, and after feeding will follow one all over the camp, and at times are rather a nuisance in their desire to be taken up and petted.

The male beaver has, to a certain extent, the protective instinct that dogs possess, but not of course so highly developed. I had no knowledge of this until one day I happened to be resting on my blankets on the floor after a trip—a common custom in the woods—and lying with his head on my shoulder was a six-months-old buck beaver. An Indian friend came in, and busied himself in some way that brought him close to my head, on the opposite side from my furry chum. Immediately the latter crossed over and stationed himself between the man's feet and my person. My friend found it necessary to pass around me, and the beaver made a quick short-cut across my face, and again took post between us. Noticing this, and thinking it might be coincidence, my companion returned to his former position, and the beaver returned also, again using my face for a runway, blowing and hissing his disapproval. It is the more remarkable in that the man was a frequent visitor, and on the best of terms with both animals, playing with them by the hour during my absence.

Another time I received a visit from a passing hunter, and on his entrance, the female beaver, always more docile than her mate, must needs go over and make an inspection of the newcomer. The male also went towards him, with every sign of disapproval, and, on the stranger stooping to pat the other, reached out with his hand-like forepaw, and endeavoured to pluck her away.

Beavers are far from being the dumb creatures that most animals are. While working they are continually murmuring and muttering, even if alone, and if some distance apart occasionally signal their position by short, sharp cries. It is very rarely that speaking to them does not elicit some kind of answer.

They have a large range of distinctly different sounds. The emotions of rage, sorrow, fear, joy, and contentment are expressed quite differently, and are easily recognised after a short period of observation. Often when a conversation is being carried on they will join in with their vocal gymnastics, and the resemblance to the human voice is almost uncanny to those not accustomed to hearing it, and has been partly the cause of their undoing, as they are a very easy animal to imitate. When in trouble they whimper in the most dolorous fashion, and become altogether disconsolate. They have an imitative faculty of a sort, as any kind of bustle or quick moving around results in a like activity on their part, entailing a good deal of unnecessary gathering and pushing and dragging.

In common with most animals when tamed, beavers will answer to a name. In Canada an Irishman is known as 'a Mick', and the Indian word for beaver, Ahmik, is identical in pronunciation. So I gave my pair Irish names, of which the two most notable were McGinty and McGinnis, names they got to know very well, and they were suitable in more ways than one, as they both had peppery tempers, and would fight anything or anybody, regardless of size, always excepting each other or myself.

My camp became known as 'The House of McGinnis', although McGinty, whimsical, mischievous as a flock of monkeys, being the female, was really the boss of the place.

In the spring they become very restless, and nothing short of confinement in a wire pen will hold them. If allowed to go they will travel far and wide; they do not forget their old home, but will return after three or four weeks, and feed all around the camp, using it as a headquarters and eventually settling in the vicinity.

I turned the two Mc's loose last spring and they made

themselves a small house and a dam on a pond in a little valley back of a mountain called the Elephant, and would come when called and enter the cabin, which practice they have continued till the present time. They would always answer at intervals all the way down the lake, a not loud but very clear and penetrating sound, much like two notes of a violin sounded together, which changed to the 'hoo! hoo!' of welcome as they landed. They have ventriloquial powers, as have some other creatures in the forest country, and at times it was impossible to tell the direction from which they were coming. This no doubt is a protection against the prying ears of certain beasts with a taste for beaver meat.

Domesticated beavers will under no circumstances bite a human being, and if annoyed they will hold a finger between their dangerous teeth, exerting only just so much pressure, screeching with rage meanwhile. At a sharp exclamation they will release their hold. They are no mean adversaries in a fight, striking a series of quick raking blows with the heavy pointed claws of the front feet, and they have been known to kill dogs with one slashing bite of their razor-edged teeth, aimed always at the throat.

In the wild state they mate for life, and in captivity they show the same fidelity to the hand that reared them. They are a 'one-man dog', accepting neither food nor favour from strangers, puffing and blowing their dis-satisfaction at the near approach of one they do not know; yet this little beast, with the mind of a man and the ways of a child, can work his way very deeply into the affections of those who get to know him, and I have been offered sums of money out of all proportion to their actual value, but cannot bring myself to sell them into captivity.

From *Men of the Last Frontier.*

CHAPTER THREE

JELLY ROLL AND RAWHIDE

JELLY ROLL

One unhappy day, McGinty and McGinnis wandered away and were never seen again. Grey Owl searched for them in vain, and at last he had to accept the fact of their loss; meantime he had found another kitten beaver, and she soon became his close companion. Here is a picture of her when she had grown up.

Hunting season passed and the woods became again deserted and we, this beaver and I, carried on our preparations for the Winter each at his own end of the lake. The outlet, near which my cabin was situated, passed through a muskeg, and the immediate neighbourhood was covered with spindling birch which I was rapidly using up for wood. Jelly had by far the best part of it so far as scenery was concerned, being picturesquely established at the mouth of a small stream that wandered down from the uplands through a well timbered gully. Here she lived in state. She fortified her burrow on the top with mud, sticks and moss, and inside it had a fine clean bed of shavings (taken from stolen boards), and had a little feed-raft she had collected with highly unskilled labour, and that had a very amateurish look about it. But she was socially inclined, and often came down and spent long hours in the camp. When it snowed she failed to show up and I would visit her, and hearing my approach while still at some distance, she would come running to meet me with squeals and wiggles of welcome. We had great company together visiting back and forth this way, and I often sat and smoked and watched her working, and helped in any difficulties that arose. After the ice formed her visits ceased altogether, and becoming lonesome for her I sometimes carried her to the cabin on my back in a box. She did not seem to mind these trips, and carried on a conversation with me and made long speeches on the way; I used to tell her she was talking behind my back. She made her own way home under the ice in some mysterious manner and always arrived safely, though I made a practice of following her progress along the shore with a flashlight, to make sure she did. This distance was over half a mile and I much admired the skill with which she negotiated it, though she cheated a little and ran her nose into muskrat burrows here and there to replenish her air supply. One night, however, after going home, she returned again unknown to me, and in the morning I found the door wide open and her lying fast asleep across the pillow. Nor did she ever go outside again, evidently having decided to spend the Winter with me; which she did. So I bought a small galvanised tank for her and sunk it in the floor, and dug out under one of the walls what I considered to be a pretty good imitation of a beavers' house interior.

Almost immediately on her entry, a certain independence of spirit began to manifest itself. The tank, after a lengthy inspection was accepted by her as being all right, what there was of it; but the alleged beavers' house, on being weighed in the balance was found to be wanting, and was resolutely and efficiently blocked up with some bagging and an old deer skin. She then dug out at great labour, a long tunnel under one corner of the shack, bringing up the dirt in heaps which she pushed ahead of her and painstakingly spread over the floor. This I removed, upon which it was promptly renewed. On my further attempt to clean up, she worked feverishly until a section of the floor within a radius of about six feet was again covered. I removed this several different times with the same results, and at last was obliged to desist for fear that in her continued excavations she would undermine the camp. Eventually she constructed a smooth solid side walk of pounded earth clear from her tunnel to the water supply, and she had a well-beaten playground tramped down all around her door. Having thus gained her point, and having established the fact that I was not going to have everything my own way, she let the matter drop, and we were apparently all set for the Winter. But these proceedings were merely preliminaries. She now embarked on a campaign of constructive activities that made necessary the alteration of almost the entire interior arrangements of the camp. Nights of earnest endeavours to empty the woodbox (to supply materials for scaffolds which would afford ready access to the table or windows), alternated with orgies of destruction, during which anything not made of steel or iron was subjected to a trial by ordeal out of which it always came off second best. The bottom of the door which, owing to the slight draught entering there, was a point that attracted much attention, was always kept well banked up with any materials that could be collected, and in more than one instance the blankets were taken from the bunk and utilised for this purpose. Reprimands induced only a temporary cessation of these depredations, and slaps and switchings produced little squeals accompanied by the violent twisting and shaking of the head, and other curious contortions by which these animals evince the spirit of fun by which they seem to be consumed during the first year of their life. On the few occasions I found it necessary to punish her, she would stand up on her hind feet, look me square in the face, and argue the point with me in her querulous treble of annoyance and outrage, slapping back at me right manfully on more than one occasion; yet she never on any account attempted to make use of her terrible teeth. Being in disgrace, she would climb on her box alongside me at the table, and rest her head on my knee, eyeing me and talking meanwhile in her uncanny language, as though to say, 'What are a few table legs and axe handles between men?' And she always got forgiven; for after all she was a High Beaver, Highest of All The Beavers, and could get away with things no common beaver could, things that no common beaver would ever even think of.

When I sat on the deer-skin rug before the stove, which was often, this chummy creature would come and lie with her head in my lap, and looking up at me, make a series of prolonged wavering sounds in different keys that could have been construed as some bizarre attempt at singing. She would keep her eyes fixed steadily on my face all during this performance, so that I felt obliged to listen to her with the utmost gravity. This pastime soon became a regular feature of her day, and the not unmelodious notes she emitted on these occasions were among the strangest sounds I have ever heard an animal make.

In spite of our difference in point of view on some subjects, we, this beast with the ways of a man and the voice of a child, and I, grew very close during that Winter for we were both of our kind, alone. More and more as time went on she timed her movements, such as rising and retiring and her meal-times, by mine. The camp, the fixtures, the bed, the tank, her little den and myself, these were her whole world. She took me as much for granted as if I had also been a beaver, and it is possible that she thought that I belonged to her, with the rest of the stuff, or figured that she would grow up to be like me and perhaps eat at the table when she got big, or else that I would later have a tail and become like her.

Did I leave the camp on a two-day trip for supplies, my entry was a signal for a swift exit from her chamber, and a violent assault on my legs, calculated to upset me. And on my squatting down to ask her how the thing had been going in my absence, she would sit up and wag her head slowly back and forth and roll on her back and gambol clumsily around me. As soon as I unlashed the toboggan, every article and package was minutely examined until the one containing the never-failing apples was discovered. This was immediately torn open, and gathering all the apples she could in her teeth and arms, she would stagger away erect to the edge of her tank, where she would eat one and put the rest in the water. She entered the water but rarely, and after emerging from a bath she had one certain spot where she sat and squeezed all the moisture out of her fur with her forepaws. She did not like to sit in the pool which collected under her at such times, so she took possession of a large square of birch bark for a bath-mat, intended to shed the water, which it sometimes did. It was not long before she discovered that the bed was a very good place for these exercises, as the blankets soaked up the moisture. After considerable inducement, and not without some heartburnings, she later compromised by shredding up the birch bark and spreading on it a layer of moss taken from the chinking in the walls. Her bed, which consisted of long, very fine shavings cut from the flooring and portions of bagging which she unravelled, was pushed out at intervals and spread on the floor to air, being later returned to the sleeping quarters. Both these procedures, induced by the requirements of an unnatural environment, were remarkable examples of adaptability on the part of an animal, especially the latter, as in the natural state the bedding is taken out and discarded entirely, fresh material being sought. The dish out of which she ate, on being emptied she would shove into a corner, and was not satisfied until it was standing up against the wall. This trick seemed to be instinctive with all beavers, and can be attributed to their desire to preserve the interior of their habitation clear of any form of débris in the shape of peeled sticks, which are likewise set aside in the angle of the wall until the owner is ready to remove them.

Any branches brought in for feed, if thrown down in an unaccustomed place, were drawn over and neatly piled near the water supply, nor would she suffer any sticks or loose materials to be scattered on the floor; these she always removed and relegated to a junk pile she kept under one of the windows. This I found applied to socks, moccasins, the wash board and the broom, etc., as well as to sticks. This broom was to her a kind of staff of office which she, as self-appointed janitor, was for ever carrying around with her on her tours of inspection, and it also served, when turned end for end, as a quick, if rather dry lunch, or something in the nature of a breakfast food. She would delicately snip the straws off it, one at a time, and holding them with one end in her mouth would push them slowly in, while the teeth, working at great speed, chopped it into tiny portions. A considerable dispute raged over this broom, but in the end I found it easier to buy new brooms and keep my mouth shut.

Occasionally she would be indisposed to come out of her apartment, and would hold long-winded conversations with me through the aperture in a sleepy voice, and this with rising and falling inflections, and a rhythm, that made it seem as though she was actually saying something, which perhaps she was. In fact her conversational proclivities were one of the highlights of this association, and her efforts to communicate with me in this manner were most expressive, and any remark addressed to my furry companion seldom failed to elicit a reply of some kind, when she was awake, and sometimes when she was asleep.

To fill her tank required daily five trips of water, and she got to know by the rattle of the pails when her water was to be changed. She would emerge from her seclusion and try to take an active part in the work, getting pretty generally in the way, and she insisted on pushing the door to between my trips, with a view to excluding the much dreaded current of cold air. This was highly inconvenient at times, but she seemed so mightily pleased with her attempts at co-operation that I made no attempt to interfere. Certain things she knew to be forbidden she took a delight in doing, and on my approach her eyes would seem to kindle with a spark of unholy glee and she would scamper off squealing with trepidation, and no doubt well pleased at having put something over on me. Her self-assertive tendencies now began to be very noticeable. She commenced to take charge of the camp. She, so to speak, held the floor, also anything above it that was within her reach, by now a matter of perhaps two feet and more. This, as can be readily seen, included most of the ordinary fixtures. Fortunately, at this late season she had ceased her cutting operations, and was contented with pulling down anything she could lay her hands on, or climb up and get, upon which the article in question was subjected to a critical inspection as to its possibilities for inclusion into the rampart of objects that had been erected across her end of the camp, and behind which she passed from the entrance of her dwelling to the bathing pool. Certain objects such as the poker, a tin can, and a trap she disposed in special places, and if they were moved she would set them back in the positions she originally had for them, and would do this as often as they were removed. When working on some project she laboured with an almost fanatical zeal to the exclusion of all else, laying off at intervals to eat, and to comb her coat with the flexible double claw provided for that purpose.

Considering the camp no doubt as her own personal property, she examined closely all visitors that entered it, some of whom on her account had journeyed from afar. Some passed muster, after being looked over in the most arrogant fashion, and were not molested; if not approved of, she would rear up against the legs of others, and try to push them over. This performance sometimes created a mild sensation, and gained for her the title of The Boss. Some ladies thought she should be called The Lady of the Lake, others The Queen. Jelly the Tub I called her, but the royal title stuck and a Queen she was, and ruled her little kingdom with no gentle hand.

From *Pilgrims of the Wild*.

RAWHIDE

With the coming of Spring, Jelly Roll no longer slept indoors; but now a new arrival caused some excitement.

Just before the leaves came I set a trap for a marauding otter, on a stream some distance away. Jelly, on account of her optimistic outlook on life, would fall an easy victim. One morning on visiting the trap I found it gone, and projecting from under a submerged log saw the tail of a beaver. On pulling the chain I found resistance, and hauled out a living beaver, an adult. He had a piece of his scalp hanging loose, and half-drowned and scared almost to death, he made little attempt to defend himself. I removed the trap and took him home with me, tied up in a sack. His foot was badly injured, and being one of the all-important hind, or swimming feet, I decided to try and repair the damage before I liberated him. For the first twenty-four hours he hid himself in the Boss's late apartment, emerging only to drink, and he ate not at all. At the end of that time he came out into the centre of the camp with every appearance of fear, but I was able to pick him up and speaking kindly to him, offered him an apple which he took. I worked on him all night doing my best to inspire confidence, and succeeded to the extent that, crippled as he was, he commenced a tour of the camp, examining everything, including the door, which he made no attempt to bite through. In the course of his explorations he discovered the bunk, climbed into it up Jelly's chute, found it to his liking, and from then on ate and slept there, occasionally leaving it for purposes of his own, such as to dispose of his peeled sticks or to take a bath. He slept between my pillow and the wall, and nearly every night he became lonesome and came around to sleep in the crook of my arm till daylight, when he went back behind the pillow.

Although the weather was still cold I dared light no fire in the camp, as the noise of the stove drove him frantic; tobacco smoke caused him to hide away for hours. The operation of dressing his foot singlehanded was an undertaking of no mean proportions. It was swollen to an immense size, and two of the metatarsal bones projected through the skin. His teeth were badly shattered from his attempts to break the trap, and it would be weeks before they were again serviceable. The loose portion of his scalp had dried, and hung from his head like a piece of wrinkled hide, so I severed it and named him after it, calling him Rawhide, a name he still retains and knows.

For two weeks I worked hard to save the injured foot, and to a certain extent succeeded, although I believe the antiseptic effect of the leeches which clustered in the wound on his subsequent return to natural conditions, completed a task that taxed my ingenuity to the utmost. Whether on account of the attention he received, or because labouring under the impression that I had saved his life, or from very lonesomeness, I cannot say, but the poor creature took a liking to me, hobbling around the camp at my heels, and crying out loudly in the most mournful fashion when I went out. These sounds on one occasion attracted the attention of the Boss who forthwith raced up into the camp to ascertain the cause. On seeing a strange beaver she nearly broke her neck trying to get out of the camp, running in her haste full tilt into the door, which I had closed. She then reconsidered the matter, and returned to give the newcomer the once over. She at once decided that here was somebody who, being disabled, would be perfectly easy to beat up, which kind and chivalrous thought she immediately proceeded to put into execution. After a considerable scramble which ended in my having to carry the would-be warrior bodily down to the lake, objecting loudly, quiet was restored. She apparently resented the presence of a stranger in the home, no matter whose home; she ruled here as queen and had no intention of sharing her throne with anybody, it seemed, and I had to fasten the door from then on to keep her out.

On my patient becoming convalescent I bid him good luck and turned him loose, not without some feelings of regret, as he had become very likeable and affectionate. The next day, on visiting the domicile of the so-militant Queen, I saw a beaver and called it over. The animal answered and swam towards me, and my surprise can be well imagined, when I recognised the now well-known voice and lines of the cripple. He came to the canoe with every sign of recognition, followed me down the full length of the lake, and crept behind me into the camp. While there he lay for a time on a deerskin rug, and whimpered a little and nibbled gently at my hands, and presently slipped away to the lake again. And this practice he continued, sometimes climbing, with assistance, on to my knees and there conducting an assiduous and very damp toilet. He had nothing to gain by these manœuvres, and could have left at any time for parts unknown, had he been so minded. While I cannot go so far as to say that he was grateful, there is little doubt but that the treatment he had received while sick and confined to the cabin had had its effect on him, for he haunted me and the camp environs, unless driven away by the Boss, whose treatment of him was little short of brutal. She was insanely jealous and drove him away from the camp repeatedly, and would not allow him to approach me if she were present. On more than one occasion she chased him far down the stream below the outlet, where I could hear him crying out; but he always stuck to his guns and came back. In spite of her hostility he followed her around and did everything she did, hobbling on his injured foot emitting plaintive little sounds, and seeming almost pitifully anxious to fit into the picture and be one of the boys. He even succeeded, after several failures, in climbing into the canoe, only to be thrown out by the Boss, on which I interfered. He somehow gave the impression that he was starving for companionship, and Jelly refusing his advances he turned to me. He did all these unaccustomed things in such a dumb and humble way, yet with such an air of quiet resolution about him, that I always took his part against the more flamboyant and self-sufficient Jelly Roll. And by this very quiet insistence, this inflexible yet calm determination, this exercise of some unexpected latent power within him, he overcame one by one the obstacles imposed on him by his new environment and found his place at last, and eventually took control and became no more a suppliant but a leader.

The Boss had for me the friendship that exists between equals; we were rough and tumble playfellows, old-timers together who could take liberties with one another and get away with it. But the stranger, for all his harsh sounding and rather unsuitable name of Rawhide, seemed to want only a little kindness to make him happy, and was as gentle as the touch of the night wind on the leaves; yet I once saw him, driven to passion by too much persecution, shake the Boss like she had been a paper bag.

And I think she owes it to him that she lives to-day.

A rogue beaver, old and watchful and wise, his colony no doubt destroyed by hunters, now gone bad and ranging far and wide, descended on these two while I was away and tried to take possession. On my return I found Jelly laid out on the landing before the camp. A thin trail of blood led to the door but she must have been too weak to enter, and had dragged herself back to the water's edge to wait. Her throat was torn open, some of the parts protruding; her bottom lip was nearly severed, both arms were punctured and swollen and nearly useless, and her tail had been cut completely through at the root for over an inch of its width and there were besides a number of ugly gashes on the head and body. There was nothing I could do save to disinfect the wounds. Meanwhile she lay inert, her eyes closed, moaning faintly, while her blood oozed away into the mud of the landing she had so stoutly maintained as her own; and in her extremity she had come to me, her friend, who could only sit helplessly by, resolving to let her quietly die beside her pond, where she had once been a small lonesome waif, before she was a queen.

I sat beside her all night, and at intervals fed her with milk from a glass syringe. Towards morning she seemed to draw on some hidden resources of vitality and bestirred herself, and slowly, painfully, crawled up into the cabin;

for I did not dare to pick her up for fear of opening up her now clotted wounds afresh. She stayed with me all that day, leaving again at night, in bad shape but with the best part of two cans of milk inside her, and apparently on the mend. Only the marvellous recuperative powers possessed by wild animals and man in a state of nature, brought her around. I did not see her again for a week, but often passed the time of day with her through the walls of her abode, and heard her answer me. By the signs I discovered around the lake and from what I saw of him another time, the visitor must have been of enormous size, and there is no doubt that had she been alone she would have been killed. Rawhide also bore marks of the encounter but to a less degree, and I am sure by what I have since seen of his other abilities, that his assistance must have turned the tide of battle.

From then on the two of them lived in perfect harmony, and have done ever since.

From *Pilgrims of the Wild*.

THE KEEPERS OF THE LODGE

Grey Owl's success in befriending the beavers attracted the notice of the Canadian Government, and it was decided to establish him in the Prince Albert National Park, Saskatchewan. So off he went with Jelly Roll and Rawhide to their new home, Beaver Lodge, beside a lake. The beavers soon turned part of the log-cabin into half of their own home with the other half outside by the lake.

By this time Jelly Roll and Rawhide had become mates, and as time went by the cabin became the headquarters of several generations of their offspring.

It was not all fun sharing a log-cabin with such a large and energetic family, as the following description will show.

For the past two months I have been trying to write a book. Whether it is a good book or not I leave you to judge. But if it isn't, I can give you a number of very good reasons why.

About the best of these is a bumping, banging, thudding noise, accompanied by wailing, screeching and chattering in what sounds like a foreign tongue from some obscure corner of the earth's surface. This is caused by a number of beavers of assorted ages from one to seven years, expostulating with each other over the ownership of a pile of stovewood that I have, in a weak moment, left before the door of Beaver Lodge. The wood is mine of course, but this in no way lessens its suitability for material to be added to the already impregnable defences of the beavers' house that has lately been built a short distance down the shore. The only real difficulty seems to be that of deciding who is to have the honour of removing it. There are sounds of strife, sounds of anguish, sounds of outraged sensibilities, and sounds of supplication. When a beaver wishes to be heard, he is not without the means. Up to three years, the age of maturity, each generation has an intonation all its own, and every individual has a different voice. As a tribe, or race (or whatever division they come under), they step heavily, pound violently, haul, push and heave vigorously, and are fanatically determined in the carrying out of any project they have decided, at all costs, to complete. Hence the noise.

I try to concentrate, to marshal my ideas for your approval. There is a fresh sound, a loud clattering as of a tin dish being thrown with monotonous and devilish persistence against a stone. I am trying to write about beavers, but begin to feel a good deal more like writing something vivid about a bull-fight. So, I put down my pen and go outside. I see at a glance that I am a little late; the wood is nearly gone. It appears that while the second and third generations have been squabbling over who is going to have all the wood (the fourth is too young to do much but squall), the first, or largest generation has been quietly getting away with most of it. They are moving up and down, one coming and one going, with that clockwork regularity that makes two beavers engaged in transportation work look like an endless chain. I like my food cooked, but not at this price; it will be cheaper to eat it raw. So I push the remainder of the stove-wood into the lake, so that there will be no further discussion. This makes a difference, the difference being that the fun will now take place inside the cabin. Three of the yearlings, finding themselves temporarily unoccupied now that the wood is satisfactorily disposed of, come bustling in through the door, bringing their potentialities for mischief along with them. They wander around for a while, peering into everything, fairly dripping with curiosity and exuding wilfulness from every pore, eventually entering into a spirited contest over the remains of a box of apples, with the usual sound-effects. Having pacified and bribed them, with an apple apiece, to go away, I pick up my pen and resume my work, although I have not yet been able to determine the cause of that exasperating tinny clattering; the only tin dish outside is the one used to hold the beavers' rice, and it is still in its place, full and intact.

I have just got nicely started when, in the middle of a word, there comes another sound, a kind of a rich, satisfying sound, as of some keen-edged tool of tempered steel cutting into very good timber; it also sounds not unlike a beaver's teeth going into a canoe. I put down my pen, go out and investigate. It is, indeed, a beaver's teeth going into a canoe. You see, an overturned canoe looks a little like part of a tree, and offers the same excellent opportunities for idle teeth; the canvas looks something like bark, is the same colour and comes off as easily, with the nice, interesting sound mentioned above. Of course, even if you are a beaver, you can't eat green paint and canvas, but it's great fun and you can always spit out the paint. After a short altercation I put the canoe on the rack out of reach, soothe injured feelings with an apple, and go in again. I pick up my pen and complete the unfinished word.

I write uninterruptedly for perhaps fifteen minutes. Then commences that infernal clattering again, as though someone were dropping a tin plate repeatedly on the hard ground. It is now broad daylight, so I take my observations through the window, and am enlightened. A beaver of the third generation, old enough to be effectively mischievous, is alternately lifting and dropping on the ground the tin dish of rice. Those of the younger beavers who haven't yet learned to eat out of a receptacle, are content to dump the rice out on the ground; they can get at the rice easier that way. They then throw the dish in the lake, to join a number of other articles, besides dishes, that they have consigned to a watery grave. But this fellow has another notion, apparently. I watch the process interestedly. He picks up the dish with his teeth, keeping it right side up, and tries to walk away with it; he wants, for some reason best known to himself, to take the whole works home with him. The container is large, and he is not a very big beaver, and as soon as he stands upright it overbalances and falls. He picks it up and tries again, and it falls again, and so on, so many times to the minute. I begin to count them. The clang of the now empty pan seems to amuse him, and he keeps experimenting, until at last he discovers the way. He finds the point of balance, stands erect with the dish in his mouth, and placing both his hands under it to support it, starts to march down the incline to the lake. Seeing my dish about to be sacrificed I rush out, whereupon the young scallawag slides down the slippery approach and throws himself, dish and all, into the water. The pan rocks for a moment or two and sinks. The beaver birls round and round in the water, in celebration of his success, and also disappears, and I am left in complete possession of the empty landing.

This is a pretty fair example of the perseverance of these animals, who will try every possible means to accomplish their ends, until they have either succeeded, or proven the project to be impossible.

And I think you will agree that any man who will attempt to write a book whilst surrounded by a number of these exceedingly active and industrious creatures, can claim to have learned from them at least the virtue of patience. And this is no idle alibi, for at the moment, even as I write, a full grown beaver has just burst open the door and entered, bringing in, as an addition to the beavers' house that stands here beside the table, a stick six or seven feet in length. And it is no unusual thing for beavers, walking erect with loads of mud supported in their arms, to pass around my chair on their way to further plaster this house within a house, and not infrequently I am obliged to cease my work, lift the chair out of their way, and stand aside until their job is done.

*   *   *   *   *

The beavers, in their immunity, have become over bold, and instead of disappearing from view at the first unusual sound, and abolishing themselves from the landscape as though they had never even existed, they now stand waiting curiously to see what they are to run away from, long after their less cultured brethren would have been in the lake, sunk and out of danger. The cuttings are often far from water, and ever I must haunt the beavers' works, armed against possible and very probable marauders such as bears, wolves, coyotes, and even great horned owls that might try for a straggling kitten. And as the mediæval watchman passed along the streets of cities calling, 'All's well—All's well,' so, as I go, I take up my own monotonous cry, 'A-a-a-all r-i-i-ight—A-a-a-all r-i-i-ight.' This is my signal and identification, and well known to them, and without such utterance I never venture forth, so they may know that any unannounced approach is not I, and therefore dangerous.

One night on checking up, as I do almost hourly, after an intensive and widespread search I could find neither hide nor hair of Jelly Roll. Bears are numerous here, and tragedy lurks always threatening in the shadows. Unable by any means to find her, I decided to remain at my original stand, and commenced to send out certain searching calls such as she only would respond to. Patiently, but with growing uneasiness, I sent out my S.O.S. at intervals, casting the beams of a powerful electric torch in all directions. I kept this up for some considerable time and was beginning to feel the least bit anxious, when all at once I felt a tug at my leg, and turned the light downward to see standing at my feet, erect and looking up at me, the missing Jelly Roll. She was bone dry, and beginning to be impatient, and must have been there all the time. I didn't blame her for being out of patience, in a way. No doubt she and Rawhide, figuring that they own me, talk me over between themselves, and I had a feeling that this fresh stupidity of mine was, to her way of thinking, only one more example of my lack of culture and training; and I sometimes imagine that they both must be at times a little disappointed in me, after all the trouble they have been to, getting me into shape.

I have sat beside her on guard whilst she, confident in

my protection, tired and weary with her working, slept in the moonlight that flooded the mouth of a runway. This often happens, and as she lies there with her head on my knee as in the old days, making soft murmuring noises in her dozing, she is no more Queen of the Beaver People, but is just Jelly the old-timer—the Tub. If I move she will clutch at my clothing to keep me there, and make sounds I hear from her at no other time.

Despite her affection and the disarming innocence of her softer moments, Jelly Roll is the most self-willed creature in all the world. She knows what is forbidden, and constantly attempts to outwit me; but on being caught red-handed, as she nearly always is (she is the most guile-less, transparent old bungler imaginable when it comes to artifice), she flops down and flounders around in an apparent agony of fear, though she must know that she had nothing to fear but my disapproval and reproach, to which she is very sensitive indeed. On being comforted (a little later, of course), she will jump up at once and start to frolic; yet the lesson is not forgotten—not that day, any-way. A scolding from me puts her in the greatest misery, but a peremptory word or two, or an overt act, from another, causes instant and sometimes very active hos-tility. She has a strong instinct for protection towards her young, as has her partner. This is a trait possessed by most animals but, like some dogs, she goes further and without training of any kind, stands with threatening attitude and voice between a stranger and myself, should I happen to be lying down. However, if I am standing up, I can darned well take care of myself. She herself has no fear whatsoever of strangers, and will face any crowd, and go among them, inspecting them and taking charge with the most unshakeable aplomb.

She still polices the estate, as before, and should someone unknown to her be in the canoe she quickly gets to know about it, and knowing that I will not allow her to approach the canoe too closely when someone else is with me, she will play sly and swim beneath the surface, bobbing up suddenly alongside from nowhere at all with a deep, explosive grunt, not always of welcome. She cannot climb into this high-sided canoe unless her diving board is attached, but she will stick pertinaciously to the canoe, swimming underneath it, getting in the way of the paddle and doing everything possible to retard our progress; failing this she will escort the canoe ashore in the hopes of getting a chance to investigate the newcomer. This intention I must of course frustrate, as my guest will have only my word for it that she does not mean business, or that taking a leg off him is not her idea of good clean fun. Her perception of what is going on about her is very keen; she undoubtedly knows what it is all about, and takes a lively interest in many things not supposed to be of interest to animals. So also does Rawhide, though in a less obvious manner; yet on occasion arising he shows a matter-of-fact familiarity with many things about him, that his indifferent and sphinx-like demeanour would seemingly have left him unconscious of; evidently a keen observer in a quiet way. At times genial, almost affable, withal somewhat of a busybody and stuck into everything, there are occasions when Jelly Roll carries about her something the same air of disapproval one detects in the presence of a landlady with whom one is a little behind with the rent.

On his visits to the cabin Rawhide acts exactly as if he could not hear the radio, even closing his purse-like ears, as beavers are able to do in order to exclude water, shutting them tight against any programme of which he does not approve. But Jelly takes in this machine the almost feverish interest she has in anything new, standing sometimes stock-still, listening, with hands and fingers making queer aimless little movements, a stiff, brown column of intense attention. During one broadcast she was present at, the characters in a play became engaged in a fight and one of them was killed. The sounds of battle had a strong effect upon her. Her eyes began to stare, her hair became erect and she commenced to blow loudly. On the woman of the cast falling unconscious, the resulting uproar had such a strange effect on her, and she stood so stiffly and unnaturally, and showed, in the unmistakable way she has, such a strong disapproval of the whole business, as to be rather alarming. She began to weave and totter back and forth, and I wondered if she too were not about to faint—though actually she had more than half a mind to join in the conflict. So to save the radio from being wrecked I gave her an apple and broke the spell. She is still a paper addict, and I keep in the cabin for her special convenience a bag full of nice crackling papers, the very sound of which drives her frantic with joy, and this she always looks for in its accustomed place on her visits. These occur, in fine weather, almost hourly, and whilst on deck she likes to stir things up; she weighs all of sixty pounds, and can stir up very effectively when so minded, and her entry into any gathering that may be assembled here, injects into the proceedings all that feeling of delightful uncertainty that one has in the presence of a large fire-cracker that is liable to explode at any moment.

She has often stolen papers of some value to me, and gets all the envelopes from my correspondence, which is considerable. She has a preference for periodicals, as the advertising pages are on stiffer paper than is the reading matter, and they can be induced to make a more deliciously exciting noise, and when she gets hold of one of these she is beside herself with happiness, shaking her head back and forth as she walks out of the door with it, her whole person emanating triumphant satisfaction. Once, at the request of an onlooker who thought that her patriotism should be tested, I placed before her three separate magazines, Canadian, English and American. After giving each one a searching examination, she chose the Canadian periodical and walked out with it. The visitor was rather taken aback, and still believes that I made some secret sign to her that she acted on. Pure accident, naturally, but the effect was quite good. Sometimes the sober Rawhide joined in these escapades, a few of which were positively uncanny, had they not been so utterly ridiculous. Beavers like to have dry cedar on which to exercise their teeth, it being nice and crunchy. As there were no cedars in that particular area, I took a bundle of shingles that had been left over from the roofing of my new cabin, and left them down on the shore for the beavers' use. Next morning I found that the fastenings had been cut off and neatly laid to one side, and the whole of the shingles removed. I wondered what was the purpose of this wholesale delivery, until, the next afternoon a man came to see me, who wanted very much to see the beavers at work. It was a few minutes' walk to the beavers' house, and as we drew near to it I noticed that it had a strange appearance, and arriving there we, this man and I, stood perfectly still and stared, and stared, and *stared—one side of the beavers' house was partly roofed with shingles!*

At length my visitor asked in a hushed voice: 'Do you see what I see?' I replied that I did. 'Exactly!' he agreed. 'We're both crazy. Let's get out of here.' We retired, I remember, in awe-struck silence, went to the cabin and drank quantities of very strong tea. I asked him if he didn't care to wait and see the beavers themselves, and he shook his head. 'No,' he answered, 'I don't believe I do. I'm not long out of the hospital and just couldn't stand it, not to-day. Some other time——' and went out of there muttering to himself. The explanation is of course quite simple. Beavers will seize on any easily handled material they find, and make use of it for building purposes (this includes fire-wood, paddles, dish-pans, clothing, etc.), and seized on the shingles at once, and being unable to push the shingles, owing to their oblong shape, into the mesh of the structure, had just left them lying there on the sides of the house.

But the star performance was one of Jelly's very own. One afternoon, shortly after the affair of the shingles, I heard a woman's scream, long and piercing, from the direction of the beavers' dam. Beside the dam ran the trail that led to my cabin. Now Jelly is a real watch-dog when I am not around, and at that time, in her younger days would lie in ambush, waiting for people so she could chase them (a practice since abandoned), and thinking she had caught somebody in her ambuscade and was scaring them to death, I hustled down to the dam to see about it. I found there a woman, evidently badly frightened, who exclaimed: 'Do you know what I have just seen?—a beaver going by with a paint brush!' 'A who going by with a what?' I demanded. 'A *beaver* going by with a *paint brush!*' she affirmed. 'Oh, I know you won't believe me, but that's what I saw.' Accustomed though I was to the hare-brained exploits of these versatile playmates of mine, this rather floored me, so I simply said: 'Oh!' and led the woman to the cabin. I left her there and went to the stump on which the man who had been painting the new roof had left his paint brush. Sure enough, it was gone, removed by busy fingers whose owner was always on the watch for something new. So I told this to the lady, and the matter was explained. But it never was explained to me why, later in the evening, I should find lying at the foot of the stump, with the fresh imprint of four very sharp incisor teeth upon it, the missing paint brush. Why was it returned? Your guess is as good as mine.

And reader, believe it or not, all during the latter part of this last paragraph, a beaver of the third, or inexperienced generation, finding that his efforts to open the door have been persistently disregarded, has been trying to get in through the window. It will I think, be cheaper, in the long run, to open the door. I have opened the door, and there are three beavers; I'll be seeing you later, reader.

To resume. To-day there were a large number of visitors here. The moose, a great bull with his antlers half developed, but for all that wide and formidable-looking enough, obligingly stalked down within a distance of a few yards and had a look at the crowd. They also, with mingled feelings, had a look at him. But Jelly Roll, after all the complimentary things I have written about her, let me down rather badly. Having demolished a chocolate bar offered her by a lady, she turned her back on the entire assemblage, took a branch I proffered, smelled it, threw it to one side, launched herself into the lake, and was no more seen. This behaviour is not usual with her. In fact, at times she is rather difficult to get away from, and is one of those ladies who do *not* take 'No' for an answer. She is very self-assertive, and has no intention of being overlooked when there is any company around or anything especially good to eat to be had. At these times she is very much to the fore, assuming a bustling and extremely proprietary manner, and whether excited by the presence of strangers or on account of the reward she has come to know that she will get, or from sheer devilment, I cannot pretend to say, but she will very often stage a little act. She first inspects, one by one, the visitors who, by the way, are seated well out of the way in the bunk—she thoroughly enjoys a taste of good shoe leather—and if pleased, which she generally is, she commences her show. This consists in trundling back and forth the bag of papers, the removal perhaps of the contents of the bag, with resultant rumpus and mess, the replacing of sticks removed by me from the beavers' house for that purpose, and various other absolutely unnecessary evolutions. And all this with such an air of earnestness and in such breathless excitement, and with such manifest interest in the audience and such running to and fro to them between the scenes, that those present could be excused for supposing it to be all for their especial benefit. We have, of course, a slight suspicion that the anticipated reward may have some bearing on this excessive display. But a good time is had by everyone present, and that is all that really matters. Speaking to her conversationally attracts her instant, if casual attention, and often elicits a response. She has come to understand the meaning of a good deal of what I say to her; but this faculty is not confined by any means to her alone. The beaver is an animal that holds communication by means of the voice, using a great variety of inflections, very human in character, and the expression and tone indicate quite clearly to human ears what emotions they are undergoing; and this resemblance makes it fairly easy for them to understand a few simple words and expressions. I have made no attempt to train them in this, or in anything else; everything they do is done of their own free will, and it has all been very free and easy and casual. I do not expect them to knuckle down to me, and I would think very little of them if they did; nor do I let them dominate me. We are all free together, do as we like, and get along exceedingly well together. Rawhide I know, for one, would not tolerate for a moment any attempt to curtail his freedom or to curb his independent spirit. He is rather a solemn individual, and he ignores nearly everything that is not directly connected with his work and family. Yet even he has his times to play, and carries always about him an undefinable air of 'howdy folks and hope everything's all right and it's a great world.' The obstinacy of a beaver when opposed by any difficulty, also applies if you try to get him to do anything against his will, but personal affection has a great influence on their actions, and given sufficient encouragement and a free hand they will learn, of themselves, to do a number of very remarkable things quite foreign to their ordinary habits. Rawhide, for instance, has learned to kick open the door when walking erect with a load in his arms. He built his house inside mine, and will climb into a canoe and enjoy a ride, as does his life partner. Jelly Roll is able to open the camp door with ease from either side, pushing it open widely to come in, and making use of a handle I have affixed to the bottom of the door to get out again. And as the door swings shut of itself, she has succeeded in creating the impression that she always closes the door behind her, which is all to the good. Though he rarely answers me as Jelly does, Rawhide listens closely, with apparent understanding, when I talk to him, and dearly loves to be noticed, often rushing up to me when I meet him by chance on a runway, and clasping my fingers very firmly in his little hands. But his old, wild instincts are very strong in him, nor do I try to break them; and he has not bothered to learn very many of Jelly's tricks, being, it would seem, quite above such monkey work. But he will come at my call, when disposed to do so, and can be summoned from his house upon occasion, he selecting the occasion.

In the more serious matters, however, Rawhide plays a more notable part, being direct in all his actions, and rather forceful in his quiet way, and in family matters is something of a martinet. For instance, he took a strong objection to Jelly Roll sleeping in my bed, at a time when they lived together with me in the cabin. She had been always used to sharing my bed and no doubt expected to keep it up all her life. But when he would awaken and find her absent from his couch, he would emit loud wailing noises, and come over and drive her away into their cubby-hole. To see him pushing her ahead of him, she expostulating in a shrill treble of outraged sensibilities, was about as ludicrous an exhibition as I have ever seen, and when with childish squeals she would break away and rush to me for protection from this unwelcome discipline, her wonted dignity all gone, she would stick her head in under my arm and lie there like the big tub she is, imagining herself safe but leaving her broad rear end exposed to his buffeting. And this ostrich-like expedient availed her very little, for Rawhide is about the most determined creature I ever knew, and always gained his point. And from then on, not wishing to be the cause of further family discord I discontinued my habit of sleeping on the floor.

But don't get the impression that Jelly only plays and never works. She does both with equal enthusiasm. Jelly, when on labour bent, fairly exudes determination. She will arrive at a runway under a great head of steam, and on striking shore there is no perceptible pause for changing gears; she just keeps on, out, and up, changing from swimming to walking without losing way. Her progress on land is not so much a walk as it is the resolute and purposeful forward march of a militant crusader, bent on the achievement of some important enterprise. Her mind made up, without further ado she proceeds immediately to the point of attack, and by an obstinate and vigorous onslaught will complete in a remarkably short space of time, an undertaking out of all proportion to her size. Sh accepts my occasional co-operation right cheerfully, but being, as she is, an opportunist of the first water, instead of making a fair division of labour she sees her chance to get that much more work done, and attempts to haul sticks of timber or move loads that are more than enough for the two of us, attacking the project with an impetuous violence that I am supposed, apparently, to emulate. Her independence of spirit is superb, and she blandly disregards my attempts to set right any small mistakes I think she has made (a practice I have long ago desisted from). She is pretty shrewd and belongs to that rare type of worker who finds the day all too short for his purpose.

For a resting-place she has a little, low pavilion backed by a large fallen tree and roofed with spreading spruce limbs. This bower looks out upon the lake, and in her spare time here she lies and gazes out across the water, and heaves long sighs of pure contentment. I have often caught her talking to herself in a low, throaty little voice, which on my approach would drop to the deep-toned sound of welcome. Beavers are the most articulate of any beasts I know of and perhaps I can best describe the sounds they make as being very nearly those I imagine a child of three would utter, if he had never learned to talk in any language; and Jelly Roll's attempts to make herself intelligible to me are often quaint and childlike, and not a little pathetic. Rawhide is not nearly so talkative as some, and is much given to working apart from the others, and this is characteristic of most heads of beaver families. Although he has, in his own quiet and unassuming way, adapted himself very thoroughly to camp life, he retains nearly all the characteristics of a wild beaver in so far as his work is concerned. He looks with a jaundiced eye on my attempts at assistance, and is expert beyond the power of even Jelly to attain to; whether as a result of his early training, or because the female is naturally more care-free, does not appear. On the rare occasions when he rests, he will sometimes share with Jelly her piazza, and with both of them my approach to this retreat is always acknowledged by some small sound of greeting, and is often the excuse for a frolic or even one of those rare sentimental spells, absurd but touching evidence of an affection that seems so firmly rooted yet is so deeply sub-merged, save at infrequent intervals, by the demands of a vigorous life. Though not very demonstrative, Rawhide has his softer moments too, and in a way that seems so very humble, as though he knew that Jelly had some method of expression that he can never have but does the best he can. But this is only when everything is properly squared away and he has time on his hands. For he is methodical in this as in all his ways. And if he does permit himself a little space for play, it is not for long, and be-coming suddenly serious, as though he felt that he had committed himself in a moment of weakness, he walks or swims very soberly away. He has a fine regard for the niceties too, and never interferes in conversation or speaks out of his turn, as Jelly often does. A visitor once said that Rawhide reminded him of some old man who had worked too hard when very young, and never had his childhood.

This methodical beast is something of an unsung hero; not that he does actually a great deal more than Jelly, but he is less spectacular and attracts less notice. Yet most of the undertakings that have been completed here, bear the stamp of his peculiar methods and devising. His studious attention to what he deems to be his duty, his quiet com-petence, and his unruffled and unconquerable poise, are on a different plane to Jelly's violently aggressive, but none the less effective programme. And as he sits some-times so motionless, regarding me so steadily with his cool and watchful eye, I often wonder what he thinks of me.

Jelly Roll, jovial, wayward and full of whims.
Rawhide, calm, silent and inscrutable.
These two; King and Queen of All the Beaver People,
These are the Keepers of the Lodge.

From *Tales of an Empty Cabin.*

CHAPTER FOUR

FILM STARS

Outside a window from which the sash has been removed stands a man, alert, silent, watchful.

The cabin beside which he keeps post faces out on to a lake, its frontage at the water's edge. The slopes of the surrounding hills are covered with a heavy forest, the tall grey poplars and giant spruce standing close in a dark and serried palisade about the camp.

The water is calm and unruffled; the lake appears to sleep. There is no sound and no movement save the desultory journeyings of a squirrel, engaged in salvaging cones he has been dropping from the spruce tops.

In front of the man, and directed through the aperture into the building, is a motion picture camera, trained on the door, which is closed. The interior of the building is equipped with the rude but comfortable furnishings and the simple utensils of a woodsman's home, for the greater part of the dwelling is given over to human occupancy, and is a permanent abode, although it has one peculiarity. Across one end of it is a large erection having the appearance of a massive earthwork, shoulder high and occupying easily one-third of the floor space.

Outside, in strategic positions commanding the door and the approach from the lake, are other men, holding cameras. Inside the building a man sits in a chair, waiting. Suddenly:

'All right! here he comes,' cries a watcher. The man at the window sights his machine afresh, makes small adjustments and stands poised, ready. There can now be heard, approaching the entrance, a heavy measured tread. The camera-man's face becomes suddenly tense, the camera commences to whirr and simultaneously with a resounding thump the door is thrown widely open and there steps over the threshold, not the leading lady of a cast of players, not the handsome hero of a screen romance, nor yet the villain, but a full-grown beaver, erect, and bearing in his arms a load of earth and sticks.

Walking upright like a man, steadily, purposefully, looking neither to the right nor to the left, past the stove, round the table, between the benches, he pursues his undeviating way towards the earthwork, advancing with the resolute step of an unfaltering and unchangeable purpose. The camera swings, follows him, grinding. But for that sound and the thudding of the beaver's heavy steps, there is silence. Straight up the side of the lodge, for such the earthwork is, the beaver marches, deposits his load, tamps it in with his hands; he pushes in a stick to bind it, cuts off the protruding end and potters at some small repairs. At this moment another and a larger beaver enters hauling a six-foot stick which she skilfully manœuvres through the opening, drawing it over to the house and up the side of it. The two animals work with the heavy pole, placing it; they are very particular and take some time at this. Meanwhile the man in the chair rises, shuts the door and resumes his seat.

The camera drones on.

Another beaver, small, brisk, business-like, emerges from a hole in the side of the lodge, places two sticks very carefully, looks around, becomes fidgety and scampers in again. The operator's face is a study; he is getting it all. Yesterday he got a moose passing through the door yard, the day before a group of musk-rats.

The two big beavers at last finish their job to their complete satisfaction; and now their purposeful, sober mein deserts them. On all fours and at a little trot, they run over to the seated man and stand erect beside him, looking up at him. Their enquiring faces reach waist high on him as he sits. They must weigh one hundred pounds between the two of them. The larger one, the female, plucks at his sleeve trying to attract his attention. The camera grinds steadily and the beavers undoubtedly hear it. But they pay no heed; this is their fourth year at the business.

The man strokes the animals' heads.

'Well! how is it going to-day, old-timers?' he asks.

A series of short, sharp, ejaculations from the larger one as she pulls impatiently at his hand with her forepaws.

'All right, here's your apple,' says the man, and seizing the offering, she runs, hops, and trots over to the door, opens it inwards, with a quick pull at a leather loop, and runs outside. The other, her consort, patient, more sedate, gently takes his apple, and slips quietly out.

The camera at the window stops. Outside other machines click and drone according to their kind, as the expert passes from one to another of his sentries; for down at the so-lately deserted water-front, a scant thirty feet away, are more beavers, swimming, playing, eating.

All at once one of them stands upright, sniffing the air, listening, a stiff brown pillar of attention; a foreign scent has drifted down from that dark unknown forest with its threat of a thousand dangers. Without warning the beaver leaps into the water with a terrific plunge, slaps his tail. Immediately there is a violent commotion, cries, splashes, heavy thudding of broad flat tails, and in a moment not a beaver is to be seen.

From *Pilgrims of the Wild*.

III

ON THE TRAIL

CONTENTS

CHAPTER ONE

THE RIVER TRAIL

If you are staunch of heart and strong in small adversities, and can face the sun and wind; if you would like to try sleeping in a tent on a bed of fragrant balsam brush, and sitting on the ground to eat, and if, above all, you have an abounding sense of humour, we'll take a voyage down this so impetuously autocratic river, you and I.

*   *   *   *

That night we sleep in the tent allotted to us, and just after we have got nicely to sleep, someone slaps smartly on the canvas door and shouts in a loud, unsympathetic voice: 'Shake a leg there! Daylight in the swamp!' A muffled grumbling from one of the other occupants of the tent asks: 'What the heck time is it?' 'What do you care what time it is?' comes back this inexorable voice. 'It's away after three o'clock. Going to stay in bed all your life? Get after your canoes'—Boyd Mathewson, brigade chief, at his best. Red Landreville, who is in our tent, suggests that the canoes must be awful wild when a person can't wait for daylight to catch them but has to creep up on them under cover of the darkness. And certainly the daylight *does* look a little thin.

Those hard-driving, pitiless chiefs! How we hated them, loved them, thumbed our noses at them (metaphorically speaking, or if otherwise, most discreetly from well-selected cover), and broke our backs to fulfil, and sometimes exceed, their orders. How we bragged of having worked for them and boasted over our 'miles a day' and 'pounds a trip' on a portage.

But we are not here to boast; there's a two hundred and
fifty mile journey to be made after breakfast, and we are
going to see some speed. No, brother, we are not going to
do it all to-day, nor even this week. This is more or less of
a pleasure trip, thirty miles a day, or forty at the most—
what'll we do the rest of the day? Say, you're quite a
humorist too, ain't you—you'll get along, I guess.

Breakfast is soon over, and canoes are loaded and
trimmed. There is the minimum of bustle and no confusion whatsoever, as loads have been assembled and
lashed the night before and there is nothing to do but pack
the grub-boxes, one for each canoe, two men to a canoe.
The only fanfare that heralds the starting out of one of
these expeditions, some of which last six months, is the
laconic 'Well, boys, let's go' of the chief.

And go we do. Paddles dip in unison, backs bend and
sway, canoes leap forward at the rate of four miles to the
hour. The great sun rises, goes on up, getting smaller but
hotter as it goes, and becomes a burning red ball that
beats down on unprotected heads and hands and faces.
As the day advances the air becomes more torrid; the
lakes lie like seas of molten glass, and the palpitating
landscape is immersed in a screeching, scorching glare.
High overhead in a metallic sky the sun, like a burnished
copper gong, beats a fierce tattoo to which the whole face
of Nature quivers, and to whose tune the rows of jack-
pines topping the distant ridges writhe, and swing, and
sway in the steps of a fantastic sun-dance, reeling
drunkenly in the shimmering waves of a merciless,
breathless heat. But we don't let a little warm weather
bother us; this is August, and the hot weather is about
over in this North-country. The odd hot day gives the
boys a break—sweats some of the infernal laziness out of
their hides, says Charlie Dougal—resting softens a
man—!

So, speed, speed, speed, grip the canoe ribs with your knees, drive those paddles deep, throw your weight on to them, click them on those gunnels twenty-five strokes to the minute; spurn that water in gurgling eddies behind you, bend those backs, and drive! Sternsmen, keep your eyes on the far objective far off in the blue distance, and take your proper allowance for a side-wind, don't make leeway like a greenhorn! Thus, eyes fixed ahead, watchful of everything, breath coming deeply, evenly, backs swinging freely from the hips, paddles dipping and flashing, we drive her—fifty miles a day or bust. Some have busted, but not this outfit. You thought you heard me say thirty miles a day? Perhaps you did, but Dougal is running this brigade, not me. We are to make the first hundred miles in two days, he says, which is sense; we want to get out of the lake country while we have a fair wind to help us; the Indians say the wind is going to change, and so slow us up.

A duck flies in before the canoes, and taking the water, flaps along in front of us as though hurt. She has young ones hidden somewhere and is trying to decoy us away from them by this offer of easy capture, keeping just far enough ahead to be out of reach. Her ruse succeeds quite well, because we don't want her brood in the first place, and we are not going their way anyhow. She continues this pretence of disability until we nearly catch up to her, when she suddenly recovers, flies a short piece ahead, and commences the performance all over again. She does this, time and time again, with a maddening persistence and an unnecessary expenditure of energy that, in this heat, makes us burst out into renewed streams of perspiration just to look at her—and all for nothing. We are just beginning to regard her with the greatest repugnance when, having lured us, as she supposes, to a safe distance, she flies back home, pursued by the objurgations of the entire brigade; except the Indians, who show no emotion whatsoever and pass no comment, though they watch the duck's every move intently, as they do everything else that is seen.

On the portages the leaves hang limp and listless, and the still air is acrid with the resinous odour of boiling spruce gum. Here men sweat under enormous burdens; earlier in the Summer, clouds of mosquitoes and black-flies would envelop them in biting swarms. But it is August, and the fly season is over, and those that are left are too weak to do any damage, and sit balefully regarding us from nearby limbs of trees. Pattering of moccasined feet on the narrow trail, as men trot with the canoes, one to a man, or step easily along under their loads; and in a miraculously short space of time everything is over to the far side. Canoes are re-loaded expertly, and we are away again. But out on the lake there is a change. A welcome breeze fans us, cooling us off, while it dries the sweat—also our throats. Someone commences to sing in a high, thin tenor, this seeming to be just the right note for a desiccated throat; the refrain is, aptly enough 'How dry I am——'. We all laugh and join in the chorus. We begin to enjoy ourselves, to rejoice in the fluid rhythm of the canoes, to feel the ecstasy of this wild, free, vigorous life that seems all at once to be the only life worth living. The free wind of the open has by now blown away a thousand petty thoughts of profit, or of desire to prevail over some-one, or of device or stratagem whereby to gain preferment. For this is not a life of dodge and subterfuge, save only where necessary to gain, not what another may have possession of, but only what Nature offers for the means to live, to carry on.

And we carry on; there is no let-up. Any faltering will draw meaning looks, and perhaps meaninger remarks from our decidedly humorous, but quite remorseless and entirely inflexible chiefs—Blood-for-Breakfast and Quick-Lunch Dougal and their piratical crew are headed for the River, men obsessed by the purpose of covering Distance, disciples of speed, knight-errants of the canoe, devotees of the Trail. And we must needs follow; you must stay with it, my friend. Here is where the rich man's riches buy him nothing, and where a parading of his business acumen will only get him in wrong with his guides. And it is no use audibly admiring the scenery (not unless you are doing your share, however little it may be), because you can't curry favour with the landscape. This, Mister, is the real thing, and no moving-picture set. You are asking me why all the hurry, and where *is* this so-famous Mississauga River? Well, it is just seventy-five miles in from town, including sixteen portages. No, sir, we are not trying to do it all in one day, though it has been done. This is to be an easy trip, on account of our guest, that's you, and we will consume all of a day and a half. You decide that further speech seems unnecessary, futile, in face of the facts.

And so, in a continuous alternation of lake and portage, dazzling sea of glare and oven-like, leafy tunnel, we go on. When do we eat? thinks you—or do we eat? You begin to wonder. But, sooner or later, noon comes and we prepare a much needed meal. The cooking is not complicated. There is only one precept to abide by, so Augustus, the financier, informs us, and that is to put salt into everything except tea and jam; that way, he says, you can't go wrong. But we soon find that this Gus fellow is also something of a humorist, because there is no jam, and nobody ever puts salt in tea. So the matter becomes quite simple. On talking the matter over with this financial expert, we are told that it is not good economy to carry stuff you don't need; it doesn't pay. But he has a great nose for his own advantage, and being German, is well provided with *urbswurst*, and with it he makes a very palatable soup, which he shares around.

Gus's pleasantry concerning the non-existent jam, brings up the subject of provisions. Limited to a canoe-load of supplies for each two men for five months—the duration of some of these trips—and with no trading posts, in this area, at which to replenish, the provision list is shorn of all luxuries and frills. And although this is more or less of a light trip, the dictates of established custom are adhered to, so we have not only no jam (because it has an uncomfortable fashion of coming open and mixing with the soap and matches), but also no potatoes, eggs, caviare, nor canned lobster. The last two items are entirely legendary in character so far as we are concerned, and we do not miss them. But we have flour, salt and baking powder with which to make bannock, a kind of large scone cooked over hot coals; this delicacy is of Scotch origin, having been introduced by the Hudson Bay people who were largely Scotsmen. It is also known as Indian loaf. It is going to be your principal article of diet, so take a good look at one—yes, you are right, it makes no attempt to float out of your hand; but don't drop it on your foot; it doesn't bounce. It stays right with you. We have long ago exploded the theory that ordinary bread is the staff of life. We almost never eat it, and have managed to thrive to quite a size without it. No one wants to kill a large animal like a deer or moose, and have the meat spoil; we have no time to spend drying and smoking it as the Indians do. Instead we bring along several sides of very salt pork which have to be parboiled, in slices, before it can be fried and eaten; it comes in large, corpse-like slabs that go under the various titles of sow-belly, long clear, and rattlesnake pork. The flavour indicates the last name as being the most applicable. We have also tea, sugar, white beans, which latter have a very high nutriment value, a few dried apples, and soap, matches and tobacco. This frugal but stimulating fare is eked out with fresh fish, of which we have the very best and lots of it, and also berries in season. The idea, of course, is to get as much solid eating material for as little weight and bulk as possible; hence the elimination of potatoes and canned goods.

This list seems rather limited, you think. Well don't say it aloud. These men, used to self-denial and hardship of all kinds, would think you were complaining. Remember, reader, you are away back in the days of the pork and bannock regime, when a man who brought along milk or breakfast bacon was deemed to be lowering the standard of manhood. Butter was taboo, not only because we never even thought of it, but also because its unlucky owner caused delay and friction as he fussed around in his futile attempts to preserve it and keep it from turning to oil in temperatures of ninety or a hundred in the shade. A man who was found to be in clandestine possession of butter, was considered to be lacking in force of character, and it was suspected that his morals were rancid. Goods labelled 'Canned roast beef' and 'Tinned dinner' were contemptuously referred to as 'Horse,' and the libertine who was caught eating them was said to be digging his grave with his teeth. And this was not all mere caprice, as such things were heavy for their size, didn't last long, and took up a lot of room in a canoe that could have been put to better use, and when after a few weeks these whimsies had been consumed, the culprit had perforce to beg donations from the meagre supplies of his fellow travellers, so that one having these luxurious tastes was something in the nature of a menace to society, or a public enemy. To-day it would be impossible for me to live that way, and I fear, too, that my speed limit has been much reduced.

Eating, under ordinary circumstances, is merely a

means of sustaining life, at least in our severely simple and unpolished social state. Yet after a long, hard siege at the paddle, the pole, or the tump-line, a meal can become the sum total of the recreation, the relaxation and the entertainment of the day, and be an event of some importance; assuming under these circumstances, a dignity and significance out of all proportion to the short time spent in cooking it, or the fifteen minutes' enjoyment that it gives. And then the cool, lazy smoke in the shade afterwards; that is even better. Stretched out beneath an umbrella-topped jack-pine, his pipe going, contented, with that feeling of satisfaction that comes of labour successfully accomplished and the thought of congenial labour yet to do, quietly glorying in his strength and fitness and proficiency, as much a part of his environment as the tree he leans against, your true voyageur would trade places with no king. There are different ideas of comfort; to some it consists in a feather bed, or in the personal service given, for pay, by 'lesser' men; to us it means getting outside of a full meal, or having our feet dry, or in fly season, having an hour's surcease from the mosquitoes; or, greatest of all, in experiencing the unutterable sense of relief, the feeling of luxurious ease that possesses a man's soul when he puts down a burden after carrying it, maybe, up three hills, or for a long distance on the uncertain footing provided by a lot of loosely-fitting boulders that move and wobble at every step. There's nothing just like it.

The dinner hour doesn't last long; it isn't even an hour before we are ready to go again. Fires are carefully put out, for the menace of forest fire hangs constantly over us, an ever-present threat. Quickly we resume our paddles and are away again. In the interim the sun has moved and, having been well burned on one side, we are now to be nicely browned on the other. This is no relief of course, but is at least a change; and after all there is something to be said for symmetry. We pass over a series of small, still lakes, where the arabesque tracery of the foliage is reflected as in a looking-glass. We pass historic places, thick with legend and tradition; the remains of an ancient Hudson's Bay post, relic of an older, wilder day. It's timbers can still be seen, and on the knoll behind it is a primitive Indian graveyard; we pass the Place-of-Crying-Mink, where sometimes is heard the desolate, awful wailing of a phantom mink; to the South lies Woman Portage where a woman long dead walks at the full of the moon. There is a camping ground shunned by the Indians, because a ghost beaver who lived nearby once stole a hunter's paddles, and with very unghostly perspicacity cut them up and thoughtfully hid the pieces. This left the hunter stranded until he had made new paddles, upon which he immediately left the country. A steep bank is pointed out, where the May-May-Gwense, Indian elves, slide up and down in the moonlight for amusement. Some claim to have watched them and if you don't believe it, there is the little trail, plain to be seen. Back in the hills hereabouts, there is known to have been found, by an Indian named The Cat, an enormous footprint of a man. It is said to have been that of an Iroquois, one of those warriors who ravaged this country about a century ago, and are remembered by one or two still living; he is still supposed to be lurking in the vicinity.

In a narrow strait that joins two lakes, we meet an old prospector; he has an Indian guide, because he is not a water dog, as a canoeman is termed, but a desert rat from Nevada, and therefore has no knowledge of water travel. The Indian says that this desert man carries a water-flask everywhere he goes—in a country that is more than half water—and fills all available vessels with water before going to bed at night. Conversation reveals that he knows his rocks very well indeed; but everything else here is new to him. He has noted our speed, and does not approve. He is never in a hurry, he tells us. His theory is, that life is short and we'll be a long time dead; so what's all the fury about? We smile gently and tolerantly at this inexplicable foible of an old man, and wishing him lucky prospecting, with a wild halloo, which he answers with a Piute war-whoop for a send-off, we race forward on our way. We pass Indian camps where dogs that are more than half wolf, bark at us menacingly, and high featured, tawny faces framed in lank black hair, peer out at us with eyes that are veiled, inscrutable, yet strangely penetrating.

On the next portage we have our first mishap. Baldy is carrying, defiantly, against expressed public opinion, one of his outsize loads when the tump-line, an old one, breaks. The sudden release throws the little fellow forward on his face, and his nose is bleeding. Self-conscious as usual, he sets out to explain. 'My tump-line was no good; they don't make 'em that way any more. A good man can't get the stuff to work with any more.' He goes on to say, with the blood dripping from his chin, that the world in general is hell-bound; even the mosquitoes are not what they were. Charlie (Quick-Lunch) Dougal agrees, with heavy sarcasm, that the fly crop was a black failure this year; Red Landreville says yes, it's only too true, even gangsters don't use machine-guns these days—they are reduced to carrying concealed razor blades; it's a tough world. Zepherin, arriving on the scene, is in one of his Pistolian moods, and affecting to misunderstand the state of affairs, roars at the gore-stained Baldy, 'Ha! Me blood-stained bucko! Fightin', eh? And you with the best man in the world at your heels—you vampire! you ravaging scorpion, you!—you hideous monster, to be consortin' with decent men——' while Baldy stands in the silent dignity of forbearance and asserts, very obviously, that he is no monster, hasn't fought and doesn't want to fight, and only needs a new tump-line. This is forthcoming, with advice not to let it (the tump-line) get him down, and not to carry *all* the load at once as there is another day to-morrow, reminding him that there is too much rock here to bury a man decently, and that a corpse won't keep in this weather, and so forth.

Soon after this, at an improvised landing of logs, someone, picking up a canoe by the centre (the proper way) knocks Matogense, usually so sure-footed, over into the quaking bog the timbers are supposed to bridge, out of which he presently scrambles, covered with an evil-smelling coating of slime. Everybody at once remembers, inconveniently for Matogense, the story of his daughter who was fed the live fish to help her learn to swim, and it is suggested that he be given a bull-frog to eat so that he will be able to get around better in the mud. It is characteristic that his load, which he has fallen in with, is salvaged first while he is left to shift for himself, the argument being that he can crawl out and the provisions can not; and it is the concensus of opinion that a man has to be dragged in the mud a couple of times before he is worth a damn, anyway. But these are two mishaps too many. Men are getting tired; their movements are not so sure. Things are slowing up, and it is getting late. So it is to our intense relief that Aleck L'Espagnol, with a glance at the rapidly darkening sky and the now rising mists, sagely suggests that we call it a day and make camp. Surprisingly, that devastating speed-fiend, Dougal, and the terse-spoken, adamantine Mathewson both agree; and in this they show the best of judgment, for Aleck is held in general esteem for his wisdom.

Camp is quickly made within an encircling grove of giant red-pines, whose crenelated columns, all ruddy in the firelight, stand about the place like huge pillars that support a roof so high above us as to be invisible, reaching up to unknown heights into the blackness, giving us the feeling that we are encamped in some old, deserted temple. While all around us is the interminable, unfathomable forest, whose denizens live in impenetrable privacy, and in the dark recesses of which a thousand shadows lie in ambush all the day, awaiting only the coming of night to creep out and slowly, silently invest the whole world of trees, and rocks, and water, and the sleeping camp. But the camp is not sleeping yet; bannock has to be made for the next day's consumption, and other preparations completed for the morrow's journey. Everything is quickly disposed in its proper place, the whole camp a standing model of neatness and well-contrived arrangement.

And then comes that hour of rest and quiet contentment, when there is no sound save the light crackle of burning wood and the odd murmur of a voice, when all the face of Nature is immersed in that brooding calm that comes down like an invisible curtain with the falling of night. Besides the central fire most everyone has settled down to sit and smoke, or sit and talk, or just to sit. Talk turns to earlier days, and of men, great men, and mighty men, and men who were remarkable, in times gone by. Any conversation among a bunch of woodsmen will inevitably work its way round to these biographical anecdotes, which invariably take the form of reminiscences commencing with such introductions as 'I mind one time ——', or 'In the early days——', or ' 'Way back in '05, I think it was——', and are given with a great wealth of detail. And it is to be noticed that these are all tributes; the mean, the trifling, and the base have been forgotten, and at any ill-advised mention of them, a sudden silence is apt to fall upon the group. We hear of Joe McLean, the Indian, who in a storm at night, the canoe swamped and no longer able to hold two men, shouted good-bye to the tourist he was guiding, and letting go of the canoe, disappeared into the darkness and was never seen again alive. Many are the tales of Billy Friday who, on a bet, carried six bags of flour, one hundred pounds in each, from the wharf on Temagami lake up to the station, a distance of a hundred yards, part of it up-hill. We are told, too, of the famous Larry Frost, another Indian, who fought on one occasion with nine men at once, and trimmed them all.

Then there was Joe Seiderquist, the white trapper, who did everything in a big way, and undertook a friendly wrestling match with a half-tame bear. Towards the close of the second bout he bit the bear so badly that they had to be separated. 'He was,' stated the narrator, 'a hearty man; you should have heard him eat!' Joe, we are informed, borrowed a dog team from Dan O'Connor, who was the Big Shot at Temagami in those days; he was known as the King of Temagami. Joe kept the dogs all Winter, and brought them back safe and sound. But when the dogs arrived back in town Dan didn't recognise them, not having had the dogs very long in the first place. So Joe, for a joke, told Dan that he had lost the original team through the ice, paid for them, and sold Dan's own team back to him at a nice profit. This same Dan O'Connor was a man of rare ability, and performed prodigies of pioneering in that North country in the face of almost insuperable difficulties, all of which he overcame. He owned some hotels at the tourist resort that sprang up by the lake after the railroad came through, and would employ almost any means by which to boost his beloved town of Temagami. His resourcefulness was proverbial, and if there was any possible way of getting a thing done, he would do it; as for instance, when an important railroad magnate wished to examine into the game possibilities of the region, with a view to establishing a tourist traffic.

This would be valuable, and Dan wanted it. But this official required duck shooting for his patrons, and he was coming at the one time of year when there were no ducks, in the middle of Summer. Dan decided to supply the ducks. This wouldn't be cheating, as there were always plenty of them in the proper season. So Dan had a crate of ducks sent up from the distant city. On their arrival Dan had an Indian take them over behind an island opposite the hotel. The magnate also arrived in due course, and sitting with O'Connor on the veranda after supper, began to ask about ducks. About that time the Indian sauntered up, and held a desultory conversation with O'Connor in Indian. This was according to plan. The Indian had a gun, and presently moved off with it and was seen paddling over to the island. 'Where's he going?' asked the magnate. 'Duck hunting,' replied O'Connor. 'Do you suppose he will get any?' enquired the interested railroad man. 'Sure he will,' asserted the invincible Dan. Presently there was a fusillade behind the island. Shortly afterwards the same Indian paddled across to the landing before the Hotel, and as he walked slowly by, this astonished official was treated, in a wilderness removed a hundred and fifty miles from any farm, to the astounding spectacle of a round dozen of common barnyard ducks, tastefully arranged upon a pole.

Dan was wont to boast that he had brought 'steamships to Temagami on snowshoes!' This was almost a statement of fact, as he had taken some Indians and broken a trail through the snow-bound bush and over frozen lakes forty miles to Ville Marie in the dead of Winter, on snowshoes of course, leading on his return journey a procession of teams, each bearing a component part of the first wood-burning steamboat that ever sailed on Lake Temagami. He it was who, greeting Lord Charles Beresford on the occasion of his visit to that country, remarked that it was a momentous occasion, the Lord of the British Navy meeting the Lord of Temagami—two Lords so to speak—'So he'd feel at home,' said Dan afterwards.

And now the talk becomes desultory, dies down. The men retire, and soon all sound ceases. And the fire begins to burn low, and from it a thin, white, wavering column of smoke ascends, up into the pine-tops, far above. The night-mist from off the water hangs in wisps and mingles with the smoke; until the fire dies at last, and the waiting shadows take final and complete possession, once and for all.

*   *   *   *

Morning comes early with Boyd Mathewson, and once he is up, it is quite impossible for anyone else to sleep. Men stagger stiffly from their tents, and we all have a touch of that stale dryness, that washed-out feeling that comes on the morning after a forced march of any kind. And there is to be another one to-day, lasting to noon when, if there are no accidents or adverse winds, we will have arrived at the Mississauga River. Dougal, having already had a quick and very sketchy breakfast, is stepping around, bright as a new dollar and as smart as a particularly aggressive cricket. To the others he is, of course, nothing but an infestation and is earning, by his disturbing activities, some black looks and very pointed and uncomplimentary comment, none of which he heeds. Beside the fire squats Boyd, glowering in caustic silence at the leisurely movements of the men; by the process of raising one eyebrow while heavily depressing the other, and holding a fork at a kind of expectant angle over a suggestively empty frying-pan, he has managed to achieve an appearance of almost malignant preparedness. The men, meanwhile, pretend an elaborate and maddening indifference to all this and continue, speedily enough, with

K

the work of breaking camp, chuckling among themselves. Red Landreville expresses himself, under his breath, as being by no means in love with these blood-for-breakfast ideas; but Zepherin, in a loud voice intended to be over-heard, allows that for his part, he is glad somebody woke him up, as he had slept so hard he nearly broke his neck, that three in the morning is as good a time as any to get up, as it gave a man time to have an appetite for dinner, and that he liked long days because he could do more work. In fact, he liked work so well, he stated, that he could easily lie down and sleep beside it. A cold silence from the direction of the fire greeted these well-chosen remarks.

However, after a short time these minor and half-jocular irritations pass off, and everybody is soon busy around the fire with their cooking apparatus, one tea-pail and a frying-pan to every two men. Billy Mitchell, who is a pretty good cook and quite justly proud of it, has prepared what he calls 'community pancakes' for the entire crowd. This is by way of asking the whole bunch out to dinner, so to speak, and it is much appreciated, and as Billy sets them out, he says: 'These pancakes look pretty good, by gosh,' which brings an immediate chorus of dissent—'They don't look any too good to me'; and 'What's so good about them, the colour?'; and 'Whatcha ma'em with, a shovel?' and 'Their looks won't help them; better take a good look at them, you're seein' them for the last time!' But very soon they are all gone, which is about the best compliment they could have got.

Tents are folded, canoes are loaded, and we are away again. Paddles dip and swing (no, they don't flash—there is no sun, and won't be for another two hours) and canoes shoot ahead. You seem to ache in every joint, stiff from yesterday's gruelling drive, and muscles feel like rusty springs; but soon you burst into a profuse perspiration, which cleanses and lubricates the machinery and releases the hidden forces of energy for the day. It is fine weather to-day again. We are lucky; and the wind is with us, too. There are few cabins back in here; everyone (we haven't met anyone yet) lives in tents and a log camp is only a place to keep a cache of provisions, or a good place to go into out of the rain; and as these shelters are very far apart, it sometimes rains between cabins.

What do we do then? Well, we can't do a thing about it, so we let it rain. An ordinary shower stops nobody, but there are often days when sheets of driving rain, the dull skies, the dripping trees, soggy moss and streaming rocks blend in a monotonous monochrome of grey; when it is wise to stop and put up tents where there is plenty of wood, light a huge fire and make as merry as possible under the circumstances, drying off before the cheerful blaze beneath a canopy of tarpaulins. Sometimes a sudden storm, which you saw coming, but took a gambler's chance that it would pass a few miles to the Westward, catches you unprepared, and under the scant shelter of a hastily overturned canoe, its one end reared above the ground to give you room, you sit for hours and shiver yourself warm until the rain stops. You don't as a rule take these chances when on the Trail, but you do when you are with Mathewson or Dougal. Let's hope it doesn't rain, says you. And you're right. The infrequent camps we encounter are, you notice, open and generally contain supplies; nothing is hidden. In this country, a man who conceals his cache or locks his camp is considered to be an outlander, and is looked on with suspicion as one who would steal—it seems to follow; and not till easy transportation brings in a few of the wrong kind of people, is this unwritten law ever broken.

As we approach the head of the River, the lakes become smaller and, because you can see most of every part of them at a glance, seem to be intimate and friendly. In such places we occasionally see moose, huge beasts, upwards of six feet at the shoulder, who stand and stare at us curiously as we pass, perhaps the first humans they have ever seen. Mostly they are in the shallows near the shore, digging up water-lily roots, and often having their heads completely submerged, presently come up for air with a mighty splurge, and seeing us, stand a moment to watch, the water pouring in small cataracts from the pans of their wide antlers. Invariably deciding that we are not to be trusted, they spin on their heels with surprising agility for so large an animal and lurch away at a springy, pacing trot that is a deal faster than it looks; and the noise of their going, once they hit the bush, is something like that of a locomotive running loose in the underbrush.

At noon we arrive at the Rangers' Headquarters on Bark Lake. This is a large body of water, beautiful with its islands, inlets and broken, heavily timbered shores. At various points a number of streams enter the lake, and to follow the shore-line and discover all of them would take a week or more. Numerous routes, navigable by the methods we are using, lead off in all directions, and this lake is the gateway to an immense, little-known territory. From its outlet there flows the Mississauga River, small as yet—but don't worry; you'll find it big enough later on. So we got here, you see; we have made seventy-five miles in a day and a half. Not bad, admits Dougal, but if we'd have been getting up in decent time these last two mornings, we'd have been a lot farther. It's been fun, hasn't it. And now the serious work is about to start. After dinner we run, in quick succession, a number of small rapids. There is not much to them. This is only the beginning; the River is as yet young.

We pass several small lake expansions, and that night we camp besi swiftly running water, on the banks of the

River proper. And all night, whenever we awaken, we can hear, in the distance, a dull, steady, ceaseless roar. Our first real white water, with all its unknown possibilities, lies just ahead of us. The next morning we arrive at the head of this. Part of the load is disembarked at the portage, as we will run with half-loads, taking only stuff that can stand a wetting. For this is a tough spot, and we will ship water, inevitably. We go to centre of the stream again, set the canoes at the proper angle for the take-off. The canoes seem to leap suddenly ahead, and one after another, with a wild, howling hurrah, we are into the thick of it. Huge combers, any one of which would swamp a canoe, stand reared and birling terrifically beside us, close enough to touch. The backlash from one of these smashes against the bows and we are slashed in the face by what seems to be a ton of water; we are soaked to the skin, blinded by spray—on one side is a solid wall of water, there is a thunderous roar which envelopes us like a tunnel, a last flying leap and we are in the still pool below, safe, wet, and thrilled to the bone. It was a short, wicked pitch, and we have taken much water, in which we are now kneeling, but we have saved two loads on the portage, so it paid us well to run; and for you, I think the experience was worth the wetting. We go ashore, unload and empty out, carry the remaining stuff over the portage, load up and are away again—happy, with a great, new-found sense of self-reliance, and looking for more thrills. There are plenty.

The current has much increased in volume and power. Rapid succeeds rapid in quick succession. Most of them we run, some full loaded, others with half loads, saving a lot of work on portages. A few are more in the nature of low waterfalls, or else too filled with stones, and are impossible. There is a marvellously picturesque cataract, running through a chasm in a series of chutes and sudden drops, that is worth the trouble of going off the portage to see. This spot is known as Hell's Gate. The old rapid is too dangerous to run with any load, and the canoes go down empty. No useful purpose is served in attempting these places, it being done only for the excitement to be got out of it. In such spots, brother, we leave you on the shore, and I think that the skill and daredeviltry, the utter disregard for personal danger with which a good canoe-man flings (there is no other word) a good canoe from place to place through a piece of water in which it seems impossible that anything could live, will furnish you with a spectacle that you will be a long time forgetting. And you may sometimes, too, remember the narrow plot that is a grave, surrounded by a picket fence, at one of them. A man was drowned here a few years ago, an old, ex-perienced trapper, who made perhaps only this one mistake in all his life. Some rivers have their private graveyards, to which they add from time to time. But Mississauga is not considered dangerous; there are portages round all bad places. We are only running them for the fun of it. We get wet quite often, and occasionally we have to step ankle-deep in water to make a landing. But things like that begin not to matter to you; it's all part of the game. You are by now becoming so used to these small hardships that to be too comfortable gives you an uneasy feeling of guilt. You say you have a sinking feeling at the pit of the stomach at the head of every piece of bad water; but I notice that you shout as loudly as the rest of them in the middle of it. Between rapids the river runs sometimes smooth and deep, at other places widens out into noisy shallow reaches, with scarcely depth enough to allow the passage of a loaded canoe; in such stretches the men get out and lead the canoes like horses. Frequently, a rapid stops abruptly to quieten down in a pool, deep and still and flecked with foam, where the River seems to pause awhile to reflect and lay new plans for the next wild and turbulent course.

We see no more moose but plenty of deer, and more than once we see a number of them together, standing ahead of us in a shallows, craning their necks, and weaving back and forth with very human curiosity, to get a better view. Sometimes they wait until the canoes are almost upon them before bounding through the shallow water with prodigious leaps and a great clattering and splashing, as they make for the safety of the tall timbers. One, a half-grown fawn, was encountered crouching in a pool, evidently in distress, and a wolf was seen hovering in the underbrush on shore. A stop was made and the wolf routed, while the exhausted fawn was tied by all its feet, and transported to a safer neighbourhood and turned loose again. Wolves, having chased a deer down to a river, not infrequently separate, and one of them having crossed over at another point, is there to meet the deer when the latter swims across. Twice we see wolves; one of them is swimming, and a frantic but unsuccessful attempt is made to catch him before he lands, but he has too much lead on us. We come suddenly on another whilst he is drinking, and before he goes have time to note that he does not lap the water, as does his kinsman the dog, but drinks like a horse, by suction. He makes stupendous bounds, far exceeding those of a deer in length, for a deer leaps up and down, and a wolf leaps ahead—which is one reason why a wolf can catch deer; persistence and a rather high order of intelligence, as well as an aptitude for learning by experience, being the other contributing factors. In all this he much resembles a dog—what's that? You object to this comparison; you say all wolves are poltroons, cowards? Don't let the boys hear you; they don't feel that way about it. I'll tell you: to them a wolf is just another hunter, like they themselves are. Only those who know nothing about wolves can hate them so very much. And as for cowardice, did you ever hear a badly scared man tell how he was chased by wolves when all he heard was one wolf, so spent a night in a tree and arrived home swearing to God that he ran eight miles with a dozen wolves after him before he climbed a tree to save his life? The wolf is no fool, and plays safe; but so does the man who goes into the woods armed to the teeth and shoots an animal that has no chance against his high-power rifle, and if the animal turns on him in self-defence, the beast is called ferocious, and the man clamours for his immediate extermination because his own hide has been endangered—he is ready to hand it out, but can't take it! Yes, I agree wolves kill lots of deer, but then so do the sportsmen; I kill them myself, who am no sportsman, but a hunter, though there is this to be said for the wolves and myself, we may not bring home the head, but we *do* eat the meat. And those who do most of the hollering about the wolves destroying these 'beautiful creatures' (which they certainly are), are those who don't like to see the wolves killing something they want to kill themselves. I read where they shot seventy thousand of these 'beautiful creatures' in one season, for sport. The wolf does do harm in small restricted Wilderness areas, and to farmers' stock; so kill him if you like, or can—but don't revile him behind his back. He has his place in the scheme of things, like everything else here. Did it ever strike you that when the white man first struck this country, both deer and wolves were in an exceedingly flourishing condition? Everything fluctuated in those days, and the balance was kept perfect. Yes, I know, we have to kill lots of wolves; I've killed my share. But the wolf is no more to be denounced for following his natural instincts than is a beaver for cutting down a tree, or the whale for eating up the sardine crop (if that's what they eat). Man need find no fault with

Nature's methods while he continues to turn whole territories into howling deserts by improper agricultural methods, or burns yearly millions upon millions of the finest and most valuable forests in North America for no good purpose, but just on account of carelessness. And now what? You don't believe that the dog and the wolf are so closely related? Did you know that the celebrated police dog, very nearly the most intelligent of his kind, is pretty close to being a domesticated European wolf? Sure, we may kill the next wolf we see, as a matter of expediency, but he is not the contemptible creature you think he is. Don't be prejudiced, my learned friend; fair play and justice are better for the health. Of course I've got to give you this, as you say, this chasing and tearing down of a defenceless animal is brutally cruel; but while I won't defend it, you must know that Nature is sometimes as cruel as sin. And we have a parallel in the highest civilisation, where people chase a fox with the assistance of a round dozen of dogs, and get the greatest satisfaction out of seeing the unhappy creature torn to pieces before their eyes. So what!

Well, we had our first argument, you and me, and I suppose we both learned something. Oh, that's nothing unusual. Sometimes everybody gets interested and the whole brigade stops and argues like nobody's business, about something that not one of them knows anything whatever about. Just to be different. Anyhow, we made two or three miles in the meantime—and say, there's a couple of bears, no, three of them, an old lady and two cubs; get out your camera. They won't do us any harm, naturally. (You'd best get that bug-a-boo of 'wild' animals out of your head; they're just being themselves, same as us.) The little fellows are all alive with curiosity to find out what we are, but their mother isn't even interested. Clowns of the woods, these black, woolly boys, with a thoughtless, rollicking, good-natured disposition, though it must be admitted that they are often thoughtless enough to go rollicking through someone's provision cache; but their heart's in the right place—it's just a way they have. No, I wouldn't get out of the canoe and pet the cubs if I were you; the old woman is probably not a mind reader, and she'd likely think you were going to hurt her youngsters and slap you down. Good way to start a bear story, but it will do you no good. Bears are quite a common sight here, swimming, or walking along on sandy beaches.

There are incidents. At a stop, where we are to make tea, Shorty, always unfortunate, sticks the tea-pail pole into a hornets' nest. The mosquitoes may not be what they were, but the hornets prove to be as good as ever, and we move away from that place. One of the canoes has its canvas badly cut on a sharp stone. The leak is a bad one, and the crew hustle their craft ashore, where the puncture is mended, temporarily, with soap. Gus, the financier, explains that this is the real reason why we carry soap; but don't listen to him—remember how he caught you on the jam question? But the outstanding presentation is the one provided by Zepherin when, carrying a canoe up a steep bank, he begins to slide backwards, canoe and all, towards the river again. He struggles futilely to regain traction, and being an active man he puts on quite a show, and goes through the most extraordinary gyrations to regain his footing. All hands are gathered at the landing, and the exhibition is watched with the greatest interest. Zepherin is a heavy man, the place is steep and slimy, he has a good start, and we all know that he hasn't the chance of a snowball in Egypt. He has a canoe with him, so if he falls into the river it will be quite all right with us. Zepherin, red in the face, feeling as ridiculous as a car-load of circus clowns, and still sliding, gasps out in desperation: 'Simmering Cimmerean centipedes! None of you guys goin' to help me? see a fella' slide into this jee-hovally crik!' and goes on sliding, until near the edge he throws the canoe from him with a terrific imprecation and shouts: 'I'll not go in! I won't go in!' and still he keeps on sliding, waving his fist at the scenery and bellowing 'You can't put me in! You can't pu——' and slides, with an uncommonly good display of footwork, over the brink and into about three feet of water. Spluttering like a walrus, he scrambles to his feet immediately, and standing submerged to the waist he shakes his two fists above his head and roars in a terrible voice: 'Put me in, did yuh?—but you can't keep me there, by cripes!—and I'll get out when I'm dam' good and ready, so I will! Try and stop me!!' and with a blood-curdling whoop he surges ashore. By this time we all begin to feel the least bit uneasy as to how he is going to take this, like small boys who have only too successfully defied the authority of a policeman. But Zeph has never actually killed a man—yet, and it is with some relief that we see him sit down upon a stone, as he enquires in his fog-horn voice: 'Why didn't some of you mugs push me in so I could get it over with?' And then he laughs and laughs until he can laugh no more. So we laugh too, if you know what I mean—keeps him from feeling self-conscious, don't you see? Dougal, who enjoys, among the more superstitious, the doubtful reputation of having once been seen at both ends of a portage at the one time, now puts in an appearance, just when he isn't wanted, and has observed the latter part of our little true-life drama. Ever a man who could ill brook delay or accident, he shoulders his way up to Zeph and asks him what in the name of all that is blind, black, and holy, was he fooling around in the water for. Zepherin looks at him for a moment in stunned silence, his cavernous mouth agape. 'What was I fooling in the water for?' he repeats in a voice weak with astonishment, and then louder: 'What for, you say?' and then in a roar: 'Foolin' in the water, me! Why, you pollusive, reptilian rapscallion—g'wan, you runt yuh, or I'll make a pile of dog meat out of yuh, that two short men couldn't shake hands over, so I will'; and addressing the surroundings, one hand raised in a supplicating gesture towards high heaven, he asks: 'Did yuh hear that one, did yuh?' and calls on all the powers to bear witness that he is an innocent man. Whereat Dougal, unable to remain serious any longer in the face of such an absurd situation, bursts into laughter with the rest of us. Such is our discipline, the kind that will, with the right men, move mountains.

*   *   *   *

And so, day succeeding day, we go forward. And as we penetrate deeper and ever deeper into this enchanted land, the River marches with us. More and more to us a living thing, it sometimes seems as if it were watching us, like some huge half-sleeping serpent that observes us dreamily, lying there secure in his consciousness of power while we, like Lilliputians, play perilously upon his back. Until, to our sudden consternation he awakens, as though some austere, immovable landmark that you had passed a thousand times before, should rise one day and look you in the face and ask you what you did there; so does this serpent, that is the River, turn on us unexpectedly, and writhe and hiss and tear, and lash out at us in fierce resentment at our audacity.

Here and there along its course are mighty waterfalls, some with rainbows at the foot of them; and one of these thunders down a deep chasm, down two hundred feet into a dark swirling eddy, seemingly bottomless, that heaves and boils below the beetling overhang as though some unimaginably monstrous creature moved beneath its surface. And in the vortex of this boiling cauldron there stands a pinnacle of rock on which no creature ever stood, crowned with a single tree, for ever wet with the rainbow-tinted spray that in a mist hangs over it, while the echoing, red walls of the gorge and the crest of the looming pines that overtop them, and the all-surrounding amphitheatre of the hills, throw back and forth in thunderous repetition the awe-inspiring reverberations of the mighty cataract. And as we stand and watch it, it is borne home to us what a really little figure a man cuts in this great Wilderness. Even Landreville has no story to fit the occasion.

Long stretches there are of smooth, slow-flowing water where everything is quiet. Here the shores are level and in wide spots there are low alluvial islands covered with tall, yellow, waving grasses, with blue irises standing in amongst them, showing brilliantly against the darker, gloomy back-drop of the heavy timber. The River winds and twists much in such places. The bends are not far apart and the curve of the banks shuts off the view before and behind at no great distance, so that we are constantly walled around by trees and move inside a circle that never really opens up but goes with us, as if we were passing through a series of high-walled, tree-lined pools in some old, forgotten moat, that looked every one the same, save only for the ever-changing character of the timber that enclosed them. We pass the cavernous, high-vaulted forests of the hardwoods, full of long, shadowy vistas that seem, in their pale, green dimness, to be peopled with uncouth and formless shapes, and that stretch vaguely off in all directions in an unending labyrinth of counterfeit roads that lead on to nowhere; then, the sepulchral gloom of spruce woods, muted corridors, that beyond a short distance from the River, had resounded to no sound of human voice; and more pleasant, the poplar ridges with golden pools of sunlight on their floor, and interspersed with huge individual pine trees, austere, towering and magnificent.

On the shores of the shallow, grassy lake we find the remnants of an ancient Indian town. A once proud flagpole had fallen in the midst of it and lay rotted beside the mouldering timbers, and good-sized trees grow within the moss-grown rectangle of what once had been Old Green Lake Post. On a low hillside, facing West, there is a graveyard and on one grave there stands a willow wand, and tied to it there is a tiny offering wrapped in yellow buckskin. It looks to have been quite recently placed there and arouses speculation; but we lay no finger on it and leave it quietly swaying there above its dead. And this evidence of remembrance and simple faith subdues even the rougher element among us. We wander round a little, and wonder who it was that lived here in those distant days, what trails they laid, and how the hunting was, how many of them there were who called this place their home. And the answers all lie buried in the grave-yard, below the grasses on the sunny hillside, their secrets, and the swinging, beaded token, guarded by a regiment of pines.

Not far from here we meet a lone-fire Indian. He comes ashore as we are eating and drifts on soundless, moccasined feet over to our fireplace and stands there for a moment, very still. 'I am Sah-Sabik,' he says. 'The white men call me Yellow Rock.' He is ancient, and says that he had known the Post when it was young. Kebsh-kong he calls it, Place-Walled-in-by-Rushes; which it was. We had never seen him before but he knows us all each by name and reputation, by means of that old and very efficient line of communication, the moccasin telegraph. We suspect that the offering on the grave is his, but do not ask. He has no English, but some among us know his language; but he tells us little. He talks not so much to us but to himself, and speaks not of the present but of the past, the very distant past, and of the men beside whose graves we had so lately stood. So we give him some tobacco for a present, and in return he offers some strips of dried moose meat in a clean, white linen bag, which we accept. He allows us to give him some tea too, and some flour, provided, he says, that it is a very little. He doesn't want to get a taste for it, because he has no means of getting any more. He lives the old way, asserting that the modern Indians eat too many soft foods (does this sound familiar?), have strayed from the way of their fathers, have become unmanly and have not guts. Hearing him, we wonder do all nations, tribes and generations of men so lament the ineptitude of the generation that follows them. His own meagre resources suffice him, for your true Indian uses sustenance merely as an engine uses fuel. For Northern wild life, waters and the Wilderness are his existence and apart from his few human relationships, the phenomena and inhabitants of the wild lands are his only interests, his perpetual occupation in which his physical appetites are almost entirely satisfied. His kind is rarely met to-day. A shadow amongst the shadows in this Shadowland the Indian recedes, as silently and as mysteriously, and as incalculably as he came, and will soon be gone. And so we leave the old man to his musing and his lonely re-collections.

To-night, the travelling being easy down a steady, uninterrupted current, we journey far and take our supper late, and travel on by moonlight. And now the forest that borders all the River becomes an eerie place of in-determinate outlines and looming, unfamiliar objects that come and go, and rear themselves up before us only to disappear on close approach. In the darker spots the canoes become invisible and can be only placed by the soft swish of the paddles; but where the moonlight filters through the trees there are pale shafts of illumination through which they pass like ghost-craft, or things impalpable, seen only for a moment, to disappear again. The spruce trees look like witches with tall, pointed bonnets and sable cloaks, and the white birches that flicker here and there among them as we pass, shine whitely out like slim, attenuated skeletons and in the shifting, garish moonbeams seem gruesomely to dance. In these shrouded catacombs the fire-flies glow on and off with pallid phosphorescence, little lambent eyes that wink and blink at us like lights on dead men's graves; while ever beside us loom the crowded legions of the trees, and there is that feeling that we pass before an endless concourse of motionless onlookers, unmoving and unmoved, shadowy spectators who watch with a profound and changeless apathy from the tall pavilions of the pine trees. And the brigade seems to move in a world of phantasma and unreality, as though the River were some strange, unearthly highway in another world where tall, dark beings, shrouded and without faces, gaze featurelessly from the river-banks upon us and stare and stare, or loom over us with ghostly whispering, while some, to all appearance, beckon with impish, claw-like hands to stay us, with a hideous suggestion of blind men reaching for us in the dark; while behind them lies a vast Kingdom of Gloom of which they are the dark inhabitants, and in whose shadowy thoroughfares untoward events lie crowded, imminently, ready to happen.

And we pitch camp in a moonlit glade and make a bonfire, which drives away the wraiths and goblins and brings us back to commonplace reality, and we discover then that we are tired. So we go to bed and sleep till noon next day. The afternoon is spent overhauling canoes, putting an edge on paddles, so they will cut sharply and without splashing or resistance in a heavy current. Dry

Wa-Sha-Quon-Asin

Rawhide
(*see page* 88)

Grey Owl and his Beaver Lodge. Sajo and Shapian did not live in
such a grand log cabin, but their home was amidst similar scenery

Grey Owl feeding a kitten-beaver by bottle

[*Courtesy of National Parks of Canada*

Grey Owl and Jelly Roll. Notice the tail underneath her

A beaver house. It is 22 ft. long, 18 ft. wide and 8 ft. high, and was built by two beavers in less than two months

Jelly Roll

[Courtesy of Canadian Official News Bureau]

Grey Owl and Jelly Roll at home. Notice the beaver lodge which
occupies part of the cabin

[*Courtesy of National Parks of Canada*

Moose calf browsing, in Riding Mountain National Park

A whiskey-jack eating from Grey Owl's hand

spruce poles are cut ten feet long, are trimmed and smoothed and driven into short sockets known as poling irons that give weight to the pole and will grip a rock, and are used both in descending and in climbing rapids, in water where a paddle is of no avail.

These preparations are suggestive and a little ominous, though you would not think so to hear the crowd roaring with laughter as Red Landreville tells the one about the calf that was born with a wooden leg. But I don't hear you laughing, brother; you say you feel that something is about to happen? Well, you are right, something is—the smooth, uneventful stretch is over. To-morrow we hit Seven League Rapids, the Twenty Mile. What's that? You say it needn't have come on quite so sudden, but that's what you came for, isn't it? And you can't go back, so you've got to go ahead. And besides, this is the high-light of the whole trip, and you'll enjoy it—and if you don't, you'd better not admit it.

Before second smoke the following morning, its deep voice is carried back to us by the South wind. The time of day is right, and the sun is in a good position for running; everyone is expectant, and iron-shod poles and extra paddles are placed firmly in position where they will not be jarred overboard, but can be snatched up at a moment's notice. For it will be fast work at times, in some spots a matter of split seconds.

The distant mutter of the rapids, as we draw on it, swiftly becomes a growl, grows louder, and increases in volume by the minute, moving swiftly towards us, rising up the scale of sound until it becomes a thunderous uproar. A hundred yards ahead the River suddenly drops abruptly out of sight, breaking off in a black, horizontal line from which white manes and spouts of foaming water leap up from time to time; below that—nothing, apparently, and the tree-lined banks fall away at what, from

L

that distance, looks to be a most alarming angle. But now we feel the tug and pull of the tow. No more talk.

The current, smooth as oil, deep and swift, carries us in its irresistible suction towards the dark V of deep water that marks the channel, and the canoes, driven a little faster than the current to gain steerage-way, are worked almost broadside on into this and at railroad speed, one after another, are flung like chips into this raging inferno of water. Are we going down sideways on this dangerous curve in these light flimsy craft at twenty miles an hour! Crossways, into this seething vortex!! Yes, yes, we must, to fight the current, to escape it and catch an eddy, for just ahead is a standing rock against which the full force of the River hurls itself in ungovernable fury, striking with terrific impact; and towards this the canoes are dragged by the deadly pull of the undertow, inevitably, inexorably. Crossways in the current, canoes headed towards the opposite bank, the crews dig deep with heavy, powerful strokes, faces set, eyes intent on some object they are using for a marker, using all the skill they know and straining every muscle to tear loose from the grip of the current that is dragging them, inescapably it seems, towards destruction. Inch by inch we are gaining the necessary leeway—comes a sudden, sharp crack, faintly heard above the racket—a broken paddle! A canoe, out of control, whirls towards the rock—swiftly the man (he is alone), grabs another paddle. His life depends on how quickly he moves—now his bow is farthest out, still sideways, and going fast—Look at that! he throws himself forward into it thus gaining a canoe's length, lifting the stern out of the current as his weight drives deep the bow—the canoe swings completely around and out, hurtling by the death-trap with only inches to spare. And then with a wild halloo the other canoes swing into line, head on, right to the edge of the current, and with whoops and yells of exultation the paddlers drive home into the thundering white water. A drumming sound passes swiftly, now it is far behind us—the rock—we have no time—confusion—an outrageous, dizzying medley of sound and furious action—snarling waves with teeth of stones, sheets of flying water, back-lash and hissing spume, the hoarse shouts of the white men and the high-pitched ululations of the Indians piercing the rolling drum-fire of the rapids. Men twist and heave and jab, and thrust with good maple paddles, throwing the canoes bodily, almost, from one strategic point to another, prying prow or stern aside from sure destruction. For this is Men against the River and all must run successfully. To fail means death. The bowsmen throw themselves forward, sideways, backward, the sternsmen sometimes standing, sometimes crouching in the bottom, reaching forward or behind, the paddles of both cutting the water like knives, their blades beneath the surface for half a dozen strokes. Each man senses his team-mate's every move, and each responds with lightning speed and the lithe quickness of a cat, as the canoes careen and plunge and pitch and the scenery goes reeling by, the trees an endless palisade on either side resounding, echoing and re-echoing with the roaring of the waters, a mighty close-packed concourse of immovable spectators, onlookers to the wild pageant of the River that races on between them in triumphant progress, decked with banners of white water and flashing crests of spray, and leaping waves like warriors, barbaric, plumed and shouting—this is the Twenty Mile.

And down its mad course go the Rivermen, carefree and debonair, wild, reckless, and fancy-free, gay caballeros riding the hurricane deck, rocketing down the tossing foaming River; a gallant, rollicking, colourful array, my trail companions; Men of the Mississauga.

From *Tales of an Empty Cabin*.

CHAPTER TWO

THE WINTER TRAIL

Out from town; the warmth, the laughter, the comfort left behind. Past half-finished barns, and snowy deserts of burnt stumps; past the squalid habitations of the alien, while the inmates stare out with animal curiosity; and so beyond the works of man, to where the woods become thicker and thicker, and all is clean, and silent, and shining white—the winter Trail.

Trees filing by in endless, orderly review, opening up before, passing on either hand, and closing in behind. That night a camp under the stars. Then, the hasty breakfast in the dark, breaking of camp in the knife-edged cold of dawn; shivering, whining huskies squirming impatiently whilst numb fingers fumble with toboggan strings, and the leather thongs of dog harness. Then away!

Strings of dogs swinging into line; a couple of swift, slashing dog fights, the shouts of the drivers, cracking of whips, and an eventual settling down to business. The swing and soft sough of snowshoes in the loose snow, the rattle of frame on frame. Then the sun rises. Glittering jewels of frost shivering on the pointed spruce-tops, like the gay ornaments on Christmas trees. The breath jets into the crackling air like little clouds of smoke, and steam rises off the dogs. Onward, onward, speed, speed, for the hands are still numb, and the cold strikes the face like volleys of broken glass; and we have far to go to-day.

So, for an hour; we begin to warm up. Suddenly ahead, the thud of a rifle, the answering crack leaping with appalling reverberations amongst the surrounding hills.

Shouts up front; someone has shot a caribou. Good! fresh meat for supper.

Two of the more lightly laden teams drop out, and their owners commence expertly to skin and dress the kill; as their hands become numb they will plunge them to the elbows in the warm blood for a minute, and resume their work.

More hours; steep hills where men take poles and push on the load ahead of them, to help the dogs; on the down grades, tail ropes are loosed, and men bear back with all their weight, some falling, others dragged on their snow-shoes as on a surf-board, amidst the shouts and yells of the brigade and the excited yapping of the dogs as they race madly to keep ahead of the flying toboggan. Meanwhile the Trail unwinds from some inexhaustible reel up front, passes swiftly underfoot and on behind, while the trees whirl swiftly by.

Then another stop; what is this? 'Dinner,' say the trail breakers; well, they ought to know, they are bearing the brunt of the work. Quick, crackling fires, tea made from melted snow, whilst the dogs take the opportunity to bite the ice balls off their feet; most of them are wearing moccasins, evidence of thoughtful owners; for men, red or white, have always a heart for a dog. Pipes are lighted, and all hands relax utterly and smoke contentedly—for a few minutes.

Meanwhile, a word for the husky. Lean, rangy, slant-eyed and tough as whalebone, hitched in teams of four; over muskegs and across frozen lakes; tails up, tongues hanging, straining against the harness, bracing themselves at the curves, trail-wise and always hungry, these faithful animals haul their loads all day for incredible distances. Not overly ornamental in appearance, inclined to savagery and deadly fighting, and thieves of no mean ability, these half-bred wolves are as necessary to transport in the North as horses were in the West in the early days. On more than a few occasions, they have been the means of saving life by their uncanny knowledge of ice, and unerring sense of direction.

And now the short rest is over, and we swing into position as the teams go by, and are away. Hours, miles, white monotony, and a keen, steady wind; lake and portage, gully and river bank; sometimes the crest of a bare hill from which a fleeting glimpse of the surrounding country is obtained. Limitless, endless, empty distance before, behind, and on either hand.

Later a trail turns in from the left, a thin winding ribbon, dwindling to a thread, to nothingness, across a lake, the far shores of which show but faintly, coming from out of the Keewaydin, the storied, mystic North. The trail is well packed by snowshoes of all sizes, men, women and children; Indians.

Good going now; the trail breakers, glad of the respite, drop behind. On the hard trail the snowshoes commence to sing.

Smoke ahead; teepees, windbreaks; the Indian camp. Sharp vicious barking, howling, and then an unspeakable uproar as a herd of wolf-dogs swoops down on the caravan. Shrill scolding of squaws, who belabour lustily with burning sticks, restoring comparative quiet. Black-eyed, round-faced children stand aloof, whispering in soft voices. Maidens with head shawls peep from canvas door-ways; buxom old ladies declaim loudly, as they cook at open fires. A tall spare man with Egyptian features, and long black hair, intones gravely in an ancient language, and we understand that we are invited to share the camp ground; the place is well sheltered, and we are told, there is much wood, moose meat. But we cannot stay; the mail is with us, and travels on schedule; to-night we camp at Kettle Rapids, to-morrow at Thieving Bar.

'Will we take tea.' We surely will, for who can refuse tea on the Trail? Large steaming bowls, and strong.

Away again; more hours, more miles. The teams with the meat have caught up, and the party redoubles its speed; it is getting colder and the men commence to trot. The snowshoes sing shriller now as the *babiche* tightens in the frost, and speed, and more speed is the slogan. Another lake; long, narrow, and bordered by glittering spruce trees garbed in white; the great sun, hanging low above them, dyeing their tops blood red.

And as the sun goes down, the shadows creep softly out of the woods to the feet of the runners, and beyond. The wind drops and the cold quickens. One man drops out; there is blood on his moccasins. Incorrectly dressed, his feet have chafed with the rub of the bridles and have been bleeding for an hour. Another man steps aside and joins the first; as no one of the brotherhood of trail runners can be left alone in distress; an unbreakable law. But the mail man is satisfied, so all hands stop for the night.

Out axes and after the dry wood, boys! A mighty clamour of steel biting into wood. Large piles of spruce boughs make their appearance. Semicircular windbreaks of canvas stretched over poles cluster before a central fire, eight feet long. Smoke billows up to a certain height, to open out in a spreading, rolling canopy over the camp. Dogs are fed with frozen fish or moose meat, this their only meal in twenty-four hours.

It has now been dark a long time, but wood is still being cut; eventually quiet settles down and the men sleep; but not the dogs. It seems they never sleep. One of them finds a morsel of something eatable; a swift rush and he is fighting at least six others. Howls, snarls, sharp shrill yapping as of wolves; then curses, shouts, thuds, and silent scurrying retreats; for your husky does not yelp when beaten, but is a skilful dodger.

Once more, quiet. And then the moon rises, pale, and very large, and seemingly no farther away than the back of the next ridge, the ragged outline of the shrouded trees standing sharply out across its face.

From around the fire, where each takes his turn at replenishing, come sounds of sleep. The bizarre shadows cast by the shifting flames dance in and out the tree trunks, and white snow-shoe rabbits appear and disappear silently within the circle of light, unseen by the dogs who have crept up near the fire, dozing with the eye nearest it.

The moon rises high and resumes its normal size. The cold grips the land with the bite of chilled steel; trees crack in the frost like scattering rifle-fire. Then, later, as the moon sets, a thin wailing comes stealing across the empty wastes, wavering in strophe and anti-strophe, increasing in volume as voice after voice takes up the burden; the song of the wolves.

A little later the mail man gets up, scans the stars, and pronounces it time to rise. An hour and a half, or less, and all is ready. As the day breaks, the last team disappears around a bend in the trail. And nothing remains but a few bare poles, flattened piles of brush, and a dead fire, and, stretching either way into the chill, white silence, the Trail.

Such, in normal circumstances, is the Trail in winter. A few days' soft weather, however, or a rain-storm, may bring conditions which make travelling virtually impossible. Yet a man caught out in such shape must do the impossible; he must go on. Goaded on by the knowledge of a rapidly diminishing food supply, or the certainty of more bad weather, he must keep moving; for this is the Trail, and will be served.

One season, having located a pocket of marten and lynx, which, being within a short distance of the railroad, had been overlooked, another man and myself hunted there all

have subscribed for a shrine at the place, in honour of some saint or other; as it was we said nothing, but seized the unfortunate beast, and quickly stripping the tump-line off the toboggan, with multiple knots fashioned a dog harness, and hitched up our new-found friend. Showing no regret for his interrupted hunt, he hauled along right manfully, whilst we, unable to do enough for our deliverer, kept the toboggan on the trail, as far as was humanly possible, with poles. About that time, the wind changed to the North, the sky cleared, and it commenced to freeze, and with all these things in our favour, we made the remainder of the trip with ease, having spent seventeen and a half hours of misery to cover about ten miles up to that point.

In the woods nothing can be obtained except by effort, often very severe and prolonged, at times almost beyond human endurance. Nothing will occur of its own volition to assist, no kindly passer-by will give you a lift, no timely occurrence will obviate the necessity of forging ahead, no lucky accident will remove an obstruction. Of course, a man can always give up, make fire, eat his provision, rest, and then slink back to camp, beaten and dishonoured; but that is unthinkable.

As you sit on your load to rest, searching the sky-line for some encouraging indication of progress, it is borne home to you most irrefutably that all the money in the world cannot hire a single hand to help you, and that no power on earth, save your own aching feet, will cause the scenery to go sailing by, or take one solitary inch off the weary miles ahead. And as you sit in chill discomfort, your body bowed down from the weight of your load, your mind depressed by the incubus of the slavish labour yet to do, you realise that the longer the rest, so much longer you remain on the Trail. The thought goads you on to further efforts. Those packs will never move themselves, and the fact that they may contain skins worth a small fortune obtains for you no respite.

In civilisation, if you showed your peltries, attention would be showered on you: willing hands would lift you to your feet. Deep in the forest your valuable pack becomes a useless burden, except for the pinch or two of tea and the few bites of greased bannock it may contain, which are worth, to you, more than all the gold in Araby.

At times you are fain to give up, and abandon your hardly won treasure, of which you would give the half for one mile of good footing, or the privilege of going to sleep for an hour. But you must struggle on; exhaustion may be such that further movement seems impossible, or you may have injuries that cause exquisite torture with every movement; but that trip must be finished, or in the latter event, fire must be lighted and camp of some kind made.

The beautiful marten stole gracing the shoulders of the elegantly dressed woman in Bond Street or on Broadway might, if it were able, tell a tale its owner little guesses.

From *Men of the Last Frontier*.

CHAPTER THREE

RISKS OF THE TRAIL

The hardships and privations of the trapper's life have developed in him a determination, a dogged perseverance, and a bulldog tenacity of purpose not often necessary in other walks of life. At the outset, before the commencement of the hunt, the trapper may have to spend one or two months in getting supplies to his ground, after spending most of the summer searching for a likely spot. His exploration work is of great value to those who follow him, but it is all lost time to him. He expects, and receives, nothing for his labours, but counts it all in the day's work, and hopes his ground will produce the goods. On such trips these men are sometimes called on to perform seemingly impossible feats, and probably no trip coming inside my recollection would illustrate this better than the journey undertaken by a white man and an Indian, three winters ago in Northern Quebec.

These men came from further south and, having made no allowance for the difference in climate, on their arrival found the freeze-up already in progress. Travelling during this period is considered by even the most enduring as being almost, if not quite, impossible.

Nothing daunted, these two hardy souls commenced their pilgrimage, for it was nothing less. Each had a canoe-load of about 600 lbs. On the first lake they found ice, which whilst not capable of bearing a man, effectually prevented the passage of a canoe. This had to be broken, the two men armed with poles first breaking a channel in an empty canoe, from one expanse of open water to another. This entailed the unloading of 600 lb. of baggage on any kind of shore, into the snow, and the reloading of it on the return of the empty canoe; work enough, if frequently performed. They proceeded thus at the rate of about three miles a day, carrying the loads and canoes over seven portages. It snowed steadily day and night, increasing the difficulties on portages, making camping out a misery, and preventing at the same time the ice from becoming thick enough to walk on.

For five days they continued this struggle, making camp every night after dark, soaking wet and exhausted. It now turned colder, and this did not improve the ice under its clogging mass of snow water, while in the channel so laboriously broken, the cakes of ice and slush often cemented together, during the return trip, into a stronger barrier than the original ice had been. Held up at length on the shores of an eight-mile lake by these conditions they passed around the entire shoreline of one side of the lake on snowshoes, the ice being too weak to carry them otherwise, and even then, within a few feet of the shore, driving their axes through the ice at one blow every few feet. A full day was consumed on the outward journey, and they returned by the light of a clouded moon, splashed to the head, their garments freezing as they walked. But they were well repaid, as the water flooded the ice around the holes they had cut, and slushed up the snow on it. The whole mass froze through, forming a kind of bridge, over which they passed in safety, wing the canoes and loads in relays on improvised sleighs.

This style of progress, alternating with the usual portages, continued for several more days, one man going through the ice in deep water, and being with difficulty rescued. The men were in no danger from starvation, but wrestling with hundred-pound bags of provisions under such trying conditions, and carrying ice-laden canoes over portages on snowshoes, was too severe a labour to be long continued. Worn-out and discouraged by their seemingly hopeless task, too far in to turn back, not far enough advanced to remain, faced by the prospect of passing the best part of the winter on a main route denuded of game, these companions in tribulation plodded with bitter determination, slowly, painfully, but persistently ahead.

Mile by mile, yard by yard, foot by foot, it seemed, those mountainous loads proceeded on their way, as two steely-eyed, grim-faced men opposed their puny efforts to the vindictive Power that vainly inhibited their further progress.

Their objective was a fast-running river, some forty miles in from the railway, knowledge of which had caused them to retain their canoes, in the hopes of finding it unfrozen. This proved to be the case, and on its current they travelled in ease and comfort, as far, in two days, as they had previously done in the two weeks that they had been on the trail. When the water no longer suited their direction, they camped several days to rest up; and winter coming on in real earnest, they cached their now useless canoes, and making sleighs moved on into their ground by easy stages.

From *Men of the Last Frontier*.

*   *   *   *

On a night in mid-winter, eleven years ago, I stood on my snowshoes with my back to a small tree in a raging blizzard, and ate what was left of a small cache I had expected to find. The birds had stolen the most of it, and there remained only two tiny pieces of salt pork and a chunk of bannock. These were all frozen solid, and when knocked together gave out a clinking sound, like stones.

It was about thirty degrees below zero and, snowing at such an unusually low temperature, the volleying snow-flakes lashed my face like white-hot sand as they whirled around and past the not very large tree, which covered little more than the centre of my back.

I had travelled hard, in five feet of snow all day. There had been nothing to eat since breakfast, and it was now well after midnight. I had twenty miles or so to go. In such circumstances, and with the terrific drain on the physical resources that such conditions imposed, all this meant something—might mean anything before morning. Making fire in such a tempest, in a country so exposed as this was, would be utterly out of the question, and later, having got fairly on my way, I would not care to stop—would not dare to, perhaps. So I thawed the pork by putting it in my mouth for a spell. At first it froze lightly to my lips, but the warmth of my breath soon thawed it loose, and presently a gooey coating formed on the outside of it. This I scraped off with my teeth, and the resulting product burnt its icy way down my famished gullet like molten lead. The bannock was more obstinate, and responded to treatment only when it had been industriously whittled into chips with an axe on the edge of a snowshoe frame. Sounds simple, but it isn't—not in the dark, in a blizzard, and a man numb, exhausted and spent with hunger. It all took a very long time. The fires of vitality can burn very low at such times. And some of the bannock chips were lost; I would as soon have thrown away a bucket of diamonds.

Eventually the bannock and pork were thawed and munched and stowed away where the birds couldn't get at them any more. After this grotesque and unspeakable meal I left there feeling a good deal better, not at all uncomfortable, and in excellent spirits, arriving at my main camp in very fair condition, considering.

So perhaps comfort can after all be found in nearly anything, provided we need it badly enough at the time.

From *Tales of an Empty Cabin.*

*　　　*　　　*　　　*

A timely sense of humour has taken the sting from many a bitter misfortune, for out on the endless Trail, the line between tragedy and comedy is very finely drawn. A look, a word, anything that will crack a laugh in faces drawn with anxiety, no matter at whose expense, will often make a burlesque out of what would otherwise be an intolerable situation.

For instance, no one could ask for a more humorous and elevating exhibition than I myself once gave, before an interested audience of sixteen Fire Rangers. Upset by an unfortunate move, for which my partner and I were equally to blame, I swung out of the canoe as it capsized, keeping hold of the stern, and going down the rest of the swift water like the tail of a comet, amidst the sarcastic comment of the assembled Rangers. My bowsman was wearing heavy boots instead of moccasins, and in a kneeling position, the usual one in a canoe, his stiff foot-wear had become wedged beneath the thwart. He must have been almost a minute under the overturned canoe, unable to extricate himself, and in grave danger of drowning, when, with what little assistance I could give, he somehow got loose. Bewildered, he climbed on to the canoe, which being old and heavy, immediately sank and me with it.

I am an indifferent swimmer, if any, and this was a dangerous eddy, and deep; there were no hand holds to speak of. So although it rolled and twisted considerably in the cross current, I stayed with the canoe, on the chance that it would float up, as without it I would be a dead loss anyhow; and soon my head broke water again. The attentive concourse on the river bank, who were in nowise disturbed, evidently thinking we were giving an aquatic performance for their benefit to lighten the cares of a heavy day, were highly diverted, until my companion, on my return to the surface, swam ashore, where his condition apprised them of the true state of affairs. In a matter of seconds a canoe was racing towards me, whilst its occupants shouted encouragement. About this time I was in pretty bad shape, having taken much water, and my hold on the canoe was weakening; so I commenced to shout lustily, suggesting speed. To my horror, one of the men suddenly ceased paddling and commenced to laugh.

'Say,' said he. 'Why don't you stand up?'

And amidst the cheers and shouts of the appreciative assemblage, I stood up in about three feet of water. I had been floating with my legs out ahead of me, and had drifted backwards within a few yards of the shore.

Then there is the official whom I saw sitting in a canoe which had run aground and filled. Wet to the waist, he sat in the water with both feet elevated above the gunwales.

'What are you doin' there?' angrily demanded his assistant, who stood on the rock, submerged to the knees.

'Keeping my feet dry,' replied the official with chattering teeth.

Many of the prospectors are old 'desert rats' and plainsmen, used to horses and knowing but little about canoes. One such, not realising the chances he was taking, attempted the negotiation of a difficult piece of fast water with the loaded canoe, whilst his companion crossed the portage. Unable to distinguish the channel, the prospector ran foul of a swift shallows; and, on getting out to lighten the load, he was swept off his feet and nearly carried away. The canoe swung sideways and filled, to the gunwales, and, with part of its contents, was salvaged only after an hour's hard work. An inventory was taken of the remaining goods, which were found to be thoroughly soaked. The man who had walked did not berate his crestfallen companion, who was responsible for the mishap, merely remarking disgustedly:

'We needn't have gone to all that trouble, we could have got that stuff just as wet letting it down on a rope.'

From *Men of the Last Frontier*.

* * * *

It is a serious misfortune, nay, a catastrophe of sweeping proportions, for a trapper to be burnt out, or see his territory going up in smoke. I know whereof I speak, having had the distress of seeing the greater portion of a well-loved and familiar landscape destroyed by a fire in the space of forty-eight hours, I myself and several others barely escaping with our lives, and this necessitated my moving out of the district entirely. I was in the Fire Service at the time, and on going out to the village for provisions was detained by the Chief, as smoke had been observed in a district with which he knew me to be familiar. That same evening an Indian, having paddled fifty miles without stopping, save for portages, came in and reported the exact location of the fire, which had come from somewhere south and west, and was fast eating its way into my hunting ground.

The next day a gang of hastily hired rangers and Indians started for the scene of the trouble. The main route was very circuitous, and more than once my fortunate knowledge of the presence of beavers enabled us to make use of several short cuts, the dams being in good condition, and the shallow creeks, otherwise unnavigable, being well flooded. With these things in our favour we arrived within ten miles of our objective late on the first day and we began to hear the roar of the fire. That night, as we camped, sparks and large flakes of dead ashes fell into the tenting ground, and the sky was lit up by the terrible, but beautiful and vivid, glare of a sea of flames. Much delayed by numerous portages, it was not until noon the next day that we were within measurable distance of the conflagration. There was a considerable mountain between us and the fire, and along the foot of this we tugged and hauled heavily loaded canoes up a shallow river, plugged with old fallen timber. Sparks, brands and burning birch bark fell about us unheeded. Sweating white men cursed and heaved, and passed scathing remarks on the owner of the country who did not keep his rivers in shape—myself. Patient, silent Indians juggled canoes and their loads with marvellous dexterity from one point of least resistance to another. Men of four nations waded in mud to the knees, broke paddles and ripped canvas from canoe-bottoms, unreprimanded by an eloquent and forceful Chief.

At his desire I described a short route to the fire area, and he swiftly made his plans and disposed his forces. My allotted sector, with two Crees, was the mountain, at the foot of which a couple of men made camp. Once up the mountain, from which we had a plain view of the camp, we separated, each taking a different direction, in order to get three observation angles on the fire from the eminence. Once alone, and in a fever of anxiety concerning my possible losses, I plunged ahead at full speed, angling towards the greatest volume of sound. I must mention here, that being used to moccasins, I was much hampered by a pair of stiff hard-soled larrigans which I had donned for fire-fighting purposes, and in which at times I was at some pains to keep on my feet.

I was suddenly startled by the sight of a bear which lumbered by me, bound for the river. A rabbit raced almost between my legs, then another and another. The roar had become deafening, and the heat almost unbearable, and I strained every muscle to attain the western, or far, crest of the mountain, before it became untenable for my purpose. I saw another galloping rabbit, and noticed curiously that it was passing from the left, when it should have been coming head on. A partridge flew, again from my left, struck a tree, and fell to the ground, scorched, blinded, and gasping. It I killed in mercy.

Just then I detected a sharper undertone of sound underlying the deeper heavy roar ahead of me, and on looking to the left and behind me, towards the line of flight of the bird, from whence it seemed to come, I saw the thin crackling line of a ground-fire creeping swiftly towards me like a molten carpet, now within a hundred yards of me, and backed at no great distance by a seething wall of flames. The fire had met me more than half-way, and had thrown out a flanking party. I was neatly trapped.

I turned and incontinently fled, making for the widest part of the V of flames, as the main conflagration had now caught up. And here is where my hard-soled packs came in. Unused to boots, I found I could not run on the slippery jack-pine needles without losing time, and it took all of whatever will-power I may possess to tone my movements down to a swift walk, and curb my desire to race, and scramble, and tear my way regardless of boots, direction or anything else, just run—run. The flames were now on three sides of me, and my clothes were becoming brittle. Fortunately the intense heat kept the smoke up so that if I could keep my distance I was in no danger of suffocation; the danger lay in a very probable enveloping movement by the enemy.

I saw some harrowing sights. Dumb creatures endeavouring to save their lives from the one element against which all are helpless, some succeeding others not.

I saw tiny partridges in huddled groups, some lying on their backs with leaves in their claws, beneath which they deemed themselves invisible, realising that there was danger somewhere, and using the only protection that they knew. And—I know of no greater love that a mother can have than this—I saw the hen bird sitting dumbly by, unable to herd the little creatures to safety, waiting to burn with them.

The smoke darkened the brightness of noonday, but the cavern of flames lit up the immediate surroundings with a dull red glow. I was keeping ahead of the fire but my direction began to be a matter of doubt. 'Follow the animals', I kept thinking; but all that could had gone by, and now there were no more. I forced back my terrible fear. I caught myself saying: 'You can't make me run, you—you can't make me run,' and there I was running and slipping and stumbling in my deadly footwear; and with a jerk I slowed, or rather accelerated, to my swiftest walk.

More partridges, eyeing me dumbly from low limbs, and the chicks huddled beneath: oh the pity of it! Two more rabbits: follow them, follow them, fast! A small muskeg showed up; I raced for it expecting a pond: there was none. Past the muskeg and on. The growth of small cypress that cluttered the forest here became very thick. Surrounded by smoke, now commencing to billow down with the back-draught of the fire, my brain reeling with the heat, with the horror of what was too probably to be my funeral pyre driving me on, I scrambled desperately ahead, with no thought but to keep the advancing flanks of the destroyer behind me.

My feet seemed leaden, and my head a shell, light and empty, as I squirmed with desperate contortions to force a way through the continuous barrier, like a cane-brake, of small trees. I could no longer keep any specific direction, but knew I must now be far past the camp. I thought momentarily of my two companions; I had long since passed the area they had been assigned to. And then, breaking at length through the last of the barrier of saplings, I burst out on the eastern brow of the mountain. Fire goes but slowly down a hill, so I took time to breathe, and looking down could see the camp; and from its proximity I knew that my ordeal by fire had not lasted over twenty minutes, if that, though I would have sworn that it had occupied an hour.

The camp ground itself was a scene of the utmost confusion. Tents were being pulled down by main force and jammed into canoes, sometimes poles and all; pots, blankets, baggage and equipment of all kinds, seemed, at that distance, to be picked up in quantities and dumped on to the nearest craft.

I descended the mountain, the fire commencing to creep over its edge, and found waiting for me with a canoe one of the Crees who had gone up with me. He had seen me coming out on the summit, expecting me there as he watched the course of the fire. He grinned and spoke in English:

'Hot like hell, eh?'

'Some,' I replied soberly, as I felt the split and scorched back of my canvas shirt.

On the river just above the camp was a live beaver-dam, and it came as a timely assistance in aiding us to make our getaway, deepening the river so that we reached without loss of time a mile and a half portage leading inland to a large lake. This, one of my main trails, was in good shape, and we moved over it at nothing less than a trot. To check the fire was impossible without a change of wind, and in any case reinforcements were necessary.

From *Men of the Last Frontier*.

*   *   *   *

Three years ago, on a night in spring, a man went down from his camp fifty yards to the river to get a pail of water and has never been seen since.

A year before the time of writing, in this district, a deer-hunter took an afternoon stroll and was discovered eleven days later, by one of a gang of twenty-five men who scoured the woods for him for twenty miles around.

In the first case the man strayed off the water-trail in the dark, and not arriving at the shack he attempted to correct his mistake and took a short cut, only to arrive back to the river at another point. He again endeavoured to strike the camp, but, angling too much to his right, missed it. So much was learned by the finding of the pail at the river bank, and by his tracks. After that he entered a country of burnt, bare rocks, and small patches of green swamp, and he is there yet.

The second man, having killed a deer, remained where he was, erected a shelter and kept a fire. Beyond the mental strain incident to his adventure he was in good condition when found. Wherein lies the secret of the difference between being correctly and incorrectly lost.

The safest course, with night coming on, and being still astray, is for one to stop, make a fire and as comfortable a camp as maybe, and wait for daylight, with the feeling of security that it brings after the uncertainties and exaggerated forebodings of a long night. Then, perhaps, bearings can be taken to better advantage, and the sun may be shining, although it may now, after half a day of extended and aimless ramblings, be impossible for the wanderer to determine in which direction a start should be made.

From *Men of the Last Frontier*.

*   *   *   *

Hardship is a comparative term, according to habit and environment. I once was a guest in a house where something or other fused, and the electric lights went out. For those people it was a real hardship, perhaps the first that some of them had known, and very well I could appreciate this, as it was certainly highly inconvenient, if not in some degree dangerous. It was as though a person had gone suddenly blind, than which, aside from the thought of impending torture, I can think of nothing more terrifying. For I have been blind, out on a frozen lake at night, alone.

It was a matter of eight miles to the nearest human being, but eight miles is as good as a hundred if you are blind, out in the snow-bound Wilderness. Early that morning I had left from the last settlements. I was lucky enough to get a lift from some freighters who were going in with supplies for a party of surveyors. It was not at all cold, a state of affairs that made bad snow-shoeing, but was very comfortable weather for enjoying a ride, something I didn't often have. That night the freighters made camp some miles from a cabin, where I intended to sleep, and I refused their invitation to stay with them, and slipping into my snowshoe-bridles started off. There were signs of a possible storm and some of the men urged me to stay; but travelling at night, even in a storm, held no terrors for me, I supposed, and away I went. For a little time after leaving the warm, ruddy camp fire, with the congenial company gathered around it, the portage trail felt very lonely and dark and cheerless, and I almost turned back once or twice. However, with the concentrated attention to business that night travelling demands, I had little time for vain regrets and the feeling of lonesomeness soon passed. I then noticed that it was getting colder; all the better snow-shoeing, thought I; which it was.

Arriving at the end of the portage, I discovered that the wind had changed to the North. Quite a stiff breeze was blowing, but there were no clouds. The waning moon, pale and on its back, the half averted face upon it pinched and sunken like the visage of one dead, gave out a pallid illumination that helped very little to distinguish the features of the landscape. The lake was about seven miles across, and on its far shore stood the cabin I was making for, and giving my snowshoe-bridles a few twists to tighten them, I started across the wide expanse of lake.

The snow was badly drifted into hard irregular waves, and the sickly light of the recumbent moon was worse than none at all, constantly deceiving my eyes, so that I stubbed my snowshoes on the brittle crests of snow waves or else stepped out on to nothing, to land with a back-breaking jar in a trough. This was very tiring and I had to go slow at last, becoming so fatigued that I even considered going ashore, making fire and passing the night there. But the shores on either side were a couple of miles or so away, and I was now well over half way up the lake towards my destination. Moreover, the wind had now freshened and was getting stronger every minute, and I had no idea of what it might portend before morning came. It presently increased to a steady gale that was neither blustering nor boisterous, but that blew with a ceaseless, changeless velocity that had the sweeping drive of a rushing wall of water and, in my tired condition, was nearly as irresistible. This wind was from the North and blew somehow dry and brassy, hard as sandpaper, and cut like a buzz-saw, even through my stout buckskins. Between the freezing, tearing wind and the continual stumbling over the snow-billows I was rapidly becoming exhausted. My eyes began to burn, and it seemed as if the wind was drying them, so that when I shut them and walked some distance with them closed, as I was now obliged to do from time to time, they felt as though filled with hot sand.

Presently I noticed that when looking straight ahead the shore on my right was, for some reason, getting dim. Now, I knew it to be only half a mile away as, hoping for a certain amount of shelter, I had been veering towards it for some time; while the shore on my left, at least three miles away, was plainly visible out of the tail of the other eye. Before long I found that unless I turned and looked at it directly the right-hand shore showed only as a grey, shapeless wall. This struck me as strange, and not a little disturbing, and I hadn't gone very far when the other, more distant shore became dim, turned grey and disappeared entirely. I looked up. I couldn't see the moon. And then dawned upon me the realisation that I was going blind! I could still see my showshoes, and they were covered with new snow; I looked down at my buckskin shirt, it was white with snow—yet no snow was falling on my face; perhaps it was frost. I tried to brush it off; it wouldn't come. I turned up the shirt and looked inside; it was white too—that was it! my eyes were turning slowly white, everything else was turning white—eyes that could see only white—white blindness, the terrible White Death I'd heard the Indians talk about!

I stood still for a few moments and let this sink in. Then I made for the shore while I could still distinguish it. In my haste, unable to see the snow with my bleaching eyeballs, I tripped and staggered, and fell repeatedly. I wanted to get close enough so I could hear the gale roaring in the timber on the shore, otherwise if it too should disappear, I might not ever find it. I was surrounded by a wall of white save in this one direction. But I got there, just about in time, for as I approached it seemed to melt, dissolve away from either side, leaving in front of me only a narrow strip of grey, that stood upright before me. I remember thinking that it looked like a grey great bastion, and had the effect of being round as the sides fell away to where they were invisible; and this I watched as it too began to shrink, turned white and receded into nothingness. And I pawed the air to feel for it after it was gone, and I stumbled forward with outstretched hands to find it, this, my last link with the living world; and I ran a step or two and crashed into a tree and fell upon my back there, in the snow.

And I knew then that I was blind. I knew all the stark horror, the awful helplessness, and the unutterable anguish of one stricken suddenly blind. I scrambled to my feet as the ghastly, inescapable FACT roared like thunder through my reeling intellect, that it had got me, that I was blind—white-blind! My showshoes were off and hung around my ankles and as I stood I sank to the hips in the snow, and cried out, a terrible, animal sound, the agonised cry of some creature in a trap, my fists clenched above my head, staring out with my sightless eyes, trying to make them see. I must have been in a little bay, for there was no wind there, and that awful demoniacal yell came back to me and I yelled again in answer to the echo, and while my face ran with perspiration I shouted 'I am blind, blind, do you get it? I am BLIND!' And the echoes answered 'I am blind—am blind—blind—blind.' And a demon came and whispered 'You are blind,' and beat at my brain and the frenzy passed and my body became pleasantly numb and warm, and I sat down comfortably in the snow and my eyes didn't hurt any more; and I was very tired. And I thought this must be the end; the end. It seemed strange to go out in this way after having braved the Wilderness so long—so simple, and after all, so easy. And I remember thinking that if I was found, no one would ever know what it had been all about.

And then all at once I came out of my lethargy, and

muttered to myself that I was not going to be found in the Spring spread out on the beach like a dead toad, but decently, with my weapons and my snowshoes beside me, kind of natural looking. What puerile things we think of in extremity! But I had lost my rifle and axe, and I crawled around in the snow and felt for them, but could not find them. So I wallowed a little further inshore, my snowshoes dragging by the bridles, and ran into a large tree. With a snowshoe I dug a hole in the snow, at the foot of it, crawled in there, stood the snowshoes up beside it, then pulled as much of the snow in on top of me as I could. Thus I would sleep; and nothing else seemed to matter. The wind had now died down, and without it I could never find my way and would perhaps wander bewildered on the lake until I dropped from exhaustion. Better this, the cleaner way.

Reader, do not judge me, not until you have had a like experience. There was not the heat of battle, nor the heroic intoxication of some deed of valour or self-sacrifice. I had taken the field once too often against the power of Nature, had pitted my puny strength against the Wilderness; and this time I had lost. Just one more animal who must submit to the invincible decrees of the creed he lived by—the survival of the fittest. A small error in judgment had proven me unfit; I should never have started out from the freighters' camp. However, I was to get another chance.

Some hours later I awoke with a start, and stood up. At every move sharp daggers of pain shot through my muscles. I knew what that meant—I was beginning to freeze. I cursed myself for waking up. Now it had to be all gone through again. Water was streaming from my eyes and they felt as though on fire. I had tied my black silk neckerchief over them and this I now took off, and opened them.

It was with a distinct shock that I found that I could see; but that was about all. I could with difficulty make out shapes of tall grey spectres that stood about me, looking like huge columns wrapped in wool, enormously thick; these no doubt were trees. In one direction there was a faint glow, as of a candle light seen through a piece of flannel; this I supposed, was the moon. My snowshoes resembled twin tombstones and when I reached for them I missed them by a foot or so.

Well, if I was going to see, there was no use in dying. Everything was very dim and hazy and distorted, and every object appeared to be coated with wool, or of enormous size. But I could see—enough to make a fire, beside which I sat on a bed of balsam brush until my sight was sufficiently restored to move on. I worked on my eyes, opening and shutting the lids, massaging them, and mopping the stream of water that flowed from them. The eyeballs felt rough, as if corrugated. Slowly, painfully, they resumed their office, even though imperfectly. All this took a long time to do, and I found myself weak and almost incapable. A little more and I would never have got away from there.

Owing to their fictitiously exaggerated size everything I reached for eluded me, and it would have looked strange to an onlooker to have seen me clawing away at things that were six or eight inches from my hands; under any other circumstances it would have been an interesting experience.

Towards morning I collected axe and rifle and after a rather severe ordeal arrived at the cabin.

The tips of all my fingers were frozen, and I didn't see very well for several days. But I had learned a very useful lesson, and had perhaps found out the reason why men of known skill and proficiency in Winter travelling, have been found, unaccountably, dead.

From *Tales of an Empty Cabin.*

*   *   *   *   *

Whether treading bitter trails, or resting securely in warm log cabins; faltering over empty barrens with staring eyes; hollow-cheeked with hunger or with hands dyed to the wrist with the rich blood of newly killed meat; fighting for life with desperate strokes in the hungry white water, or floating peacefully along some slow, winding river; these men of the Last Frontier are toilsomely, patiently, but indubitably laying the stepping-stones by which will pass the multitudes of future ages.

On the outskirts of the Empire this gallant little band of men still carries on the game that is almost played. The personnel changes as the years roll on, but the spirit remains the same. Each succeeding generation takes up the work that is laid down by those who pass along, leaving behind them traditions and a standard of achievement that must be lived up to by those who would claim a membership in the brotherhood of the Keepers of the Trails; bequeathing something of their courage, self-sacrifice, and devotion to a cause, to those who follow.

These are the soldiers of the Border Lands. Whether recruited from pioneer stock, and to the manner born, or from the ranks of the wage earners; whether scion of a noble house, or the scapegrace who, on account of some thoughtless act has left the haunts of men, or, perchance, a rolling-stone to whom adventure is as the breath of life; each and every one is playing his allotted part in that heroic struggle which is making possible the fulfilment of the greater and more lasting purpose of the future.

We, to-day, of this generation, are seeing the last of the free trappers; a race of men, who, in passing, will turn the last page in the story of true adventure on this continent, closing for ever the book of romance in Canadian History. The forest cannot much longer stand before the conquering march of modernity, and soon we shall witness the vanishing of a mighty wilderness.

And the last Frontiersman, its offspring, driven back further and further towards the North into the far-flung reaches where are only desolation and barrenness, must, like the forest that evolved him, bow his head to the inevitable and perish with it. And he will leave behind him only his deserted, empty trails, and the ashes of his dead camp fires, as landmarks for the oncoming millions. And with him will go his friend the Indian to be a memory of days and a life that are past beyond recall.

From *Men of the Last Frontier.*

IV

CREATURES OF THE WILD

CONTENTS

CHAPTER ONE

BEARS

Waskesieu is a tent city situated on the shores of a lake of the same name, a lake the far end of which is invisible to you as you stand on the broad expanse of sandy beach, some hundred of yards in length, that stretches before this town of tents. The furthest you can see is at a point where the shores taper down from the bold, spruce-clad hills on either side, and nearly meet, forming a narrows only a bow-shot across, and even this point, in the middle distance, is visible only as a long, low line that shimmers in the sunlight of a Summer day. And far off as you may consider this, when you get there you are still only half-way up the lake.

Standing on the beach at Waskesieu, you begin to have a faint idea of the real meaning of the word Distance. Thirty miles from the camps, and beyond the distant narrows, accessible only by water, is Ajawaan Lake, where my Beaver People and I have our home in one of Canada's greatest Wilderness playgrounds, Prince Albert National Park.

Far enough away to gain seclusion, yet within reach of those whose genuine interest prompts them to make the trip, Beaver Lodge extends a welcome to you if your heart is right; for the sight of a canoe approaching from the direction of the portage, or the appearance of some unexpected visitors on the mile-long trail that winds through the forest from larger and more navigable waters, all coming to bid the time of day to Jelly Roll and Rawhide and their band of workers, is to me an event of consuming interest. Save for my animal friends I live here quite alone, and human contacts, when I get them, mean a lot, and are important.

The whole region is one vast Wilderness of lake and forest, and you may pass beyond the boundaries of the Park (if twenty-three hundred square miles of country is not enough for you) and never know the difference, and you can go East and West for unthinkable distances, and North as far as the Arctic Circle, with little interruption save that provided by the trading posts.

Every Spring the tent dwellers move into Waskesieu, and every Fall move out again, leaving this vast, un-peopled territory to the Mounted Police, the Park wardens, the teeming wild life population and myself. And perhaps the most interesting of all these Summer visitors are the bears. Waskesieu has bears of all kinds— excepting grizzlies—from little fellows of a hundred pounds or so, just youngsters starting out in life, to others that will go six hundred pounds—by no means the largest —just good, comfortable-sized bears, if you get what I mean. There are black ones with red muzzles, black ones without red muzzles, reddish brown, dark brown, and just plain brown bears, and I have seen some that were a rich bronze colour. They are inoffensive, good-natured fellows, who pay not the slightest attention to anybody, and it is no uncommon thing to meet a bear or so walking peacefully along the highway. The streets of the tent city are lighted up at night, but the lights are some distance apart, and it has been suggested that more lights be provided so the bears can see their way around and not get scared stiff by having people bump into them in the dark. They forgather around the various cook-shacks in groups of half a dozen or more, nosing around among the scraps that the cooks throw out for them, acting towards each other with an unfailing courtesy which it is very elevating to observe, and politely ignoring the sightseers, who are getting the thrill of their lives and who, at a distance of about twenty feet, get all the bear pictures they could ever wish for. Some of these bears, the bigger ones are regular visitors every year, and must be nearly worn to the bone from being photographed.

There is a seventy-mile highway between Prince Albert and the tent city of Waskesieu, that runs bang through the bush for the last forty miles of its length, and there is a spot, near the resort, where a she-bear and her cubs (one of those ferocious she-bears we hear so much about) will wait for cars, and if you stop for them the entire family will come over and beg for titbits in the most barefaced fashion. This, of course, rather discredits a lot of good old-fashioned traditions concerning bears, but the occupants of the car get quite a kick out of it, and can truthfully say thereafter that they are able to look a bear in the face.

Some of the younger set, among the newer bears, before they become thoroughly acquainted with the regulations, indulge in some rather ill-considered pranks, such as entering unoccupied tents and falling asleep there or getting their heads in garbage cans and having to be extricated, and a lady of my acquaintance entered her camp to find in it what she thought was a large black dog, who was making himself very much at home, and who regarded her entrance with supreme indifference. Somewhat nettled by this cavalier behaviour, the lady administered a severe drubbing to the intruder first with the flat of her hand and then with the broom, only to discover of a sudden that it was no dog at all, but a middle-sized bear, who behaved with admirable restraint, and allowed himself to, so to speak, be swept out of the house.

Yet another had, during his wanderings, been unchivalrous enough to annex a pair of ladies' shorts. He played with them awhile, but there was no kick in them, and quickly tiring of the pastime he moved off to fresh adventures. However, his claws had become entangled in the material and he could not detach it, and every so often he would stop and try to shake it loose, sometimes standing erect to do so, waving the offending piece of apparel at arm's length above his head, like a flag. He went through the most extraordinary contortions to rid himself of his encumbrance, and his evident embarrassment at his inability to remove it was highly diverting to onlookers. Eventually the garment flew high in the air and landed on the branch of a tree, and the bear, greatly relieved, looked at it fixedly for a moment and kept on going.

Then there is the one who is said to have attached himself to the hotel, and every day, at a certain hour, he would walk most unconcernedly into the kitchen. He being rather a large bear, the staff would walk just as unconcernedly out. Arrangements were always made for his accommodation, the odd pie and so forth being left out for him to eat, in order that he would not burglarise the premises. Having eaten he would walk out in a state of the greatest gratification, and the staff would then walk in, also with a good deal of satisfaction, and not without some feelings of relief. So everybody was quite cheerful about the whole business.

Sometimes a store-house gets broken into, but this is generally by the lower, and less educated type of bear. No real harm is intended of course, it being really the fault of the night watchman who omitted to leave the door open. However, no bear who knows his onions, or has at least a grain of self-respect, will do this, it being more ethical, and also a deal less labour, to beg his meals at the cookery.

There is a report comes from one Summer resort (not Waskesieu!) that certain bears, wrongly accused of wilful damage and being victims of misunderstanding by the grown-ups, have been caught playing clandestinely with the children. How far these misunderstood bears would go in their endeavours to make themselves better appreciated is problematical, but probably no further than to take whole parties of youngsters on their backs for rides into the country.

Your bear is really a good fellow, and will eat almost anything that you give him, or that you may inadvertently leave lying around, just to show you that his heart is in the right place. He has a humorous outlook on life, and a few minor depredations should not be allowed to detract from his character. He expects you to be very broad-minded; and why not? That bears sometimes break open provision caches and take out bags of flour, scattering the flour all over about half an acre of land and rolling in it, proves nothing except that bears are playful in disposition and like to roll in flour. I will admit that a bear who behaves in this manner should be severely reprimanded, but a judicious display of several quarters of beef, or choice ham, or a few jars of honey tastefully arranged so as to catch the eye (leave the jars closed, the bear will open them himself quite easily), will divert the bear's attention and prevent this sort of thing, for the time being at least.

Seriously, these bears give rather an atmosphere to the place, and are considered by most of those who see them, to be one of the chief attractions there. Some few timorous souls might not perhaps relish the idea of meeting a whole troop of bears on a main street, but for every one who doesn't, there are twenty that do. The bear is the clown of the woods, clumsy, and often a thief, but he is amiable enough if not abused; and it says a good deal in his favour that with bears in some numbers constantly present around the resort at Waskesieu, apart from certain ludicrous and quite harmless incidents, there has never been an accident.

Animals are very quick to appreciate a sanctuary when they find one, and will become very tame in a short time, minding their own business so long as the human being minds his. They seem to enjoy the novel and interesting entertainments that the place affords them. There are several foxes, very beautifully coloured in black and silver-grey and red, who have adopted this Summer camp ground for a headquarters. Although naturally great travellers, and given to ranging far and wide over large areas, these enterprising creatures spend most of their time at the resort, and once I was treated to the sight of a fine silver-grey mother fox and her four half-grown puppies, all black as your hat, who stood beside the road and watched me pass them. In the Winter they make regular visits to the cabin of the interpreter and guide attached to the Mounted Police, one Wally Laird, where they find food and a welcome and above all, a little kindly understanding when they feel the need of it—and it would be just too bad for the man who would try to do them harm.

My visits to Waskesieu are infrequent, and I know little of what takes place there from year to year, so it was with some surprise that I saw, walking quietly among those gathered there to see them, a little drove of deer. There were five of them stepping daintily and gracefully along in Indian file, seeming to pick each step, springy and effort-less of gait, wary and alert, wild, free creatures of the Wilderness, swift envoys from the Silent Places, emissaries from the far-flung Kingdom of the Wild. A man said: 'They are the real thing.'

And he was right; they were.

Some time before this there had been a tame deer who practically lived at Waskesieu. He had since passed on, some say from an overdose of tobacco. No, he didn't smoke it, but some animals are very fond of it and eat it, and this one was, so I am told, something of an addict. One evening when he saw a lady going for a walk along the beach, he thought it might be a good idea to go too. So he accompanied her. Being acquainted with this particular deer she raised no objection, and they walked along together, on the beach. Presently the lady, becoming tired, sat down. So did the deer. Rested, the lady decided to return home and rose to her feet. But the deer, apparently, was not yet ready to go, and pushed her down again, more or less gently, and lay down beside her. After a decent interval the lady attempted to rise once more, only to be again forced to a sitting position by her escort. This happened a number of times until, fearing to anger the animal, the woman remained where she was, with the deer beside her. As long as she remained sitting down everything was all right; this deer was not going to allow any lady to walk out on *him*. And she didn't, not until a party of her friends arrived, when the deer surrendered her quite amicably, and walked back to Waskesieu along with the rest of the folks.

These deserters from the rank and file of the furtive folk who dwell in the Wilderness that surrounds Waskesieu on every side, must be something of a pain in the neck to the regular troops who, following the old traditions, remain back in the hills, no doubt viewing this defection from accepted custom with the sternest disapproval. But they do nothing about it, and the number of recruits to the ranks of these mutineers increases year by year, and there is a not so remote possibility that eventually they will have to be included in the census.

From *Tales of an Empty Cabin*.

CHAPTER TWO

MOOSE

Still-hunting (stalking) is an art learned from the Indian, an accomplishment in which few white men excel, save only those who have spent many days in the lodges of those silent, thoughtful people, or consorted much with those who have. I can almost hear the howl of protest going up from a host of pseudo-bushmen, whose experience is confined to running moose down in deep snow, blundering on them in sections where they are numerous, or shooting them at the water's edge, which anybody can do. I repeat that the average white man is not a good still-hunter.

There are exceptions; famous guides, celebrated for their skill in 'calling,' crafty as the savage whose tricks they have acquired, men who have earned a reputation of never coming out without their moose, are to be met in bush communities in all parts of Canada; but they are as outstanding there as is a genius in a colony of artists. But all must take off their hats to the Indian. His own evasive, subtle mind fits him admirably to cope with the cunning and elusive nature of such animals as moose and deer. Indeed, it is probable that his type of mentality has been evolved by just such exercises during many generations, for the red man is primarily a hunter. Few but he are able, without snow, and in most cases even with it, to track and locate a moose without scaring the animal (in which case he is gone, and as impossible to overtake as a train would be), for no moose, unless bogged to the shoulders in snow, has ever been taken by tracking him down from behind. Not all are mentally fitted to enter into the intricacies of

move and countermove, advance, circle, and retreat
which must be studied in each case, or to guess the
necessary allowance for the changing of a scarcely
perceptible breath of wind.

Busy workers have not the time to acquire the knowledge that warns of too close an approach to a disad-
vantageous firing position, nor have they, unless they live
as close to Nature as their swarthy brethren, the instinct
that shows itself in the achievement of knowing the exact
position of the moose in relation to himself, before the last
two or three steps are to be made that will expose the
hunter, and give him his shot at a quarry that he has
stalked for an hour. And all this without sight, sound, or
indication of the presence of moose, excepting perhaps
some week-old tracks and nibbled branches, and in a
section, such as moose commonly resort to, where a man
is lucky to be able to see ten feet ahead of him.

It takes no little skill also to enter a 'yard' of moose,
padded down with tracks as numerous as those of cows in
a pasture, and make a specific set at one particular beast.
Yet this is necessary; hit or miss, rambling tactics meeting
with no more success than firing into the centre of a flock
of ducks ever does. The least carelessness of approach, the
rattle of cartridges in the pocket, the slapping of a twig
on the clothing, or even too much mental concentration
on the animal itself, causing uneasiness, will alike result in
a sudden flurry and crackling of twigs and brush, the
measured, rapidly diminishing thump of hoofs driven by
legs working like piston-rods, the distant crash as some
rotten tree gives way before the driving weight of flesh,
bone and muscle, and then utter silence. And like as not
without a hair of the quarry having been seen.

The actual shooting is child's play. More moose are
killed at fifty feet by good hunters, than at a hundred
yards by good shots. A moose is not a hard target, and

once seen, looms up amongst the undergrowth like the side of a barn. The difficult part is to get to see him. On the still-hunt the sum and substance of the hunter's efforts are to see the animal before it sees him; to closely approach a moose without his being aware of your presence is an impossible feat, as indeed it is with any other of these dwellers amongst the leaves. But like all the other types of deer, unless rendered frantic by the scent of man, his curiosity gets the better of him; he will stay until he gets a fleeting glimpse of what he is running away from. That is the hunter's only chance of success.

All animals that live in the wilderness are provided with a set of protective habits which the skilled hunter, having knowledge of them, turns to his advantage. Beavers, when ashore, post a guard; not much advantage there, you think. But standing upright as he does in some prominent position, he draws attention, where the working party in the woods would have escaped notice. Both beaver and otter plunge into the water if alarmed or caught in a trap (in this case a stone is provided which keeps them there, to drown). Foxes rely on their great speed and run in full view, offering excellent rifle practice. Deer contrive to keep a tree or some brush between their line of flight and their enemy, and the experienced hunter will immediately run to the clump of foliage and shoot unseen from behind it.

Moose feed downwind, watch closely behind them but neglect to a certain extent the ground ahead. When about to rest they form a loop in their trail, and lie hidden beside it, where they can keep an eye on it, manœuvring to get the wind from their late feeding ground. These things we know, and act accordingly. We decide on the animal we want, and make a series of fifty-yard loops, knowing better than to follow directly in the tracks, the end of each arc striking his trail, which is a most tortuous affair winding in

and out as he selects his feed. We do this with due regard
for the wind, all along his line of travel, touching it every
so often, until we overshoot where we suppose the trail
ought to be. This shows—provided our calculations are
correct, our direction good, and if we are lucky—that our
moose is somewhere within that curve. It has now become
a ticklish proposition.

We must not strike his tracks near where he is lying
down (he cannot be said to sleep), for this is the very trap
he has laid for us. If we go too far on our loop we may get
on the windward side (I think that is the term; I am no
sailor). Pie for the moose again. Probably he is even now
watching us. To know when we are approaching that
position between our game and the tell-tale current of air
is where that hazard comes in which makes moose-hunting
one of the most fascinating sports.

All around you the forest is grey, brown and motionless.
For hours past there has been visible no sign of life, nor
apparently will there ever be. A dead, empty, silent world
of wiry underbrush, dry leaves, and endless rows of trees.
You stumble and on the instant the dun-coloured woods
spring suddenly to life with a crash, as the slightly darker
shadow you had mistaken for an upturned root takes on
volition; and a monstrous black shape, with palmated
horns stretched a man's length apart, hurtles through
tangled thickets and over or through waist-high fallen
timber, according to its resisting power. Almost pre-
historic in appearance, weighing perhaps half a ton, with
hanging black bell, massive forequarters, bristling mane,
and flashing white flanks, this high-stepping pacer ascends
the steep side of a knoll, and on the summit he stops,
slowly swings the ponderous head, and deliberately, arro-
gantly looks you over. Swiftly he turns and is away, this
time for good, stepping, not fast but with a tireless regularity, unchanging speed, and disregard for obstacles, that

will carry him miles in the two hours that he will run.

And you suddenly realise that you have an undischarged rifle in your hands, and that your moose is now well on his way to Abitibi. And mixed with your disappointment, if you are a sportsman, is the alleviating thought that the noble creature still has his life and freedom, and that there are other days and other moose.

I know of no greater thrill than that, after two or three hours of careful stalking with all the chances against me, of sighting my game, alert, poised for that one move that means disappearance; and with this comes the sudden realisation that in an infinitesimal period of time will come success or failure. The distance, and the probable position of a vital spot in relation to the parts that are visible, must be judged instantly, and simultaneously. The heavy breathing incidental to the exertion of moving noiselessly through a jungle of tangled undergrowth and among fallen timber must be controlled. And regardless of poor footing, whether balanced precariously on a tottering log or with bent back and twisted neck peering between upturned roots, that rifle must come swiftly forward and up. I pull—no, squeeze—the trigger, as certain earnest, uniformed souls informed me in the past, all in one sweeping motion; the wilderness awakes to the crash of the rifle, and the moose disappears. The report comes as a cataclysmic uproar after the abysmal silence, and aghast at the sacrilege, the startled blue-jays and whiskey-jacks screech, and chatter, and whistle. I go forward with leaps and bounds, pumping in another car-tridge, as moose rarely succumb to the first shot. But I find I do not need the extra bullet. There is nothing there to shoot. An animal larger than a horse has disappeared without a trace, save some twisted leaves and a few tracks which look very healthy. There is no blood, but I follow for a mile, maybe, in the hopes of a paunch wound, until the trail becomes too involved to follow.

I have failed. Disaster, no less. And I feel pretty flat, and inefficient, and empty-bellied.

Worst of all, I must go back to camp, and explain the miss to a critical and unsympathetic listener, who is just as hungry as I am, and in no shape to listen to reason. Experiences of that kind exercise a very chastening effect on the self-esteem; also it takes very few of them to satisfy any man's gambling instinct.

*   *   *   *   *

A big bull racing through close timber with a set of antlers fifty or sixty inches across is a sight worth travelling far to see. He will swing his head from side to side in avoidance of limbs, duck and sway as gracefully as a trained charger with a master-hand at the bridle, seeming to know by instinct spaces between trees where he may pass with his armament.

It is by observing a series of spots of this description that a man may estimate the size of the bull he is after.

The tracks of bull and cow are distinguishable by the difference in shape of the hoofs; the bull being stub-toed forward, and the cow being narrow-footed fore and aft. Also the bull swings his front feet out and back into line when running; this is plain to be seen with snow on the ground of any depth; furthermore the cow feeds on small trees by passing around them, the bull by straddling them and breaking them down. Tracking on bare ground is the acme of the finesse of the still-hunt, especially in a dry country; and tracking in winter is not always as simple as would appear. More than a little skill is sometimes required to determine whether the animal that made the tracks was going or coming. This is carried to the point, where, with two feet of snow over month-old tracks, visible in the first place only as dimples, an expert may, by digging out the snow with his hands, ascertain which way the moose was going; yet to the uninitiated tracks an hour old present an unsolvable problem as to direction, as, if the snow be deep, the tracks fill in immediately and show only as a series of long narrow slots having each two ends identical in appearance. The secret is this, that the rear edge of the hind leg leaves a sharper, narrower impression in the back end of the slot than does the more rounded forward side. This can be felt out only with the bare hands; a ten-minute occupation of heroic achievement, on a windy day on a bleak hillside, in a temperature of twenty-five below zero. Nevertheless a very useful accomplishment, as in the months of deep snow a herd may be yarded up a mile from tracks made earlier in the season.

But should the herd have travelled back and forth in the same tracks, as they invariably do, we have confusion again. In that case they must be followed either way to a considerable hill; here, if going downhill they separate, taking generous strides, or if uphill, short ones. Loose snow is thrown forward and out from the slots, and is an unfailing guide if visible, but an hour's sharp wind will eradicate that indication save to the trained eye.

Assuredly the hunt is no occupation for a pessimist, as he would most undoubtedly find a cloud to every silver lining.

There are many ways of killing moose, but most of them can be effected only at times of the year when it would be impossible to keep the meat, unless the party was large enough to use up the meat in a couple of days, or, as in the case of Indians, it could be properly smoked.

In the Summer when they come down to water in the early morning and late evening, moose are easily approached with due care. They stand submerged to the belly, and dig up with the long protruding upper lip, the roots of water-lilies, which much resemble elongated pineapples. Whilst eyes and ears are thus out of commission the canoeman will paddle swiftly in against the wind, until with a mighty splurge the huge head is raised, the water spraying from the wide antlers, running off the 'pans' in miniature cataracts, when all movement in the canoes ceases, and they drift noiselessly like idle leaves, controlled by the paddles operated under water. The moose lowers his head again, and the canoes creep up closer now, more cautiously, care being taken not to allow the animal a broadside view. On one of the occasions when he raises his head the moose is bound to become aware of the danger, but by then the hunters have arrived within rifle shot of the shore; so, allowed to provide his own transportation to dry land, he is killed before he enters the bush.

In the mating season moose may be called down from the hills by one skilled in the art, and threshing in the underbrush with an old discarded moose-horn will sometimes arouse the pugnacity of a reluctant bull; but when he comes it is as well to be prepared to shoot fast and straight.

After the first frosts bull moose are pugnaciously inclined towards all the world, and more than one man has been known to spend a night up a tree, whilst a moose ramped and raved at the foot of it till daylight. Whether these men were in any actual danger, or were scared stiff and afraid to take any chances, it is impossible to say, but I have always found that a hostile moose, if approached boldly down wind, so that he gets the man-scent, will move off, threateningly, but none the less finally. Although the person of a man may cause them to doubt their prowess, they will cheerfully attack horses and wagons, domestic bulls, and even railroad locomotives.

Bull moose are quite frequently found killed by trains at that time of the year, and they have been known to

contest the right of way with an automobile, which had at
last to be driven around them. A laden man seems to
arouse their ire, as a government ranger, carrying a canoe
across a portage once discovered.

It was his first trip over, and, no doubt attracted by the
scratching sound caused by the canoe rubbing on brush
as it was carried, this lord of the forest planted himself
square in the middle of the portage, and refused to give
the ranger the trail. The bush was too ragged to permit
of a detour, so the harassed man, none too sure of what
might occur, put down his canoe. The moose presently
turned and walked up the trail slowly, and the man then
picked up his canoe again, and followed. Gaining confidence, he touched his lordship on the rump with the
prow of the canoe, to hasten progress; and then the fun
commenced. The infuriated animal turned on him, this
time with intent. He threw his canoe to the side, and ran
at top speed down the portage, with the moose close
behind. (It could be mentioned here, that those animals
are at a distinct disadvantage on level going; had the
ranger entered the bush, he would have been overtaken
in twenty steps.)

At a steep cut-off he clutched a small tree, swung
himself off the trail, and rolled down the declivity; the
moose luckily, kept on going. After a while the ranger
went back, inspected his canoe, which was intact, and put
it out of sight, and it was as well that he did. He then
returned to his belongings to find ... standing guard
over a torn and trampled pile of dunnage which he could
in no way approach. He commenced to throw rocks at
this white elephant, who, entering into the spirit of the
game, rushed him up the trail again, he swinging off in
the same place as before. This time he stayed there. The
moose patrolled the portage all the hours of darkness, and
the ranger spent the night without food or shelter.

A moose, should he definitely make up his mind to attack, could make short work of a man. They often kill one another, using their antlers for the purpose, but on lesser adversaries they use their front feet, rearing up and striking terrific blows. I once saw an old bull, supposedly feeble and an easy prey, driven out into shallow water by two wolves, where they attempted to hamstring him. He enticed them out into deeper water, and turning, literally tore one of them to pieces. Fear of wounding the moose prevented me from shooting the other, which escaped.

When enraged a bull moose is an awe-inspiring sight, with his flaring superstructure, rolling eyes, ears laid back, and top lip lifted in a kind of a snarl. Every hair on his back bristles up like a mane, and at such times he emits his challenging call—O-waugh! O-waugh! a deep cavernous sound, with a wild, blood-stirring hint of savagery and power. This sound, like the howling of wolves, or the celebrated war-whoop when heard at a safe distance, or from a position of security, or perhaps in the latter case, at an exhibition, is not so very alarming. But, if alone and far from human habitation in some trackless waste, perhaps in the dark, with the certainty that you yourself are the object of the hue and cry, the effect on the nervous system is quite different, and is apt to cause a sudden rush of blood to the head, leaving the feet cold.

Once, and once only, was I ever in any serious danger from the attack of a moose. On this occasion, needing meat, I was looking for moose-tracks. Finding some indications, I had, after only a short still-hunt, come on to two of them, a cow and a well-grown calf, at the edge of a beaver-pond. I shot the calf, which suited my requirements, it being yet warm weather, and the cow made two or three runs at me, but was easily scared away by a few shots fired in the air; I felt safe enough as I had in my pocket some spare cartridges, tied in a little buckskin bag to keep them from rattling.

Whilst skinning the kill I noticed a beaver swimming towards me, his curiosity aroused by the shooting probably, as I suppose that the crack of a rifle had never been heard before in all that region. The beaver was unprime, and the hide valueless, but, becoming interested in his movements, I sat down on the bank and watched him. Quite absorbed in my pastime I was suddenly startled by a slight crackling behind me, followed immediately by the hollow, coughing grunt of an angry bull moose. The sound was no novelty to me, but never before had it carried to my ear the note of menace that it now did. No thunderous bellowing roar of a lion could convey half the murderous intent expressed in the cold malevolence of that sound behind my back. It chilled me to the marrow and the hair crept on my scalp. I jumped to my feet and whirled with a yell calculated to jar the horns off the creature's head, but which produced not the slightest effect. He stood facing me, every hair on his body erect, his eyes red with hate. He commenced rubbing his hocks together, sure signal of a charge, and I smelt distinctly the sickening, musky odour these animals emit when about to fight.

Afraid to make a sudden movement, for fear of precipitating an attack, I reached stealthily for my rifle, jerked it to my hip, pumping as I did so, and fired; that is, I pulled the trigger, and almost before the answering click told me the gun was empty it flashed into my brain like an arrow that I had emptied the magazine in driving away the cow.

But the spell was broken. The moose moved; so did I.

He had me between himself and the pond, with a margin of about ten feet in my favour. Once in the water, my chances, I knew, would be poor; so I made pretty good time down the edge of it, and the moose ran parallel to me; we seemed to be pretty evenly matched for speed. At the end of the pond I turned, quickly jumped the creek, and made for a stretch of flat, steeply sloping rock, where I could not be cornered up; this was covered with a scattered growth of small jackpines, which, whilst not large enough to climb, offered dodging facilities. This move brought the moose directly behind me.

Still running, I got out my bag of cartridges, and pulled the string with my mouth: the knot jammed; I slackened my speed and tore at the bag with my teeth, ripping it, and spilling most of the cartridges. Ramming a shell into the breech, I spun quickly round to find that the moose had stopped also, startled at my sudden move, and at about the same distance as before. I took quick aim, ready to shoot, but his rage was spent, and his former pugnacity gave way to uneasiness. I knew now that the danger was over, although I was obliged to sting him in the flank before I could get rid of him.

*   *   *   *   *

In the course of a hunt every detail liable to have a bearing on the situation must be noted; such as the roll of the land forming pockets where the wind may eddy; the direction of the different vagrant air currents, or a shift in the wind itself, must be tested for, generally by means of wetting a finger and holding it up, the side which the wind is coming from becoming immediately cool; or if there be snow by throwing up handfuls and watching its drift.

Care must be taken that an approach is not made up a steep hill where your quarry will sight you before you can see enough of him to cover with your foresight; also that you do not stand out in prominent relief, in the full glare of the sun, or find yourself obliged to shoot into it.

I remember well seeing a much-needed buck saunter

off into the bush in plain sight, owing to the fact that I faced the setting sun on a lake shore, and every time I raised my rifle the deer completely disappeared, swallowed up in the glare.

Trivial occurrences, that would appear to have no connection with the hunt whatever, may be of the utmost importance. The cawing of a few crows once led to a kill which was the realisation of the dream of years to the sportsman I accompanied on the trip. It was in a burnt country, and my companion was unsuitably clad as to his feet in a pair of heavy, hard-soled boots, and in the dry, brittle ruck of the fire was making a terrific noise. We had heard that exciting, terrible sound, the clashing of huge antlers as two bulls fought to the death, about half a mile back; and we were now closely approaching our estimation of the position of this battle, which had ceased. I asked my companion to stand still for a moment so that we could listen awhile, and he unfortunately chose a brittle log to stand on, which gave way with a crash. Remarking meekly that he 'made more noise standing still than some people did running,' the unfortunate man urged me to try my luck alone.

Just at that moment we heard faintly a continuous, low sound, about two hundred yards to the south of us. This, after listening attentively, we made out to be the sound of crows, flocking together at some spot. This probably meant that some animal lay dead there, in all likelihood a moose, killed in a fight. My friend took courage on hearing the good news, and decided to see the thing through. As we listened, getting our bearings and testing the wind repeatedly, the sound changed to a scolding, and the birds seemed to scatter and take the air, as though disturbed. Better all the time; this argued a living moose, no doubt inspecting his victim, as they do periodically when victorious.

We laid our plan of approach and started away, and when we were within about twenty-five yards of the disturbance, the crows took flight, and we came suddenly out in plain view of a pool of water, in which lay a moose, very dead, and for a long time since, which it took no skill to determine. Seated in the water, feeding on the ill-smelling carcase, was about the biggest black bear I had seen for a long time, he being the cause of all the uproar.

Although it was not my hunt, the other man being for a moment spellbound, and with good reason, for it was a remarkable sight, I immediately shot the bear. On receiving the second bullet, he raced into an unburned patch of larches, where we eventually found him dead. This clump we circled, to find his point of egress, if any, as a wounded bear is apt to be dangerous, and we were as yet uncertain of his demise.

We had no more than half completed our detour when we heard that deep-throated gurgling cough that so thrills the hunter to the core of his being, and, it seemed, almost at our elbows. Turning, we saw two big bulls looking down on us from the top of a knoll not fifteen yards away. Here this sportsman redeemed himself. The biggest bull did not offer him a very good target, but sensibly taking the smaller one that did, he dropped his moose neatly and cleanly with a well-placed bullet.

*   *   *   *   *

Being accustomed to hunting on the plains, where the game is in pockets, in gulleys, river bottoms, or in bluffs of poplar or willows, and thus standing partly located at the outset, and where it is more a matter of good shooting than good hunting, I found the still-hunt, as practised by the Northern Indians, an entirely different proposition. I know of no set of conditions to which the ancient simile of the needle in the haystack could be better applied.

My first experience was a good many years ago, with a young Ojibway, yet in his teens. He had all the quiet and confident bearing that goes with conscious ability, moved like a shadow, and addressed me not at all. From the outset he was in no hurry, spending much time listening to the wind above, and inspecting the ground below, both apparently inconsequent proceedings as there seemed to be no wind and the only visible tracks, to the reading of which I was no stranger, were old ones and plain to be seen. However, his tardiness suited me as, coming from a territory where walking is not popular, and with the slippery, stiff-soled moccasins of the plains Indian on my feet, I was quite well occupied keeping him in sight as it was, and sincerely hoped nothing would occur to increase his speed.

We proceeded in a fairly direct line of travel for maybe an hour, when on a sudden he stopped and, motioning me to come, showed me the fresh track of a cow moose. Our progress now became more circuitous and rambling, and he wandered apparently quite aimlessly around, listening meanwhile for a non-existent wind.

It was during the Fall of the year, and I found the wonderfully coloured woods a fairyland after the bare, brown prairie, and the dry harsh mountains protruding from blistering belts of sand. I was having a good time and, moose or no moose, the gyrations of my gnome-like and elusive companion intrigued me to the limit. Presently he stopped in a glade, and looked around, smiling with the air of one exhibiting a long-sought treasure. I also looked around, but did not smile, as I recognised the spot as the one at which he had discovered the moose track. I had been twisted often enough in my calculations in the wild lands to guess what that meant.

'Ki-onitchi-kataig, we are lost,' I said.

He shook his head, and pointing to the moose track held up two fingers.

So that was it, he had in the circling discovered another moose. I had not seen him go through any motions indicative of a person discovering anything, moose or man, but supposed he must know what he was about. Maybe, I reflected, if we went around again, we could add another moose to the tally, and then surround them and make a general slaughter. The stripling now made some preparations. He took off his outside shirt and his hat, tying a folded handkerchief of indefinite colour around his bobbed hair. He hung his discarded clothing, with his blanket-cloth gun-case on a limb, and this mark of confidence in his ability to find the place again induced me also to remove and hang up my coat and hat; it seemed we must be about to hurry.

But my elfin guide stood motionless, apparently lost in thought, formulating his plans; and as he so stood, a study in black and tan, and faded buckskin, under the bronze dome of a giant birch tree, I thought that if only some great artist were there with skilful brush to commit to canvas the wondrous colour scheme, the shades, the shadows, the slanting streams of subdued light, the attitude of my primitive companion, wild, negligent, yet alert, furtive almost, like the creatures he was hunting, the masterpiece would result that could well be representative of a race, and of an epoch that will soon be with the things which are no longer, lost for ever.

The moment passed and he moved on.

Our progress was now very slow. Twice I ascertained that we were covering short sections of our previous itinerary, back-tracking in spots, making endless half-circles on a base line itself anything but straight.

On our left came a breath of sound, a slight rustle, and on the instant the boy sank into the woods like a hot knife through butter. Presently he returned, smiled his thin smile, and made the sign of a fox's tail. More half-circles. He commenced testing for the wind with a wet finger, and crumbling dry leaves in his hands allowed the dust to drift. The result was almost imperceptible. He seemed to gather some satisfactory information from the manœuvre however, as he nodded his head and went on.

Bars of sunlight hovered here and there as the trellised roof of leaves wavered and swayed, and in the more open spaces it filtered through, to lie in golden pools upon the forest floor. These he skirted stealthily, keeping in the gloom on their borders with that instinct of self-effacement which alike to the predatory or the furtive, spells success or safety.

He tested for wind more frequently now, on one occasion stopping and creeping backwards on his tracks, as though backing out of some sacred precinct that he had inadvertently entered. He circled out, and back into the same spot by another direction, a matter of yards only, and, selecting a spot in a wall of small evergreens, suddenly raised his rifle and fired.

At the same instant I saw a patch of coarse hair resolve itself into a huge brown body, as a cow moose surged through the balsams, blood streaming from nose and mouth, to sink down within twenty feet.

The Ojibway blew the smoke out of his rifle.

'Meheu,' he said, speaking for the first time. 'It is done.'

From *Men of the Last Frontier.*

*   *   *   *   *

Animals as a whole are apparently devoid of imagination, which is fortunate for them as it enables them to meet the hardships they have to undergo with greater equanimity than can a man, and without any effort of will; but

I have none the less been long convinced that, in many species, they are capable, to a more or less limited degree, of the power of thought. Even those of us having the most dim and distorted views on animal mentalities must concede something to the ape, the elephant and the beaver, and in many cases to the dog and the horse, but a long experience has hitherto failed to reveal to me any evidence of reasoning powers in any branch or individual of the deer family coming under my notice. The moose would seem to be a creature of slow mental processes, but that he is capable of using, and does, on occasion, use his head, over and above his accustomed, almost automatic reactions, has been amply demonstrated to me and to others who have seen him, by an eight-year-old bull who has been a constant, if irregular visitor here for nearly five years.

At the time of writing he is lying alongside my canoe placidly chewing the cud with occasional grunts of satisfaction. The canoe, behind which he is ensconced, offers him a certain amount of shelter from the easterly wind that is blowing, though he could get better protection from it in the rear of the cabin, where he occasionally bedded down last year. But this new position perhaps has more intriguing possibilities, as he can see all that is going on, including my own small affairs in which he seems to take a lively interest. In his present situation he is an object of curiosity and some resentment to the numbers of squirrels and whiskey-jacks that frequent this spot and he is apparently quite undisturbed by the erratic movements of these small but rather violently active creatures.

Although I knew of the presence of this bull in the district on first taking up my abode here, and often had fleeting glimpses of him, I made no attempt at any friendly overtures and adopted a policy of quiet withdrawal on sighting him.

That Summer it became necessary to fell a number of

poplar trees to provide light for photographic work, and he made furtive nocturnal visits to the fallen trees for the purpose of eating the leaves. These visits to the free lunch counter thus provided, continued as long as the leaves lasted, a matter of nearly two weeks, and during that period I made it a practice to be unobtrusively present at his feeding time. From then on, at intervals, he could be seen passing at no great distance from the cabin, and on occasion stood gazing down at it from some point oi vantage. Often I observed him hovering on the hill-tops no great distance away, as I came and went on my constant patrol of the beaver-works. He even ventured beyond the last fringe of the forest that borders the tiny clearance on every hand, and watched me cutting wood, silent and motionless as the trees themselves. I did not press the matter, nor did I abate my labours, but carried on as though unaware of his presence, as evidently his interest was already sufficiently aroused. It was noticeable that the movements of the beavers seemed particularly to engage his attention, and one evening he came boldly down and stood observing them. The beavers speedily collected in a body and treated him to a salvo of tail splashing and stirred the water to a great commotion. All this had no effect on the moose whatsoever, except to cause him to step a little closer to see what it was all about.

Now a bull moose weighs something short of half a ton and is altogether rather a staggering proposition to have around at such close quarters and could, if he chose, become the least bit unmanageable; so becoming a little dubious as to the outcome of this rather alarming intimacy I stepped out of the cabin, having so far watched the performance through a window. With no hesitation the moose spun around on his heel and fled up the hill, and I commenced calling to the beavers in my usual manner to calm them. And now occurred the most remarkable feature of this whole business. At the first sound of my voice the moose slacked down, slowed to a walk and stopped, and as I continued calling the beavers he slowly returned, coming most of the way back, and commenced feeding on a clump of alders that was handy to him. Unbelievably, the words and inflections I used to pacify the beavers, seemed to exert the same influence on the moose. On being further alarmed by my rapid movements the moose withdrew once more, but he did not go so far as before and was reassured by the same sounds, so that he again commenced to feed where he stood and spent upwards of an hour browsing unconcernedly around before he finally moved off. This, to me, unprecedented behaviour on the part of a wild animal with whom I had hardly even a bowing acquaintance, seemed very marvellous at the time and unless we are to admit that he figured the situation out for himself, an adequate explanation is hard to come by. I can claim little credit in the conduct of this affair, as the moose seems to have formed his own decisions and acted on them. I pondered long and deeply on the subject, and not yet satisfied, experimented time and again during the now frequent visits of this strangely complaisant beast and on most occasions with the same result, scaring him by a sudden appearance and easily recalling him. And each rehearsal was a further confirmation of what I scarcely could believe myself was true, that without any attempt at training or the exertion of any influence on my part this astonishing and unfathomable creature, wild, free and beholden to me for nothing, would respond willingly to my voice, and place himself in my power at a word. Fortunately this has occurred on different occasions before a number of witnesses, otherwise I would have some diffidence in committing the matter to paper, and an unusual aspect of animal psychology would go unrecorded.

Many of those who have not had the advantage of first-hand experience with wild animals accept as commonplace some of the really extraordinary manifestations of animal intelligence, and on that account it may appear to some that I stress unduly the peculiarity of this particular case. But those who have hunted moose or who reside in districts where they are common will appreciate my point of view.

Many ridiculous stories have been circulated, some of them in print, relative to the sagacity of moose and other beasts, and while recorded truth is sometimes humdrum and uninteresting, cool and accurate observation will often disclose facts or incidents that transcend the wildest flights of fiction.

There is little doubt in my mind that this bull had a pretty fair idea of my attitude towards him from the outset, and it is highly probable that he had taken careful and lengthy observations of the situation and had listened long and intently to all the sounds emanating from this place long before I was aware of it. He had thus become accustomed to the sound of my voice, formed his own conclusions as to its significance, and without any artifice of mine, had come to share in the sense of security it was intended to convey.

Most animals are equipped with some means of identification so that they may be readily recognised by others of their own species. This exists sometimes in the voice, as with beavers, musk-rats, porcupines, as well as birds. Some are marked by a patch radically different in hue from their general colour scheme, such as the white hind legs of a moose, the orange rump of the elk, the stripes of the skunk, the white flag of the Virginia deer. I, too, have made use of yet one more device from the Economics of the Wilderness and have likewise established my own method of identification by means of one word uttered at a certain pitch and tone which all the creatures that frequent here are quick to recognise. This I did all unconsciously at first, falling into the prevailing custom from long association with it and not realising how potent a spell it was until seeing its effect on an animal as extremely mobile and suspicious as is a moose. On my unexpected appearance, or on the occurrence of some unusual sound, any and all animals present, be they squirrels, musk-rats, beavers or the moose, will freeze to instant immobility, appearing like stone images of various shapes and sizes and will momentarily remain in this position of suspended animation until at the sound of the well-known word, utterly foreign sound though it is, they spring instantly to life and resume their interrupted occupations.

During the past Summer and Fall the bull spent a good deal of his time within the camp environs strolling around complacently amongst my arrangements, the woodpile, store-tent and canoes, etc. He sometimes stood outside the cabin door for long periods, close enough that some visitors were not unreasonably afraid that he might try to enter. I was not sure myself as to what lengths this enterprising animal would go, as he had already got, at the one time, all four of his feet into a small canoe and smashed it beyond any possibility of repair.* I actually had to drive him away from the door one night as his presence there, standing engaged in some ponderous cogitations, was obstructing the passage of the beavers in and out of the cabin with their building materials. By this time they no longer feared him, but were probably like myself, a little uncertain as to what his next move might be, and refused to pass him.

Every animal has its special fear, both as a species and as an individual. In the case of this particular moose, his pet antipathy was to have anyone pass between

* See also p. 229.

himself and a lighted window, throwing thereby a quick flitting shadow across him. This would cause him to break away at a run, and although he could invariably be called back, he would retire hurriedly on the offence being repeated nor did he ever become accustomed to it.

Until the beavers began at last to accept this huge visitor as a regular feature, I always received fair warning of his approach at some distance by tail signals given out by the beavers. He has now become to them, I imagine, something of a necessary evil, to be tolerated even if not to be over-effusively welcomed, and he has become so ordinary that his presence is taken as a matter of course, and warnings are no longer given. And stepping out from the cabin into the night and almost falling, as I once did, over a beast the size of a horse, is a severe trial to the nervous system of any man, however bold.

While the weather was warmer, he had a habit of standing in the water at the landing, and whilst there, was evidently something of a spectacle to the young beavers, who would swim completely round him, slapping their tails on the water and creating a great uproar, all of which he would view with a lofty unconcern.

At times the behaviour of this strange beast led me to wonder if he was not lonesome, and that having at last found company that combined the advantages of being safe and at the same time interesting, he had attached himself to the place on that account. For animals of all kinds love entertainment, and become very excited and playful on the introduction of something unusual into the monotony of their everyday lives, and they seem to get much pleasure from the contemplation of something new and strange, always of course provided that it is first proven to be safe. This theory of a desire for social inter-course on the part of a dumb brute, I have long held to be as tenable as the better known and well attested one, that in some instances individuals of the brute creation will go to the opposite extreme, and become so unsociable as to be dangerous to their own kind.

This community of interest has no whit abated the native alertness and vigilance of this animal, as on my coming upon him once unannounced from behind a knoll he rushed immediately round to the far side of the little eminence and, using it for cover, beat a precipitate retreat. I cannot believe that animals under ordinary circumstances when running from danger do so in an excess of panic and blind terror. For scared as he certainly was, he must have retained an admirable presence of mind, as on my running to the top of the knoll and calling out loudly the pass-word, he stopped within a hundred yards and eventually permitted me to approach him; but being far from camp and in a section where he was not accustomed to encountering me, I did not put his confidence to too great a test. This is by no means the only evidence I have that animals, even when in full flight and apparently panic-stricken, have all their mental faculties working one hundred per cent, and I am positive that only when dominated by the mating instinct, or driven to extremes by hunger, or on finding themselves in some utterly unnatural situation, such as unwanted confinement, do they ever completely lose control of themselves.

At the earliest view I had of him, about five years ago, this now proud bull was little more than a spike-horn. He had only two V-shaped protuberances, each about a foot long, on his adolescent brow, which, as an abbreviated moustache sometimes does to an otherwise manly face, detracted from rather than added to his appearance of virility. The next year, however, he blossomed forth with a real set of antlers, his first, provided with a good-sized pan and several assorted spikes. In the mating season he strutted around with these in some style, and issuing loud vocal challenges that I am sure he was quite incapable of backing up. Although he had been, at other times, a model of propriety and decorum, acting always the natural gentleman, with the coming of the first sharp frosts he was transformed overnight into something resembling a dangerous lunatic. He strode into view one afternoon with a demeanour greatly changed from his usual quiet and dignified bearing. He had about him all the appearance of one looking for trouble. With some idea of testing his courage, I brought out a birch-bark horn, an instrument shaped like a small megaphone and used for calling moose at this season, and gave a couple of short challenging coughs. The effect was instantaneous. With no preliminaries at all he opened hostilities on everything within reach. He tore at willows and alders, emitting hideous grunts, gouged and gored helpless prostrate trees, made wicked passes at inoffensive saplings that stood in the path of his progress, entered into a spirited conflict with an upturned stump, threw a canoe off its rack and had a delirious, whirlwind skirmish with a large pile of empty boxes. The clash and clatter of this last encounter worked him up to a high pitch of enthusiasm, and he gave a demonstration of foot-work and agility hardly to be expected from so large an animal. All this had a very depressing effect on the spectators, who consisted of several of my furred and feathered retainers besides myself—about the same effect that a crazed gunman running loose on a city street would have on the pedestrians. I tactfully withdrew with the horn, which I carefully put away. Having, after a time, pretty well subdued all visible enemies, except the store-tent which he had fortunately overlooked, this bold knight moved off to fresh fields of glory, and from the way he surged through the scenery I judged it would not be very long before he got himself into serious trouble.

I viewed this exhibition with much the same feelings that would be mine were I to see a highly respected and respectable acquaintance suddenly commence to throw handsprings in a public place, or to roll a hoop along the street, shouting. There was also a certain feeling of pity for the temporarily aberrated mind that one feels in the presence of an inebriate, with more than a little of the same uncertainty.

For a week or more he failed to show up at the camp and I began to fear that he had met his Waterloo, but one evening on returning by canoe from a trip to my supply cache, I saw in the dusk the familiar dark, ungainly form reclining at ease before my cabin. My canoe was heavily loaded and the water was shallow, so I was entirely at his mercy, but he allowed me to land and unload without any argument, merely getting to his feet and feeding on the surrounding underbrush.

He does not come so often now and stays but a short time, an hour perhaps. By his actions, I think that he has succeeded in finding himself a partner. I cannot conceive by what system he was able to obtain her in a district so populated by big experienced bulls. He has no doubt all the optimism and enthusiasm of youth on his side, and perhaps he has met a cow who is, like himself, young enough to see romance and gallantry in the mock battles which this handsome young fellow no doubt staged before her, and to experience maidenly thrills to see him vanquish make-believe antagonists. And if he has made the same use of his brains in the selection of a mate that he did in his manner of adopting my domicile for refuge, he has no doubt picked himself a good one.

As he sits without, before the window, I see that he is gazing anxiously, wistfully back into the dark recesses of the woods. Ever and anon his head turns in this one direction, ears pointing, nostrils sniffing the air. And I know that back there his cow is lurking, afraid to come down into the open and brave the terrors of the unknown.

Soon he will follow the law of all nature and follow where his consort calls; and as he stalks majestically away, he will march as to the sound of drums and martial music, with regal pride and with the bearing of a king. For he has attained to his majority, has proved himself before the eyes of all the world. He is now a finished product from the vast repository of the Wild, a magnificent masterpiece of Nature's craft, scion of a race whose origin is lost in the mists of unnumbered ages, the most noble beast that treads these Northern forests.

And I cannot altogether subdue a little, sneaking feeling of satisfaction, when I realise that without subjugation, training or confinement, and on account of no considera-tion of food or safety, but just because he is contented here, happy and above all—free, he will leave for a time his chosen mate, to rest in my door-yard for an hour.

From *Tales of an Empty Cabin*.

CHAPTER THREE

DWELLERS AMONG THE LEAVES

In a wilderness apparently without life there is a teeming population continuously on the move, yet a man may travel for days at a time and see nothing but the trees around him, and hear nothing save the sounds he himself makes. For here man is the only alien, the arch-enemy from whom all the dwellers in this sanctuary flee, as from pollution. Apprised of his approach by senses trained to register the least discordant note in the symmetry of their surroundings, they disappear long before he arrives in the vicinity. All along his line of travel this is going on and hardly ever is he permitted to see or hear the living creatures that surround him on every side.

Animals seem to be able to distinguish instantly the slightest noise made by man, from that of any other forest dweller. The laughing owls may hoot in uncouth cackling whoops; a beaver may waken the echoes with a resounding smack of his tail on the water; a tree may fall with a crash, or a moose walk carelessly along rattling the underbrush, or smashing dry sticks underfoot, and cause no more commotion than the shake of an ear or the flick of a tail. But let a man so much as break a twig or rustle the dry grass of a beaver meadow, and all living creatures within earshot will, each according to his kind, sink beneath the surface of the water without a ripple, fade soundlessly into the shadows, leap with astonishing bounds to cover, or freeze into immobility, if their colour scheme harmonises sufficiently well with the immediate background.

There are two notable exceptions to this, however; the skunk and the porcupine. The latter beast is dumb cousin to the beaver, whom he resembles very closely except for the tail, the webbed hind feet, and his bristles. But it seems that when the brains were handed out between the two of them, the porcupine was absent and the beaver got them all. With no regard for personal safety, to him strange noises or the smell of cooking are as music and ambrosia; and a camp will not be very long pitched, in a country where they abound, before a 'porky' will be over to make his inspection. Save for an insatiable appetite for canoe gunwales, paddles, leather goods, provisions of all kinds, anything made of wood, canvas, paper—or perhaps it were easier to say everything not made of iron or steel—and for a bad habit he has of leaving barbed quills lying around carelessly, he is a harmless enough beast. Skunks are also friendly, and if undisturbed are as good-natured as a cat. They also have the community spirit, but this can be carried too far, as in the instance when I awoke one morning to find a number one extra large specimen curled up on my blankets. I made several attempts to rise and on each occasion he became very agitated, so I had to lie in bed until he was pleased to go.

To the majority of the dwellers in the centres of civilisation the animals inhabiting the waste places are nothing more than savage creatures, wandering aimlessly about, with no thought beyond the satisfaction of one or two animal appetites. But closer observation reveals the fact that nearly all of them have more native intelligence than those animals that have spent many generations dependent on man, and amongst the higher orders among them their 'personal' relations are such that the word 'brute' as a term of contempt is somewhat of a misnomer. Ferocious as many of them undoubtedly are when in pursuit of their prey, they all have their lighter moments, and their lives are almost as well regulated as those of human beings living under the same conditions.

They form strong attachments amongst themselves. Beavers work in shifts, keep a clean house, and hold rapid fire conversations together; coons wash their food before eating it. Most of them keep trails, especially beavers, deer, and bears, and in the case of the latter animal they blaze the boundaries of their territories in places by biting and tearing bark off trees, and it is known that they do not encroach on each other. They will climb a tree for the express purpose of sliding down again, doing this repeatedly for no other reason that the kick they get out of it. Otter also play together, and will climb a steep bank and slide down into the water uttering sharp barks of enjoyment, climb up, and slide again, much after the fashion of human beings on a toboggan slide; they, too, travel in well-defined territories, passing certain spots every eight or nine days with the regularity of clockwork. Crows, gulls and eagles will fly into the wind during a gale, and then turning, allow themselves to be blown down wind at dizzy speed, flying back upwind and repeating the performance until satisfied. Wolves when hunting exhibit team work similar to that employed by football players, send out scouts, obey the orders of a leader, and will gambol and play on the ice precisely as do pedigreed collies on a lawn.

Man is not the only trapper in the wilderness. There are insects that dig holes into which their prey falls and is captured before it can get out. Water spiders set nets shaped like saxophones, the large end facing upstream, to catch anything floating down, and round the curve, in the small end, waits the spider. Wolves divide their forces to capture deer, and I saw one of them drive a deer across a stream, whilst another waited in the brush on the other side for him to land. I know of another occasion on which three wolves cornered a caribou on a fair-sized lake. In the timber the snow was too soft for either wolves or caribou to make much headway. It was April and the ice was clear of snow and slippery as glass. A caribou's hoof is hollowed out in such a way that it grips the ice, but the wolves had difficulty in making any speed. The caribou ran round and round the lake, a distance of several miles each trip, thinking, no doubt, to tire the wolves; but two would rest whilst one chased the caribou, taking each his turn until the deer dropped from exhaustion.

Of the creatures that inhabit the woods, by far the lesser number are of a predatory nature. The majority consists of the varieties of deer, the rodents, and the smaller birds. Nature is cruel, and the flesh-eating animals and birds kill their prey in the most bloodthirsty manner, tearing off and eating portions of meat before the unfortunate animal is dead. The thought of this considerably lessens the compunction one might feel in trapping carnivorous animals, as they are only getting a dose of their own medicine and do not undergo a tithe of the sufferings they inflict on their victims, often hastening their own end by paroxysms of fury.

From *Men of the Last Frontier*.

*   *   *   *   *

This Beaver Lodge is not only my home; it is the home, too, of my Beaver People and is the gathering place of many other creatures, denizens of the forest that encircles it on every side. They are of all shapes and sizes, these shy, elusive Dwellers among the Leaves who have broken the rules of all the furtive folk, and have come from out the dark circle of the woods to stay with me, some permanently and others from time to time. They range all the way from the small, black, woolly beaver-mouse who goes hopefully around wondering when I am going to leave the lid off the butter-dish, to the great moose, as big as a horse and having, in the proper season, antlers three feet and a half across, who, an intermittent but fairly regular visitor, does some of his heavier thinking while standing outside my window.

Though living quite alone, and far from the haunts of my fellow-men, I am seldom lonely; for I have but to step outside, and it is not long before some little beast, bedight with gay caparison of flaunting tail, or smart display of tuft or coloured stripe, goes racing by and seeing me, or hearing my low call, comes to see what I may have for him. For it has not taken them very long, these smaller fry, to discover where I live, and to find that no one ever leaves here empty-handed. The bigger beasts are not much influenced by offerings of food, as theirs is usually abundant and easily come by, but pay their visits more, apparently, for the companionship they find here; as does a woodsman who goes occasionally to town to share in the small excitements of the place.

But some of the bird population are more practical, being swayed by considerations of an economic nature; and they make no bones about it either, especially the whiskey-jacks, those companionable, impertinent grey brigands who appear, soundlessly like ghosts from nowhere, at the first stroke of an axe or first wisp of smoke from a camp fire. They contrive to make themselves welcome by an ingratiating amiability that may, or may not, be counterfeit. Their antics are amusing and they provide considerable light entertainment at times that might otherwise be dull. A man feels that their companionship at a lonely camp fire is worth a few scraps of bannock or meat, until he discovers that they want, not part of his lunch, but all of it. But these lads are pertinacious to a degree that is unbelievable, and if they do not get as much as they expected they will sit around on branches with a kind of sad, reproachful, half-starved look about them that causes the inexperienced traveller to make further and handsome contributions for very shame.

The two original whiskey-jacks who were attached to this spot when first I came here, have called in, off the endless, empty streets of the forest, all of their kin who resided within a reasonable distance, say about five miles, judging by the number of them. This assembly of mendicants follows me around closely on my frequent tours of inspection, wholly, I fear, on account of what there is in it for them, and my exit from the cabin with something in my hands, supposing it is only an axe or an empty pot, anything at all, is the signal for piercing outcries from watchful sentinels who have been waiting patiently for hours for my appearance, they calling loudly to their fellows the bird-equivalent of 'Here he is, boys!' When I stop they gather on branches on all sides, regarding me alertly, solemnly, or wheedlingly, according to the disposition of the individual, whispering meanwhile confidentially among themselves. And as they sit in mock decorum, dispersed among their various vantage points, a direct and steady glance nearly always discomposes them, causing some to turn their heads away—whether as a disclaimer of any ulterior motive (they would steal the eyes out of a brass monkey) or from a hypocritical desire to appear not too eager, I cannot attempt to divine. Perhaps they have the grace to simulate some slight feeling of shame at the means, little short of bare-faced robbery, that they are adopting to satisfy an insatiable appetite; in which case this assumed diffidence does not prevent them from keeping a keen weather-eye on every move I make, and they readily observe morsels thrown to the ground behind them, or otherwise supposedly out of sight, and are able to detect a single crumb that would be invisible to the eyes of more honest folk. Most of them have learned to alight on my extended hands, and will sit there picking daintily at their portions, while others will dive at me like attacking planes and seize their share in passing. Gourmands and thieves they undoubtedly are, but they are cheerful, good-natured pirates and good company withal, and these engaging rascals have a pleasant, plaintive little ditty that they sing, as if to please the hearer, but which I gravely suspect is but a siren song used only to charm contributions from reluctant prospects.

They will go to almost any lengths to gain their ends, and I once saw one of them, dislodged from a frozen meat-bone by a woodpecker (a far stronger bird), waiting with commendable patience until the red-head should be through. However, the woodpecker was far from expert, and using the same tactics on the bone that he would have employed on a tree, he pecked away with great gusto, throwing little chips of meat in all directions, thinking them to be wood, only to find, when he got to the heart of the matter, that he was the possessor of a clean, well-burnished, uneatable bone. This pleased the whiskey-jack mightily, for at once appreciating his opportunities, he hopped around among the flying scraps of meat and had a very good lunch, while the unfortunate woodpecker, who had done all the work, got nothing.

Birds of bright plumage are not common in the North, and the woodpecker, with his bold, chequered patterns and crimson-tufted head, provides a welcome note of brilliance on his short, darting flights from tree to tree. And he dearly loves a noise. To keep the beavers from cutting down some of the best trees near the cabin, I have been obliged to put high, tin collars around the bases of them, and these are a godsend to the woodpeckers from all over the country, who amuse themselves by rapping out tinny concerts on them with their beaks. It has long been my custom to be up and around all night, going to bed at daylight, but no sooner am I settled when, at the screech of dawn, the woodpeckers commence a rattling tattoo on the tin. The result is a languorous uproar to which salvos of machine-guns fire would be a welcome surcease, and in the midst of this unholy pandemonium I am expected to sleep—sometimes succeeding, and sometimes not. This diabolical racket takes me somewhat back to my earlier trapping days, when I had no clock, and in order to ensure my early rising, I used to freeze a piece of meat solidly into a tin dish and set it on the low roof of the shack, directly above my head. At the first streak of daylight the whiskey-jacks would hammer on the frozen meat, creating a clatter in the tin dish that would wake the dead. I believe I can claim to be the sole inventor of this very serviceable alarum; and it had one great advantage not shared by alarm clocks in general, that when the weather was bad it remained quiet, as the birds didn't show up, or if it was snowing heavily the sound was deadened, and I knew then that I didn't have to get up.

Near the cabin there lives a mama woodpecker. In a hollow tree she has a nest, with young ones in it, who keep up a continual monotonous chattering which is going on just as stridently when I get up as it was when I went to bed, and I think never ceases. They have very penetrating voices which never seem to tire, and if at any time there is a public demand for bird voices that are guaranteed never to wear out, they would have an excellent future on the radio. The jetty black-birds, very black indeed, with bright carmine patches on their wings, give another note of colour, but the most resplendent of all my bird guests is a humming bird. He is a tiny, lustrous little creature, and his feathers are so very miniature that they seem like tiny scales, and in his tightly fitting, iridescent sheath of opal, emerald and ruby red, he seems more like some priceless, delicate work of Chinese artistry, than a living thing. For a short time only he stays, hovering among the wild rose bushes, his wings winnowing at an incredible speed, so as to be a nearly invisible blur until he darts away with almost bullet-like velocity, a brilliant streak of fabulous colouration.

For several years now a brood of partridges has appeared here in the Spring. The owls get a few, but most of them survive, greatly owing to the militant defence tactics of their mother. Ducks and snipes and other waterfowl and even singing birds with nests upon the ground, will feign disability, and retreat as though badly injured, and so appear an easy prey, hoping, with pathetic optimism, to draw an intruder away from young or nest. The partridge will do this too, but far more frequently will attack even a man with reckless bravery, flying in his face with shrill battle-cries or rushing at him with outspread wings, hissing like a snake—truly, an exhibition of determined courage that should win the little bird a meed of admiration from even the most callous. In the Winter, her brood long gone to parts unknown, she stays around, sleeping warmly in a tunnel in the snow at night, and in the daytime, if it is not too cold, stepping daintily about the yard. If the weather is cool, she alternately puffs out and flattens down her feathers, so that she looks to be inflating and deflating as she walks, appearing to be first a bird, all sleek and smooth, and then a feathered football going forward on spindling, inadequate legs. She had a habit of feeding up in a good-sized poplar near the house, year after year eating the buds from it all Winter. She always picked on the same tree, until at last the tree gave up, and now is dead.

To-day an eagle swept majestically above the camp, flying very low, the beat of his great wings loud and portentous in the still air. He checked a little in his flight as though minded to stay awhile; but he changed his mind and kept going on his way. I had not seen him for two years, though his nest is not over a mile from here. An eagle is the only bird that I have so far noticed who turns his head from side to side and looks around him as he flies, and this one looked back and gave me a look of keen appraisement as he passed.

And now, of a sudden, I hear behind me a light, but furious trampling, and a squirrel hurls himself through the air and lands on my back, and clambering to my shoulder he snatches from my fingers the pea-nut I always have for him. Precipitating himself on to a shelf arranged for his accommodation on the wall of the cabin, he expertly shells his pea-nut and there eats it. He sometimes does this for a visitor, if in the mood, and whilst on his shelf keeps one very bright eye keenly on the donor. Most of his kin that visit me are content to hull the nuts, but he is more fastidious, and skins them too. Like all his kind he lives at the rate of about a hundred miles an hour, and when seen is always in a state of delirious activity. This is Shapawee, The Jumper. Vastly different in disposition and unusually sedate, is my little friend Subconscious, so named because, when quite young, he would enter the camp and roam around without apparent object, like one in a dream, or under the influence of his subconscious mind, meandering aimlessly around. He was the only squirrel I have ever met who walked, most all of the others moving at nothing less than a round gallop. Subconscious is more leisurely, and very gentle in his ways, one of the very few who have permitted me to handle them. He used to spend most of his day around my feet, monopolising my time, and when I cut wood he stuck around and different times narrowly escaped being chopped or cut in two. He was on a fair way to becoming a nuisance, when one day he ran across the top of a hot stove. Then he came no more. I mourned him for dead, and missed my merry little companion who had become almost like a familiar spirit. The yard looked a little empty without him, and his familiar trails and vantage points became snowed under, or were used by other and less interesting specimens of his kind. But this Summer he has returned, and is as gentle and friendly as ever, though he has evidently learned something of the ways of the world during his wanderings, as the appearance of another squirrel, regardless of sex or size, transforms him immediately into a little termagant.

During the absence of Subconscious, I undertook to tame another of these flying acrobats and succeeded up to a certain point. Then a third offered himself voluntarily as a candidate (with reservations), so that I now find my footsteps dogged by three of the, to each other, most unsociable, irascible and pugnacious bundles of dynamic energy ever forgathered together in any one place—three minds with but a single thought—to do unto others as they would be done by, but to do it first! Each considers the environs of the camp as his personal property and will fight at the drop of the hat, or less, any of his breed who dare set foot on, or even breathe, in his chosen territory. The squirrel is not a gregarious beast, and these territorial rights are pretty generally respected. But I am afraid that I have somewhat upset the regular balance of things by my well-meant attempts to arrange that a good time is had by all. This difficulty I have endeavoured to adjust by feeding each one in his own small district, but have failed signally. Most of what they get is not eaten, but is hidden away in tree-tops, crotches of limbs and such places, and on each cache being made the owner issues a long, quivering screech of defiance to all the world. This challenge, instead of driving away possible robbers, under present circumstances only serves as an advertisement, and attracts the attention of the other two of this militant triumvirate, who both know what it is all about. Their appearance on the scene precipitates immediate battle, the aggrieved party being always the aggressor and launching himself at his opponent as though to annihilate him on the spot. But the prospective victim is not there when his assailant lands, being already well on his way, and a lively chase ensues, carried on with shrill skirrings and chatterings of rage, and at a devastating speed. The intruder, however big, seems to feel the weakness of his case, always giving way before the onslaught of the proprietor, irrespective of size. I notice that the pursuer is always careful not to run any faster than the fleeing enemy, so that they keep always the same distance apart, and the duel is never brought to an issue; showing that they possess not only valour, but also the discretion that is said to be the better part of it.

One day Shapawee and Subconscious appeared simultaneously, one on each side of me. With some misgivings I gave them a pea-nut apiece, keeping them as far apart as possible—but they saw one another! Each at once assumed a most ferocious aspect and glared at the other with manifest evil intent. And of a sudden both turned and ran in opposite directions as fast as they possibly could, each thinking the other was behind him. It is all very harmless and entertaining; no blood is spilled and it is doubtless good exercise. And meanwhile the remaining squirrel, the whiskey-jacks, and other non-combatants, make a Roman Holiday with the caches that are being so valiantly defended. Whilst not gifted to the extent that some other creatures are, squirrels are by no means unintelligent. They have good memories too, recognising me immediately among strangers, even after an absence of a year. It is to be noticed, too, that they will test all cones dropped by themselves from the tree-tops, to see if they are good, before laying them away for Winter provision, and will bury the duds separately, out of the way, to avoid mistakes. Their strength is quite disproportionate to their size; I have seen a squirrel with half of a large apple in his mouth, jump without noticeable effort up and on to a root projecting out from a fallen tree, twenty inches above his head—equivalent to a man leaping ten feet into the air with a bushel of potatoes in his arms.

Once a family of musk-rats lived under the flooring in one corner of the camp, having reproduced an almost perfect replica in miniature, of the domestic arrangements of the beavers. They were docile little fellows, and they learned to come to my call precisely as the beavers did, and frequented the cabin with the same freedom and lack of fear, save that they were not strong enough to open the door themselves. However, they would pull at a loose board until it rattled loudly, and stand chittering outside, with the greatest impatience, until admitted. One of them, when I fed the beavers titbits, would sit humbly by waiting for his share until the bigger folk were done, and whenever I called the Mah-wees (young beavers), he thought he was Mah-wee too, and would come helter-skelter through the water along with them. Unlike his fellows he associated with the beavers, except with Jelly Roll, who was jealous of him, and if noticed by her, he would make himself, if not invisible, at least as inconspicuous as possible; though when the young musk-rats first appeared out in the open, and were sometimes abroad under the guardianship of this one (as with beavers, musk-rats of both sexes help take care of the young), Jelly Roll would swim beside them, exhibiting great interest, and make no hostile demonstration towards him. But if he was alone she would chivvy him around as often as not. These interesting and intelligent little rodents should not be called 'musk-rats', as they are not rats at all, but are first cousins to the beavers, whom they much resemble in appearance, habits and disposition. I had good company with them for several years, but much to my sorrow, a periodical epidemic which they, like the rabbits in the woods are subject to, killed every one of them. And I often wonder if their little ghosts do not sometimes swim on Ajawaan, and haunt the small, well-kept home they had, where they had been so happy while they lived.

There was a wood-chuck, a special chum of mine, who year after year made her home under the upper cabin, where she had every Spring a brood of wood-chucklets, or whatever they are called. She was an amiable old lady, who used often to watch me at my work and allowed me a number of privileges, including the rare one of handling her young ones. But if a stranger came, she would spread herself out so as to quite fill the entrance to her domicile, to keep the youngsters in, and when the stranger left she would emit shrill whistling sounds at his retreating back, very sure that she had frightened him away. She too has gone, her time fulfilled, and another has taken over her old home; a well-built, very trim young matron who stands up straight and very soldierly before her doorway, and tries to look in windows.

I must meet these losses with what equanimity I can muster, without vain regrets. Yet I miss these old-time friends of so long-time standing, each a small, humble presence that has entered, for a little time, my life and then passed on.

*   *   *   *   *

People having the dim, distorted ideas that are held by so many concerning animals can gain very little insight into their true natures. Each animal has his separate personality, easily distinguishable to one who knows him.

Among the more highly intelligent species no two individuals seem to be alike, each having an individuality all
his own. Their ways are often so extraordinarily human,
and this is especially true of the rodents. They seem at
times so rational, their movements are often so much to
the purpose, and their actions, and their manner of
expressing their emotions sometimes so childlike—the little
side-glances, the quaint and aimless gestures, their petu-
lance if unduly annoyed, their artlessness and lack of
guile, their distress when in some small trouble, their so-
evident affection for each other—I have never ceased to
regret the thousands of them I destroyed in earlier days.
Even then I never enjoyed killing them, preferring to find
them dead, refusing to visualise the hopeless struggle, the
agony, the long hours of awful misery. And to-day I feel
that however great the inconvenience they may put me to,
it can never pay the half of what I owe them. Only those
who have suffered similar tortures can have any concep-
tion of what trapping by present methods really means to
the animal population of the woods.

Perhaps you, whom I am trying to entertain, find these
thoughts a little serious. But this life I lead lends itself
not only to watchfulness, but also to heedful observation
and deep thinking. Remember, reader, that those who
live within the portals of the Temple of Nature, see far
into things that are outside the scope of ordinary existence.
There is a kind of sanctity in these forests of great trees
that makes me think of dim cloisters in old, vast cathedrals
in England, and causes the ceremonious pomp and the
sonorous insincerities of not a few theosophies to seem
cheap and tawdry in comparison.

Owing greatly to the ignorance, thoughtlessness or
intolerance of many who come in contact with them, some
really harmless creatures have been saddled with a reputation for evil that they do not deserve, and are penalised

accordingly. All that most of them need is a little sympathy, and most of all to be let alone to mind their own business. Though I must admit that sometimes this 'business' is a little ill-judged, as in the case of the skunk who took refuge in my store-tent, sleeping there regularly, and who repaid my hospitality by having, in amongst my provisions, a family of kittens, or pups, or skunklings—or is it skunklets? This was no doubt an oversight and no harm was intended, I am sure, and everything turned out all right, and no one was a bit the worse off for it. The skunk is really a natural gentleman (or lady), but unfortunately is not a mind reader, so he cannot always gauge with accuracy your intentions towards him when you bump into him suddenly in the dark. Usually they (your intentions) are hostile, and he acts accordingly, but he is slow to anger and of monumental patience; and his feelings must be badly outraged before he will turn his battery on you. Meeting him in the moonlight is sometimes startling, for then his long, white horizontal markings and white cap are accentuated and, the rest of his coat being black, are all that can be seen; so that as he turns quickly this way and that with supple movements, he looks at first like some darting white snake with a venomous head. But he is an inoffensive, happy-go-lucky beast with a fixed idea that human beings like to find him in tents, camps, and out-houses, and under the flooring of summer cottages. Even so, finding a skunk in the store-house is not nearly as inconvenient as discovering a moose in a canoe; and I once had this interesting experience, although I hasten to add that I was *not* in the canoe at the time. It was on shore, drawn up, awaiting my early departure that day for Waskesieu, thirty miles away and all by water. As I was making my preparations I heard, outside, a sort of light crackling, crushing sound, and looking through the window saw my friend the moose (previously mentioned) walking slowly, steadily, and very thoroughly, through and along my canoe. I rushed out of the cabin at him, shouting, and this seemed to remind him of something, so he extricated his feet from the various holes, where they must have felt most uncomfortable, and stood aside, surveying the wreckage with an air of rather thoughtful detachment. Now this was nothing but rank carelessness on his part, and I remember having a distinct feeling of annoyance about it. Granted that he was a youngish moose, and perhaps didn't know much, the fact still remains that a canoe is a very handy thing to have when you have a thirty mile trip to make, entirely by water. A moose is rather a terrific object to have around, being about the size of an overgrown horse, and it is as well, if your visiting list includes one, not to leave any breakables around where he can walk on them. So in all fairness I must take some of the blame for this affair, for not having carried the canoe up a tree in the first place and secured it there. So, forgiving the moose, I placed the injured craft up on a rack, intending to mend it, where, in this unusual position, it became an object of intense interest to the beavers. One night these enterprising animals, with the high intelligence for which they are celebrated, carefully felled a large tree across the long-suffering canoe, reducing it to the very best of matchwood.

None of these guests of mine stand in any need of gifts from me. With the exception of the beavers, who came with me, they fended for themselves before I arrived on the scene, and if I were to suddenly disappear, though they might disperse, no one would be a whit the worse; though I like to think that some of them would miss me. But it makes me happy to put out treats for them, and to take note of the so very different way in which each one takes his daily portion from my hand; to observe his manner of approach, and his reactions afterwards. It is great fun in the morning (or at noon in my case) to wake up and find everything gone, and to know that small forest people— and sometimes big ones—have been busy whilst I slept, running back and forth with all they can possibly carry with them of my bounty. It pleases me immensely to hear some hungry worker who has been absent for hours on a working party, mumbling his satisfaction as he eats a well-earned meal of dry bread, or an apple, or steps into a dish of rice with both hands at about a mile a minute; and in Winter I view with the deepest satisfaction a hole in the snow beneath an old root, maybe, with a tell-tale ring of rime around its rim, revealing the home of some happy little beast who has a full belly and is fast asleep.

Every one of these so-busy dwellers in the Wild Lands presents intriguing possibilities, and has a life history well worth a little patience in the studying. Even those that live in the water, or on it, and are therefore more difficult to cultivate, have an interest that is easily discovered by a little investigation; all the way from the water beetles, that leave their natural element and climb on rocks to sun themselves, to the proud, white-throated loons, greatest and most accomplished of all the divers, who run races round and round the lake with the most inordinate splashing and other uproar, and play a kind of water-leapfrog, driving the beavers to distraction with their weird, half-human laughter. These royal birds, however, cannot walk, but are strong fliers and real artists in the water. When they take their young ones out for exercise there are usually only one or two—the wee, jet black chicks sit upon their mother's back, getting a free ride while they look around in the most complacent manner at the scenery. Though they receive visitors, and I have seen as many as eight of them swimming before the cabin together, these stay only a short time, and each lake, unless a large one, provides a home for only two. And here they play and fish all Summer, winging South in early Autumn and returning every year for a period of their lives, which some say to be a hundred years. It seems probable that, like eagles and wild geese, they mate for life, and in support of this supposition is the fact that the same pair has lived on this lake every Summer since I came here, and I do not know how long before. These two know me very well, though the female is not so intimate with me as the male, who always visits near the cabin very punctually, soon after daylight every morning, and holds a conversation with me at a distance of a hundred feet or so, very noisy on his part, and quite unintelligible to me, and he hails me with a not unmusical fanfare of recognition when he sees me pass in the canoe. He is a splendid bird, and besides being highly ornamental he is very useful too, giving out a loud, unusual call should anything uncommon, or a stranger, appear upon the lake or in the timber near the shore.

Every one of these creatures had his proper function, and each, however apparently useless, serves well the purpose for which he was created. Even diminutive birds, negligible-appearing denizens of these wide solitudes, have their own appointed place to fill. Seemingly quite superfluous in the vastness of the mighty scheme about them, yet as they hop happily in little groups among the fallen leaves, seeking the wherewithal to maintain their tiny lives, competent, wise, and bright-eyed and very much at home, who that watches them will question their right to be, or doubt but what they also do their part?

Animals quickly know a sanctuary when they find one. How I cannot tell; something in the atmosphere of the place perhaps, or some kind of telepathic divination all

wild creatures seem to be possessed of, may account for
this; nor is this sixth faculty of sensing the presence or
absence of danger confined to animals alone. While some
need time in which to figure out the situation, others
will respond almost immediately to my advances,
depending on the disposition or intelligence of the
individual. Take an instance of the latter case; the time
is evening, on a day in Autumn, two years ago. I look
out of my window and see a deer feeding in the glade
upon a knoll beside the camp. I open the door without
sound, unhurriedly; with quiet, easy movements I step
out, smoothly, but without any suggestion of stealth.
The deer tenses in every muscle, raises his head and stares
at me—almost an unseeing stare, you would think. But
a squirrel passes swiftly, and inaudibly because the leaves
are wet, and with a sudden shift of his eyes (but not his
ears) the deer acknowledges the slight, momentary flicker
of the tiny beast's passage—he is watching all right; he sees
very well indeed. He swings his eyes back into line with his
ears, to me. I speak softly, soothingly. Now he flicks his
tail—that is the sign; his mind is made up—either he will
bound with high, rocking leaps out of sight, or he has
decided to accept the situation and stay—which? I speak
again, advance a little towards him, talking to him. Then,
he relaxes; the stare becomes a gaze and, supreme gesture
of confidence, he turns his back on me. He reaches down
for some jack-pine shoots a squirrel has obligingly dropped
there from the tree-tops, and nibbles at them, looking at
me casually from time to time. He is satisfied. I have
made another friend.

Seldom am I without one or another of my dependents,
even though they are not always visible. The crash of a
new-fallen tree, or a shrill outcry of adolescent beaver
voices from the lake, may disturb the sleeping echoes. The
door is thrown open and a load of mud and sticks comes in,

borne in furry arms and intended as materials for the earthen lodge that stands inside my cabin; then a light pitter-patter across the floor, as a musk-rat calls in for his nightly apple; comes the rattle of antlers among the willows —these sounds, familiar to me as are street noises to a town-dweller, tell me that I am not, after all, alone.

This region, like any other Wilderness, has its population of predatory animals, and I must be for ever on the watch to safeguard my fellow-citizens from harm. Wolves, coyotes, bears, owls and mink and weasels are all potential and very active enemies; nocturnal creatures who can operate in the daytime with the same facility that they do at night, furtive, sly and ever-hungry, could slip silently in to deal out death in a moment of time, and be quickly gone. So I have not spent a night in bed in years, and during all the hours of darkness I travel back and forth through the velvet blackness of the sombre, whispering forest. And as I traverse these imponderable halls of Silence, there comes not a sound that is even faintly audible, but my ears will register it. For these are all the sounds there are to hear. Each has its meaning, which I must determine swiftly and with unerring accuracy; for on the acuteness of my senses and the precision of my findings, may depend the lives of those who look to me; for as I heed their danger signals, so do they mine.

So that my life has become something like that of a scout of ancient days of forest warfare, and even if asleep, any unusual sound from the surrounding woods, an unwonted commotion in the beavers' house, or even the abrupt cessation of some familiar noise, brings instant wakeful-ness. Danger lies hidden in the lurking shadows, waiting for the day when the high-tuned senses of my retainers, or my less perfect ones shall be at fault; yet not without due warning can it ever strike. The wood-chuck who haunts my wood-pile, and who should be sleeping, whistles sharply, for no apparent reason, into the night; comes the discordant warning cry of a whiskey-jack, the sudden alarmed scurry and subsequent shrill defiance from a safe retreat of a squirrel—then, softly, the muffled hoot of an owl who, in his downy, sanctimonious robe of white, like the robber-priest of some false religion fattening on the community about him, broods rapaciously above them like an evil spirit—or, a breath of sound, a flicker that is quick as a flame, the sinuous, reptilian slither of a weasel, small but deadly, swift, lithe, and ruthless—gangster and cut-throat par excellence of all the Wilderness. Either one I must destroy at once; there will be no second opportunity.

Later, perhaps, as I listen, the precise, dainty stepping of a deer ceases for a moment, to break into a series of startling leaps; a nearby moose, visible to me by the light of the moon, pauses suddenly in his browsing to catch some seemingly non-existent sound, or to sniff a warning from a vagrant current of air; from the lake, the cry of a loon, pitched at an uncommon note, off-key a little, weird and alarming, strikes a jarring note of discord. And then, most portentous of all, shattering the night like a rifle shot, there crashes out the appalling detonation of a beaver's tail-slap on the water—and then falls silence, ominous and nerve-racking, surcharged with menace, as every living creature within earshot stops motionless in its tracks, crouched, or in an attitude of suddenly arrested motion, its senses keyed to an excruciating pitch of sensitivity, waiting for someone to make the first move. And then I see shifting, wavering like a disembodied spirit through the shadows, unsubstantial as a phantom, the ghoul of all the forest lands—a wolf!

And then, if the moon is right and I line my sights quickly enough, and above all, if my calculations are cool and accurate, the smashing report of my rifle will end the incident and save many a day of anxious uncertainty.

And all these things that may be seen and heard, and other things that may not be even heard, but are a kind of feeling, advise me more positively than the spoken word, are as clear to me as lines of print, telling me how it fares with my Little People, and the big ones too, reminding me, sleeping and waking, of my responsibilities towards all things both great and small that within, without, and all about, dwell here under my protection.

From *Tales of an Empty Cabin.*

V

NORTH AMERICAN INDIANS

CONTENTS

CHAPTER ONE

INDIAN WAYS

Far, far away beyond the cities, the towns and the farmlands that you are so used to seeing all about you, away beyond the settlements of Northern Canada, lies a wild, almost unknown country. If you wished to see it you would have to journey Over the Hills and Far Away, to where there are neither railways nor roads, nor houses nor even paths, and at last you would have to travel in a canoe with your Indian guides, through a great, lonely land of forest, lake and river, where moose, deer, bears and wolves roam free, and where sometimes great herds of caribou wander across the country in such vast numbers that no one could possibly count them, even if he were there to do so.

Here, in this great Northland, you would see a part of North America as it was before the white man discovered it, and as it will remain, I hope, for many many years to come. You would not see very many white people there, even to-day, for besides the few trappers and traders, the only human beings that live there are the scattered bands of Ojibway Indians that have made this land their home, calling it the Land of Keewaydin, the North-west wind. They are a race of people so ancient, and they have been there so long, that no one, not even they themselves, know where they came from or how they ever got there. Far beyond the reach of civilisation, they live very much as their forefathers did when Jacques Cartier landed on these shores over four hundred years ago. Their villages of teepees, tents and sometimes log cabins, are still to be found, often a hundred miles apart, in sheltered groves and sunny openings in the woods, or beside the sandy beaches on some pleasant lake shore. In these small towns the Indian families live, each in its own dwelling, in happiness and contentment, well-fed in good times, going a little hungry when times are bad, as is the case with more civilised people.

Everybody in these villages has work to do; even the young people must do their share. Nearly all this work has to do with travelling, as Indians are constantly on the move. Some seasons, the animals on which the Indians depend for a living disappear out of a district, and the people must follow them or find new hunting-grounds, so that whole villages have to be pulled down, and everything (except the log cabins, of course), must be loaded in canoes or on toboggans, according to the time of year, and moved for many miles. On these Winter trips little boys and girls take their turn at breaking trail on snowshoes, feeling very proud as they lead the long procession of dog-teams and toboggans and people, for a mile or two at a time. In Summer they paddle all day in the canoes with the older people, and each has his or her small load to carry on the portages. They really enjoy their work, and they are just as serious and business-like about their tasks as are their parents.

Those of the Indian children who spend their summers near a fur-post or on a reservation, have an opportunity to go to school, and often make good scholars; some, indeed, become lawyers, others doctors, writers, or artists, and are very successful. But those of them who live the year round in the wild country have an education of another kind. The forest is their school, and in it they study the lessons so necessary to their way of life. Geography, history, or arithmetic or English would be of no use to them; their studies are plant and tree life, the ways and habits of animals and how to track them; how to catch fish at all times of the year and, most important of all, how to make fire in any kind of weather, such as rain, wind or snow. They learn the calls of all the birds and beasts, and can imitate some of them very well. They are trained to observe the movements of water in the rivers and lakes, so as to become skilful in the handling of canoes, and they learn the proper use of snowshoes, guns and axes, and how to drive a dog-team besides such every-day tasks as sewing moccasins, tanning hides, and finding firewood in places where there looks to be none at all; and they must be able to cook. Such a thing as a compass is unknown to them, and they can travel anywhere they wish in the forest by means of the sun, stars, moon, shapes of trees, formation of the hills, movements of animals and many other signs far too numerous to mention here. Their knowledge of woodcraft is so great that they become very self-reliant, and are able to make long trips alone and face without fear many dangers.

The Indian life is so hard and toilsome that no one in these villages can be lazy very long without quickly running short of food, clothing or shelter; and while the people will help one another and divide up whatever they may have, a lazy person is very much looked down on. Yet in spite of all this hard work, the younger people find much time to play their simple and very active games. Sometimes, after the day is done and darkness falls, they will sit out beneath the glittering northern stars, around the blazing camp-fires, and listen to the tales of their elders. Some of these tales are about hunting trips, or far-off tribes of Indians, or about great men of long ago; others are about strange adventures in the forest. But the strangest tales of all, to them, are told by those of the grown-ups who have visited that wonderful country so far away to the south, where the white people come from; where are great sleighs on wheels that run with the speed

R

of wind over an iron trail, by which they mean the railroad, and where smoke-canoes, as they call steamboats, go nearly as fast on the water; where there are no Indians and not many trees, only rows of tall stone houses between which people walk in crowds, rushing, hurrying along, seeming to go nowhere and come from nowhere. A country, they are told, where if you have no money you cannot sleep or eat. And they find this last to be the very strangest thing of all, because in the woods travellers are always welcome to rest and eat in the camps of white trappers or in an Indian village, free of any charge. For these children, and most of the older people too, know as little about the necessities of city life as perhaps you do about their wilderness.

From *The Adventures of Sajo and her Beaver People.*

*   *   *   *

Modern influences have taken away much of the romance, picturesque appearance from Indian camps, as seen on the reserves and more easily accessible areas of the Wilderness. Their racial pride has been sapped, and, destitute and hopeless, they no longer have the ambition to keep up the old methods and traditions, so that home life is slipshod and wretched, and national character is falling into decay. Attempts at living in a poor imitation of the white man's way without the means and training, have not resulted in gaining for the Indian a reputation for cleanliness. Only those of them having a long experience and good opportunities have succeeded in conforming themselves to the limitations of a wooden house, as the ill-kept, not always cleanly establishments of the more or less mendicant Indians near the railroad, plainly indicate. Yet in the cramped quarters of a tent or a teepee they are able to conduct their household affairs with neatness and system, where a white family used to living in a house would speedily become involved in hopeless confusion. Many of the shack-living type of Indians have lost the art of camping as an all-year-round method of living, and the traveller has to journey far beyond the regular lines of bush travel, to find a band of Indians living in the primitive but highly specialised manner that has been evolved by centuries. This type of community breaks up into small movable semi-permanent villages for the Winter, the location decided by the fluctuations of the hunt. These hunting bands are not large, and consist generally of from one to four or five families, according to the possibilities of the district. Being movable all the equipment and materials are very light, and apparently quite inadequate to withstand the rigours of a Winter north of fifty-two degrees. A well-sheltered spot is chosen where wood, fish, and moose are plenty, and tents and teepees are reared on walls three or four logs high, rectangular in shape for the tents, and octagonal for the teepees. The logs are well chinked with moss and later banked with snow. Small tin stoves, generally without an oven, supply the heat in the tents. The wigwams rely on open fires inside, placed not as those used by the plains tribes in the centre, but nearer one side which is nearly perpendicular.

During the day all blankets and other materials not in use are placed out of the way in the back of the tents, or rolled back nearly into the empty space in the angle between the lodge wall and the floor. Each member of the family keeps his accustomed place, and has his or her belongings at their back, while the indoor work, including eating, is done on a deep and generous carpet of balsam brush which covers the whole floor of the habitation, and is frequently changed. Household affairs, under these conditions, are of the simplest and are carried on with a minimum of disturbance and with few implements, thus avoiding confusion. The accumulation of carcases and waste matter from tanning, skinning and other activities incidental to a hunter's life over a period of seven or eight months, are thrown out to freeze on brush piles or recognised dumps, and lie harmless until Spring, by which time the inhabitants have gone. It is the presence of this rotting waste matter in disused Winter camp grounds that is responsible for a widespread impression that Indian camps are necessarily unclean. Outside the habitations, shelves are secured between suitable triangles of trees, and high racks are erected to keep meat, fish and other eatable goods, as well as many things not supposed to be eatable, out of the reach of the ever-hungry huskies. Narrow snowshoe trails, dug out after every storm, connect the dwellings, each with its row of snow-banked dog houses of brush. Within the camps all is surprisingly snug and comfortable while the stoves are going. In the lodges open fire is maintained all night without difficulty, but in the tents, when the stoves die, it is another matter.

In Summer, after the Spring trade, a few of these communities repair to some chosen spot, generally situated in some little known region far off a main route. White visitors, or intruders of any kind, are not welcomed at these villages, some of the sites of which have been used from time immemorial. The approaches are often carefully masked, and often no indication of their presence is encountered until the chance wayfarer comes upon them unexpectedly. These camps are known to the Indians as 'Oden-na-ka-inne-hekaj,' literally 'Hidden Towns.' Such towns are no longer common, but some still exist, and in them many of the old traditions are observed, and ancient customs, long supposed to have been forgotten, are still perpetuated.

It has been my good fortune to be a not unwelcome

guest at several of these self-contained, self-supporting concealed hamlets, and on one occasion I had the remarkable good fortune to obtain entry to a typical Hidden Town with a party whose genuine and friendly interest in their red brethren led me to make the attempt.

It so happened that we camped one night within a few miles of this village, the proximity of which was known to me and the guides. Although, so far, no white people had ever succeeded in gaining admittance beyond the canoe landing, the head of the party urged me to see what could be done. I knew the chances to be poor. No select gathering of aristocracy into whose presence you have blundered unknown and unannounced, can so completely, definitely, and absolutely give you the air as the semi-civilised inhabitants of a primitive Indian village in which you are not welcome. The Chief of the band in question, Big Otter, had a well-sustained reputation for exclusiveness, and although acquainted with him, I had never so far had any pressing invitation to exchange calls. I had, however, found on a portage that Summer a well-made paddle of Big Otter's make, tagged with a sign on birch bark representing my name. This was a present of some account in a country of rough rivers, and seemed a good omen, but I did not build on it.

The next day, after a short lecture on the procedure common to such occasions, all hands but the cook embarked and headed for Big Otter's village. An hour's paddle, including some pretty stiff poling up several rapids, brought us to a beautiful sheet of water several miles in extent, a lake almost round with sandy beaches and hemmed in by precipitous hills covered with virgin pine; a forest untouched by the hands of man. Across the lake we paddled for an hour into the eye of the sun, and down a narrow bay. Behind a high protecting point we came suddenly on a row of canoes pulled up or turned over on the shore, and from them wound a narrow trail, leading up a low grade to a grove of immense red pines. Here, on the level ground between the giant boles, were scattered a number of habitations. A blue haze of smoke hung in the air of the glade, and indistinct figures appeared momentarily between the lodges, to vanish suddenly again.

No one came down to meet us; the silence was deep and oppressive—one of those thick, heavy silences. Not attempting to land, I gave the customary call, the cry of an owl, and on the instant an indescribable tumult tore the silence to ribbons as a round dozen of dogs, of strongly wolfish appearance and great lung capacity, raced down to the water's edge, there to carry on a most alarming demonstration suggestive of an unappeased lust for blood. One of the party permitted himself to wonder if they could swim.

A tall slim figure with flying hair ran down the slope and plunged into the surging, leaping huskies, belabouring impartially on all sides with a burning brand, when the savage-looking body-guard retired reluctantly and ranged themselves in skirmishing order on the slope.

The figure, who could now be recognised as the Chief himself, advanced to the sandy margin and stood there.

He raised no hand in welcome, and gave no salutation of any kind. The setting was wild enough. The immense columns of the age-old trees, the conical teepees dimly seen in the shadows beneath them, the swift furtive movements of uncertain, half-seen shapes shifting among the smoke-wreaths, the tall, motionless, forbidding figure on the lake-shore, and behind him the herd of savage huskies. Something had to be said, so I opened negotiations. 'How! Quay, quay, Kitche Negik!—Greeting, Big Otter! I have found the paddle, and must thank you. My friends wish also to make presents to the little ones.' This last offer has softened the paternal heart of many an obdurate chieftain; but this one made no friendly sign, and even at that distance he exhaled a passive but very evident visitor-resistance. 'Anoatch! Anoatch!' he cried. 'This is not well done; who are all these people? Are they Kitche Mokoman?' (The Long Knives, Americans).

The situation called for no little tact and diplomacy, and I used what small amount of them I am blessed with.

I told them how far these people had come, their genuine interest, and sincerity in their desire to pay a friendly visit, and elaborated on their fortitude in the face of the hardships of so long and difficult a journey from the railroad (a matter of ninety miles or more). The diplomatic evasions, the carefully worded compliments, the guarded statements and the discussions entered into, much resembled those 'conversations' held between the ambassadors of two countries on the brink of war, and are beyond my power to recollect. Suffice it that in time, having cross-questioned me with no little skill, and adding unfortunately as a proviso that no photographs were to be taken, he pronounced himself satisfied: 'Undush, kibaan: All right, come ashore; we will talk together.'

I surveyed the wolf-pack in the rear. 'There are women; perhaps you could tie your dogs,' I suggested in English. And audible sigh of relief went up, and not only from the ladies either. Big Otter turned and intoned a few words, and soon an old woman and some children went fearlessly in amongst those potential man-eaters and drove some and dragged others away, to which treatment they tamely submitted.

At the landing the Chief met us, gravely shook hands with each one of the party, and his face crinkled into a rare smile, his white even teeth in startling contrast to his weathered countenance.

He led the way up to the camp. The dogs, although out

of sight, voiced their disapproval and commenced to growl. One or two dark heads peered out at us blankly from canvas door-flaps; several children retreated some distance, to turn and stare curiously at us. Two or three men were present, but they regarded us not at all. No women were to be seen. The situation was decidedly strained, and there was a tendency on the part of our folk to talk in whispers. Between them and these people there seemed to exist a wall of reserve, intangible but very real; not to be seen but plainly felt.

Then Big Otter spoke a few words in smooth-flowing sibilants and gutturals, and soon a man slipped noiselessly up to us on silent moccasined feet and shook hands all around. He was young, and his handsome face was flushed with embarrassment. Other men appeared, of various ages, all with the same level gaze and soundless tread, and also shook hands, impressively, but without emotion and without speech. Women now came out from lodges and other places of concealment and performed the hand-shaking ceremony; these last addressed me as interpreter, bidding the women of the party welcome.

A buxom old lady dressed completely in Highland plaid and wearing a brilliant head shawl, and carrying a large butcher's knife in her left hand, declaimed loudly, passing apt but not unfriendly comment on the personnel of the entire party. Changing hands with the knife, she resumed her labour of removing the hair from a green moosehide.

She and the other squaws relapsed into the state of indifference common to Indian women, resuming their various tasks apparently laid down on our appearance.

Then came the children; shy, smiling faces with bright, shoe-button eyes alive with curiosity. Small boys stepped up manfully and shook hands with dignity. Little girls in head shawls and voluminous plaid skirts sidled up within measurable distance and whispered together in wonder: 'Shaganash! Kitche Mokoman!'—White people! Americans! The simple presents were distributed, busy womenfolk looked up from their work with frank approval, and the atmosphere of distrust and suspicion melted away like snow before the Summer sun. All was now well. Yet there could be sensed an attitude of watchfulness. The disposal of the dogs gave evidence of this; a belt of at least a hundred feet in width on the rear and sides of the village had been denuded of its timber and allowed to grow up in a tangled mass of undergrowth through which no creature of any size could pass without noise. Through this natural fortification, and radiating from the town, lanes had been cut, and in these approaches the dogs were tied on long leashes that gave them control of the full width of the paths, and from whence on close approach they glared out at us in open hostility, their feral eyes red with hate.

This was the twentieth century, yet in a few minutes we no longer remembered it. Time, and the influence of modern civilisation fell away from us like a discarded garment.

All around an ancient forest of trees that were old when Wolfe stormed Quebec; birch-bark teepees, old ones grey with smoke-stained tops, new ones a bright yellow, scattered beneath the dark green limbs. In the foreground a scaffold hung with split-open fish and long strips of moose-meat, under which smouldered a slow and smoky fire. Women cooking at an open fire, others working ceaselessly at half-tanned hides. Farther off near the lake shore, surrounded by a litter of shavings, two men and a woman worked on a half-finished bark canoe. Rich-looking Hudson Bay blankets, red, green, or white hung out to air on high racks, adding a barbaric note of colour. The acrid smell of smoke, and the low hum of intermittent converse in an old, old tongue. An Indian village of the old régime; in just such another town Pontiac dreamed his dreams of conquest. We had slipped back down the pages of history a hundred years in as many seconds. The sportsmen in their outing clothes suddenly seemed out of place. In spite of the official reception we had been accorded, one felt instinctively that there was a limit beyond which we dare not venture, and one became conscious of an air of secrecy and reserve that held more than a hint of savagery. Out in civilisation these people might be awkward, ill at ease, negligible and nondescript. Here, far in the wilderness, in their own domain, they were supreme. Self-reliant and efficient, they proudly maintained their rights as Citizens of the Kingdom of the Wild.

And I tried to remember that I knew these men this many years. Big Otter himself had often made me gifts of meat; who could fear the wise and humorous Pad-way-way-donc—Here-he-comes-shouting—the teller of tales, who because he has lumbago will paint red and blue triangles at the corners of his eyes, play the turtle-shell rattle all night, and jump into the river through new ice in the Fall; old Sah-Sabik—Yellow Rock—who travelled alone, spoke only rarely and then in parables; Jimmy Twenty who always moved at a dog-trot and was seldom seen walking; Mato-gense—Little Child—he is a conjurer of no mean ability, and is reputed to be able to tell the weather two weeks ahead. Although he habitually chants to the tune of his wolf-skin drum, he is a pleasant old gentleman in conversation. Pad-way-way-donc has a daughter, a wonderfully built young woman with a wealth of long hair which she wears loose. She has not been near us, but stands apart, staring at us with the eyes of a wild thing.

Big Otter presently pointed to a large teepee and said: 'Go in and rest, the women have prepared food.' This was a welcome diversion, and on entering we found ready a savoury if substantial repast of bannock, fried moose-meat, fried fish, and piping hot tea. The interior of the wigwam was scrupulously clean, and from the poles hung bunches of herbs and roots that gave out an aromatic and not unpleasant odour. Two young women were in attendance, and all the party squatted on the soft carpet of freshly gathered boughs, and ate off shining tin dishes, with modern implements, and drank tea out of porcelain cups.

To some of the party the affair was novel to a degree, and the experience of eating Indian-cooked wild meat on the floor of a smoke-stained birch-bark teepee, within the precincts of a jealously guarded secret village, was, to one of the sportsmen with us, the fulfilment of a life-long ambition.

The ladies suggested that one of the women should tell something about herself. She agreed after some per-suasion, and it transpired that she had never seen a town or a train, nor did she care if she ever did. And forthwith arose a conversation in which I became the go-between. The questions on either side concerning mostly subjects beyond the knowledge of the object of them, I found myself saddled with the somewhat delicate task of steering the talk clear of shoals. I was obliged to extemporise considerably, thereby endangering my chances in the hereafter, in order that both parties should get the answers that pleased them, and so have everybody satisfied.

In the drowsy heat and silence of the wigwam, several of the visitors, fatigued with the journey, had fallen asleep. Others sat back to trees on the red-brown pine needles, or on logs near the central fire, and smoked contentedly. A young boy, armed with a cedar bow, drifted in. He had three partridges tied to his belt. These he skinned and cleaned deftly and hung above the lazy fire to smoke.

The day drew on and the heat waned. Two squirrels raced madly through the camp and up a tree, circling round and round the trunk in mimic chase with shrill profanities. A whiskey-jack floated soundlessly here and there, lighting where he would, and no hand was raised to molest him.

Calm, repose, and an ineffable peace settled over the camp. A coolness and the damp of evening commenced to fall, and the shadows crept from behind the trees and from out the dark aisles of the forest. The day was drawing swiftly to a close, and we must now travel by moonlight. Sleepers were aroused and we embarked. No good-byes were said, but the Chief followed us down to the landing. I raised my hand in a farewell gesture, when he spoke: 'Ki sakitone na ki do mokoman—do you value your knife very much?' he asked; I was wearing an ordinary hunting-knife of good quality at the time. I replied that I valued it very much, so much so that I did not care to part with it. 'But,' I added, 'as you are my brother, I will give it to you'; which I did, belt, sheath and all.

Once away from shore we paused with one accord, held by the wild beauty of the scene. The red sun was already half hidden behind the black rampart of the western forests. Rank on rank, file on file stood the dark legions of the pine trees, reaching in mass formation into the shadows of the already darkening hills.

A pair of loons, their white breasts flashing, swam lazily on water so calm that it seemed they floated as on air. Slowly the thin columns of smoke ascended from the clustered teepees, to lie in a white pall above the town. Soon the moon rose, pale and very close, and against its broad and luminous expanse a single pine stood blackly out in silhouette. Somewhere an owl hooted once.

*   *   *   *

We moved off silently from the Hidden Town with its mystery, its customs of bygone day, and its aloof, silent inhabitants, inscrutable and unfathomable as the sombre forest that had bred them. And as we entered the narrow defile at the outlet, came the long drawn-out sobbing wail of the wolf-dogs as they saluted the full of the moon, even as their wilder kindred have done for untold ages.

And late that night there was faintly borne on the still air a sound, persistent, insistent and monotonous; the steady rhythmic throbbing of an Indian Drum.

From *Tales of an Empty Cabin.*

* * * *

It was at the time of the Fall of the Leaf, when the Hunting Winds course through the empty aisles of the sombre spruce forests, and all the Indians had left the trading post, and were on their way into their hunting grounds with their Winter supplies. Enormous quantities of provisions had to be transported over lakes of all sizes and portages of all lengths, for as far as two hundred miles, for these bands would remain, each family in its own territory, until the last trace of Winter had gone, a matter of six or seven months in the high North. Most families made two trips by relays, with their immense loads, using the ordinary sixteen-foot canoes for the purpose. But Kee-way-keno scorned such methods and took everything in one trip in a huge freighting canoe, one that it took two good men to lift, carrying it alone over each portage. He had also a small birch-bark canoe, with a lesser load, of which the two boys took charge, and which was to be used for the Autumn hunt.

Things progressed as they usually do on such ex-peditions, the party making five miles some days, twenty on others, according to the kind of going, until they eventually arrived on their Winter stamping ground. The Winter camp was erected, fish netted and salted down, meat killed and brought in, and the country, which was new to them, quickly explored and trails laid. Soon the brown grass of the beaver meadows became coated with a rime which showed the passage of foxes and lynx, and ice began to form on the edges of the marshlands. Traps were set and the hunt was on.

Now Kee-way-keno was known far and wide as a mighty hunter and a skilled canoeman; but many and various are the snares and pitfalls which abound in the Wilderness and to which even those with many years of experience to their credit sometimes fall a victim. One morning having apparently overcharged his trade-gun, and the bark canoe being slippery with ice, on his firing at a duck the frail craft upset, and the father was swept over a sixty-foot falls. The two boys, engaged in breaking camp on shore, were horrified but helpless spectators of the catastrophe. They rushed to the foot of the chute, but saw no sign of canoe or man, and as the river runs at this point for miles in a succession of falls and heavy rapids, gave up any attempt to recover the body at that time.

Such is the training of these people that these youths, of thirteen and fifteen years of age respectively, considering the recovery of their father's remains paramount, decided to return one hundred and twenty miles, over thirty-two portages, and report the occurrence to the post manager. This they would have to do by means of the big canoe which it took two able men to raise to their shoulders, and that at a time of year when, owing to ice conditions, travelling might at any day become impossible. They first had to return on foot to their main camp, having brought only the bark canoe along on the hunting trip, a two days' journey by lake and portage. But in a region where there seems at times barely enough dry land to go around the water, this distance was doubled at least. This accomplished, they set out on the return trip. In view of the short time left them before the freeze-up, they went as light as possible, took no camping outfit save an axe, and for provision only a bag containing flour, grease and tea, some matches, a frying-pan and tea pail. Thus they hoped to make the portages in one trip, a saving of days.

What followed seems unbelievable. At this time of year, heavy winds prevailed, and the huge canoe with its light crew and no load, became at times unmanageable, and was on occasion driven miles off its course. Head winds baffled them, as their course lay south-west into the teeth of the prevailing wind of the region. Beating into this with their high-riding and empty hull often became impossible, necessitating much travelling at night, when it would be generally calm, and this in a district with which they were unfamiliar, and on a route of more than a hundred miles in length over which they had passed but once.

These conditions imposed a severe enough tax on the boys' strength and ability, but it was on the portages where the real difficulty existed. The two boys would double on each end of the canoe, lifting it on to convenient fallen timber or rocks, and getting in under, each at his end, would struggle to their feet, and stagger, stumble, and at times crawl across the carry. Most of these were mercifully short, but several were very long, one being over a mile. Day after day they continued this exhausting and heart-breaking labour, eating hastily made bannock soaked in hot grease and washed down with tea, and sleeping without blankets under the canoe. On the smaller lakes ice began to impede progress, and latterly a channel had to be broken with a pole in the hands of the bowsman, at the rate of a quarter of a mile an hour, if that. There came a heavy fall of wet snow, which whilst it enabled them to drag the canoe on the smoother portages, increased their difficulties on the rough ones, as well as keeping them soaking wet all day. So that the time that should have been occupied in sleeping was spent standing naked before an open fire, drying clothes.

These delays, and the physical exhaustion that began to overcome them, shortened their daily journey to barely four or five miles, and food began to run low. They rationed themselves, and the weakness of under-nourished systems worked to the limit, reduced their progress yet the more. Eventually they ran out of food altogether. The big canoe, without which they could not move, now began to be a grim white elephant that rode them, a merciless taskmaster that was slowly grinding the life out of them. It seemed to their fevered imaginings almost like an evil creature bent on their destruction. Indians they were no doubt, and to the manner born, but just now they were only two young lads, alone in an endless empty waste without food or shelter, where the least mistake in seamanship on the windlashed surface of a big lake, or a slight error in casting the route, meant death either by drowning or from hunger and exposure. Yet in the face of these almost insuperable difficulties they lived up to the Creed of the Trail, where that which is undertaken must be finished, and where none may falter or evade the issue.

With staring eyes and hollow cheeks, minds wandering in the delirium of starvation and clouded by the black shadow of an awful tragedy, the sons of Kee-way-keno arrived at the Post after nineteen and a half days of suffering such as few boys of any race have been called on to endure. Only the intensive training to which Indian youths are subjected, together with a spartan spirit of fortitude inculcated by a life of hardship, enabled these striplings to win through where many a grown man would have failed.

From *Tales of an Empty Cabin*.

*　　　*　　　*　　　*

It was the time of first ice, and the travelling was of the best, with less than six inches of snow. We took two days' provisions, intending to return by a short-cut the third day. And here is where the mice and men, so often mentioned, sustained their well-known reputation. We were poor prophets. The second night it turned soft, and there was an unprecedented snowfall of at least two feet. The lakes slushed up and the bush was clogged with wet snow. We had brought no snowshoes, we had not killed a moose, we had nothing to eat save the remains of our last meal, and were at least twenty miles from the village; an interesting problem any way you look at it. It took us four days and a half to get back, during which time we ate one partridge and two squirrels. These last we ate raw in order to get all there was in them. Once we found a thin strip of dried moose-meat hanging on a rack at an old camp ground; it was no bigger than your thumb, and must have been old enough to vote, being much like a stick of wood.

We commenced to become weak, taking long rests which ate into our time, and when it was necessary to cross over a log larger than common, we sat on it and looked at one another for long periods. I thought frequently of the squirrel skins which we had thrown away; apart from the hair there had been nothing wrong with them. We were much tempted to commit the indiscretion of eating snow, and sometimes chewed the scrapings off the inside bark of yellow birch. This, however, induced thirst, and drinking ice-water under these conditions is sometimes fatal. In the course of our wanderings we arrived at a spot where a moose had been killed that Autumn, and we dug the bones out of the snow, scorched them for a while on a fire, broke them open, and devoured the rotten marrow with relish.

These exercises occupied four days. At noon on the next day we met a rescue party supplied with snowshoes, but we were unable to use them, as we were now deathly sick from our last meal, and had to ride the dog teams. But for an old woman who understood the use of herbal medicines we should probably have died. I can never be caught in precisely the same predicament again, as since that experience I keep my snowshoes within reach whilst there is ice on the lake.

But the pitfalls are many and various. Violent and unseasonable changes of weather may catch unprepared those who live precariously on the edge of things, and inflict severe hardship; and even Indians, who have made the weather a separate study, are not altogether immune.

Five canoes of us, all heavily laden, were caught on a river that was rapidly freezing up, and thinking to beat out the ice, we made no camp, but continued on our journey in the darkness, until, unable to break ice any further we were actually frozen in near the shore. We had to chop the canoes out by firelight, make a cache, and wait for daylight. This was only the middle of October, and one of the party froze the ends of all the fingers of one hand.

The next day, taking what we could carry, we started overland on a twenty-five mile journey to our destination, where we had camps already built, walking on good ice all of the last day. On our arrival we commenced setting traps, intending to return with toboggans, at the first snow, for our goods. We had worked only a couple of days, when the unnatural conditions changed, the ice went out with heavy rain, and we were well marooned on a large island on which the camps were situated, with but little food and no canoes.

We stayed here for three weeks living mostly on fish, until the second and permanent freeze-up released us, when we drew in our huge loads by relays, losing the early Autumn hunt in the process.

From *Men of the Last Frontier*.

CHAPTER TWO

THE SUNSET TRAIL

Many years ago I cast in my lot with that nation known under the various names of Chippeways, Algonquins, Londucks, and Ojibways. A blood-brother proved and sworn, by moose-head feast, wordless chant, and ancient ritual was I named before a gaily decorated and attentive concourse, when Ne-ganik-abo, 'Man-that-stands-ahead,' whom none living remember as a young man, danced the conjurers' dance beneath the spruce trees, before an open fire; danced the ancient steps to the throb of drums, the wailing of reed pipes, and the rhythmical skirring of turtle-shell rattles; danced alone before a sacred bear-skull set beneath a painted rawhide shield, whose bizarre device might have graced the tomb of some long-dead Pharaoh. And as the chanting rose and fell in endless reiteration, the flitting shadows of his weird contortions danced a witches' dance between the serried tree-trunks. The smoke hung in a white pall short of the spreading limbs of the towering trees, and with a hundred pairs of beady eyes upon me, I stepped out beneath it when called on. And not one face relaxed in recognition, as, absorbed in the mystery of their ritual they intoned the almost forgotten cadences.

'Hi-Heeh, Hi-Heh, Ho! Hi-Heh, Hi-Heh, Ha! Hi-Hey, Hi-Hey, Ho! Hi-Ho, Hi-Ho, Ha!' and on and on in endless repetition, until the monotony of the sounds had the same effect on the mind that the unvarying and measured markings of a snake have on the eye. The sensation of stepping into the motionless ring was that of suddenly entering a temple, devoted to the worship of some pagan deity, where the walls were lined with images cast in bronze; and there I proudly received the name they had devised, which the old man now bestowed upon me, Wa-sha-quon-asin, Grey Owl.

At that the drums changed their rhythm and the whole assemblage, hitherto so still, commenced to move with a concerted swaying, rocking motion, in time to the thunder of the drums, and the circle commenced to revolve about me. The chant broke into a series of rapidly ascending minor notes, which dropped from the climax to the hollow, prolonged hoot of the owl whose name I now bore.

'Hoh-hoh, hoh-hooooooo! Hoh-hoh, hoh-hooooooo!' The weird cries trailed off into the empty halls of the forest, while faster and faster grew the dance before the bear skull; and the drummers, and those who played the rattles, and the circle round about, moved in unison to the constantly accelerating tempo that the old man gave them, till the swift thudding of many feet made a thunder of its own, and the glade became a whirling mass of colour; and ever the chant grew louder, until with a long-drawn-out quavering yell: 'Ahi, yah-ah-ah-ah-ah,' all movement ceased, and like the dropping of a curtain, silence fell.

This band is sadly reduced. The lonely graves beneath the giant red pines are more numerous to-day; they are a fading people. Not long from now will come one sunset, their last; far from the graves of their fathers they are awaiting with stolid calm what, to them, is the inevitable. To leave them, to stand from under, to desert the sinking ship, were a craven act, unthinkable. All of whatsoever I may know of the way of the wild they have taught me.

Ne-ganik-abo, my mentor, my kindly instructor, my companion in untold hardship and nameless tribulation, has pulled back little by little, the magic invisible veil of mystery from across the face of the forest, that I might learn its uttermost secrets, and has laid open before me the book of Nature for me to read; and in my bungling way I have profited by his lessons, but the half is not yet done.

I have followed him when snowshoes sank into the soft snow half-way to the knee, mile after weary mile, to sleep at night behind a square of canvas; this for five days and nights, it snowing steadily most of the time, and with nothing to eat but strips of dried moose-meat, and teas made from boiled leaves of the Labrador sage. I have negotiated dangerous rapids under his tuition, when at each run, after the irrevocable step of entering, I doubted much that I would reach the foot alive. He has led me many hours of travel with birch-bark flares at night, and more than once entire nights in an unknown country without them. Once, soon after the freeze-up, and with the ice in bad condition, we returned late in the evening to our shelter, to be greeted by a heap of charred fragments, and bare poles on which small portions of canvas were still smouldering.

Our fire, which we supposed we had extinguished, had worked under the peaty forest soil, and sprung up in the centre of the camp, destroying every last ounce of provisions, the blankets, and the shelter itself. Greatest of our losses was that of several mink and a red fox, the latter not entirely destroyed, but now scorched black; my first black fox, and, I might add, my last. As a storm threatened, the old man started on the day and a half's journey to the village in the darkness, over ice that few would have attempted by daylight, judging it by the sound only, singing in bad spots in an undertone, a song suitable to the conditions; such as 'I see the trail like a thread, I see it, I see it,' or 'I feel water close, I feel water.' Meanwhile all I could see was the surrounding blackness, and the only thing I felt was a sinking sensation in the pit of my stomach when the tap of his pole indicated bad ice.

I have seen him, in the spring of the year, when all ice is treacherous, after half a day of juggling between canoe, sleigh, and snowshoes, walk out on to the next lake, that by all the law should have been as bad as the last one, and glancing casually across it say:

'This ice is good.'

His faculties of observation, as with most Indians, were very keen; nothing seemed to escape him. He could detect game invisible to me, yet his gaze was not piercing, rather it was comprehensive, all-embracing, effortless, as in the eye of a camera, registering every detail in a moment of time. He often made fire with bow and spindle, habitually carried flint and steel, and seemed to have knowledge of the speech of some animals, calling them almost at will in the right season. He carried a beaded pouch which contained, among other trinkets, some small beaver bones. In spite of the advances in latter years of the price of beaver skins, on account of some belief he held he would not kill these animals, even when in want; and he would stand at times outside their lodges, seeming to converse with them. Not a good shot with firearms, yet he would get so close to his quarry without their knowledge, that an old muzzle-loading beaver-gun (so called from the method of purchase) fulfilled all his requirements for game of all sizes, partridges included. For your Indian, in common with the white hunter, shoots his birds sitting; but he uses a bullet, and the mark is its head, a sporting enough proposition for a man with an empty belly. He showed me, in the course of years, did I but have the head to hold it all, what a man may learn in a long life of observation and applied experience.

He had his humorous occasions, too. With a party of moose-hunters we were standing on the abrupt edge of a hill, the face of which had fallen away and lay in a mass of broken fragments at the foot, crowned with a few small jack-pines, shoulder high. Across the valley was a ridge crested with a row of immense white pines, seedlings, perhaps in the days when the Plymouth Brethren dodged flights of arrows on their way to church. One of the tourists had shown great curiosity with regard to the venerable guide, and had pestered me with endless questions regarding him. The old man knew no English, but I think he got the gist of the conversation, for at last, on being asked his age, he pointed across to the big pines.

'Tell that man,' he said, 'that when I was a boy those trees were so small that I could reach out and shake them —so!' and grasping one of the jack-pine saplings he shook it violently back and forth.

From *Men of the Last Frontier*.

*   *   *   *

Towards evening a bark canoe drifted gently ashore at the landing-place, and with a guttural exclamation of greeting there rose before me my friend of many days— Ne-ganik-abo, Stands First.

My emotions were not a little mixed, as I had thought of him as long ago gathered to his fathers. Many years had passed since we first had bent to the paddle and slept beneath the stars together. An aged man from my earliest recollection of him, he now seemed of another day and age, which indeed he was, and changed beyond belief. Dressed in old and faded overalls and shirt, he retained only the footwear of his people, a pair of beautifully beaded moccasins, and a medicine pouch decorated with porcupine quills. His hair, now white, framed a face the colour of old mahogany, patrician in cast, and almost fleshless; the eyes alone lent life to the mask-like visage, which was seamed with a thousand wrinkles. He sat at the fire and smoked awhile, seeming to rest, for he was very feeble.

He refused my offers of food, and, it not being customary for younger men to open a conversation, I waited until he first should speak; which, his smoke finished, he did, standing, and emphasising his remarks with the restrained but expressive gestures of an Indian.

'Wa-sha-quon-asin, Grey Owl, I see you do not forget. I called, and, of them all, you came.'

Up to this moment I had thought of no such thing, but there now flashed through my mind the tales I had heard. Was this the explanation of my unaccountable urge to visit the lake? I remembered that this place had been accessible to me any day for years, yet I had chosen this particular time to come. Coincidence? I became conscious of a slight feeling of uneasiness. He continued:

'Three days have I called and none came; this is the last day, the day of Two Sunsets; to-night I go away from here; to-morrow you would not have found me. My son, I have seen many snows come and go; to me you are a young man, and most of what I say will pass by your ears like the piping of frogs, or the tapping of a woodpecker on a hollow tree; yet of all my people, you are the only one who remembers the way of our race. I was a warrior once, and fought the blue-coated soldiers on a day when a river ran red with blood, and none escaped. This is many years past. Three of us returned here; we formed ourselves into a blood-brotherhood, that of the Beaver, called after our bravest warrior, killed in the battle. Of them, I alone remain. When you were named, I made you a blood-brother of the clan; remember that.'

He looked searchingly at me for a moment. This, then, was the reason for his attitude towards these animals, and I knew that I might never set another beaver trap, did I choose to remain true to the creed of this society of the

Dead. For the old man's weakness was such that it was evident that soon, not he, but I, would be the last of the clan of the Beaver.

He said a few words in a language unintelligible to me and resumed:

'Since then I have seen many changes; I have seen the skin teepees replaced by houses; the snowshoe trail by the railroad; and now the winged canoe of the white man flies with the wild geese amongst the clouds. I am now very old. Old age is a time of rest and meditation, yet I find myself surrounded by changes that keep me moving; at no place can I rest, and ponder peacefully on the past. Long ago my people left this lake where I was born. I played as a child on this very beach, and in these forests I learned the wisdom of the Old Men. Here I will leave my bones that the Medicine Spirits may see that there is one that has not forgotten that he is an Indian.'

He paused and seemed to listen.

Came a sound, a murmuring from the distance, a wind that stirred the tree-tops overhead; the sleeping forest half-awakened, sighed, and as the sound passed onward, slept again. And all around the golden and red leaves of the birch and maples, the spots of sunlight on the forest floor; and the thin blue wisp of smoke trailing up and up from the dying fire, up through the leaves and on beyond them. And far overhead the Unseen Musician improvised a low rambling melody in the many-stringed lyre of the pine-tops, and its soft humming, and the quiet lap, lap of the wavelets on the sandy shore, mingled with the old man's voice as he intoned in soft gutturals, with all the imagery to which his language lends itself.

'I hear a sound: the wind speaks to the leaves. No! it is the spirit of an Indian, looking for a place to rest, and there is none! The sky is red at night with the fire of burning forests. The beavers are gone, and there are no more singing birds; they cannot sing in the dry limbs of dead trees, and the Indian cannot live in a land of rotting stumps. The setting sun throws a red path across the water; there lies the trail to the Land of Spirits; along it I soon must follow my people. When the deep snows come I will dance the Dance of the Dead Men in the northern sky.'

The latter part of his speech seemed only indirectly intended for me; rather he thought aloud. He spoke of his past life, his old-time friends, and of days beyond the memory of living man. He dwelt on the time when his band could count half a hundred lodges, and told of his struggles to keep his people steadfast; and he seemed to wander a little, till I got the purport of his words: he was painting the picture of a vanishing race. He seemed no longer aware of his surroundings, and somehow gave the impression of talking to an invisible audience, of which I was not one. And his voice gathered some arresting quality from his theme, so that even the motionless trees about him seemed to stand and listen. And my previous intimacy faded into the background; and he seemed no longer a man, but a prophet, the patriarchal ruler of a vanished people, a reincarnation of the fabled Hiawatha.

And from his words there seemed to spring a pageant in the air behind him, of days gone by; of mighty men, long dead, whose deeds now lived again; of lines of naked braves filing by in the crouching hop and shuffle of the war-dance; of clouds of mounted warriors with waving ghostly bonnets, passing in review to strains of wild unearthly music. Of a buckskin-coated figure, with long yellow hair, surrounded by the bodies of dead men dressed in blue, standing alone in an inferno of screaming, racing savages, painted ponies, and whirling dust-clouds; in his ears the terrible shuddering chorus of the death-hulloo; a pistol raised to his head for the last act.

His voice lost its martial note, and the fire died from the old eyes, momentarily aflame with the memory of the historic combat. And then the scene changed. Endless forests marching, marching, tops swaying to the tune of the Hunting Winds; brigades of yellow-bark canoes loaded high with skins, floating down swift rivers walled with granite; four-footed creatures, now rare, trooping by in all their rich variety; the quiet lodges of a peaceful people, lodges before whose doors stood racks of sturgeon, moose and deer-meat. Then —the coming of the railroad; unnumbered leagues of noble forest falling before a sea of flames; scattered bands of a broken, bewildered people driven like leaves before the wind and then—to-day! And as he ceased the scenes faded, and the figures were gone; and he stood again alone; a forlorn, lonely old man.

I fumbled in my mind for words to express my thoughts, when turning, he walked the few steps beyond the edge of the forest to the sandy lake shore, and stood facing the glimmering ribbon of red cast on the still water by the now rapidly setting sun. In the crimson glow, the broken, patched canoe became a thing of beauty, and the withered, time-worn figure in its tattered clothing, silhouetted against the brilliance, seemed to take on again something of the wild freedom of his youth in its posture. With the simple dignity of a savage chieftain he raised his right hand, palm out, and bowed his head, as though in benediction of the scene before him, saluting the western sky with that greeting with which the Indian met the first white man, the ancient and almost forgotten Peace Sign. And as he so stood, embracing into his audience with a single gesture, the peaceful sleeping lake, the dark legions of the forest, and the brooding hills, he cried in a loud, clear voice, as to a vast and unseen assemblage:

'I stand on the Trail of Two Sunsets. To-night the sun sets for the white man for a day. Soon another sun will set for the Indian; and it will be for ever. There is a cloud across the face of the sky, and it shadows our trail to the end.'

He dropped his head, and sitting down beside his canoe, seemed lost in reverie. And the rim of the burning sun sank behind the distant hill-tops, and the last vestige of the red beam disappeared from the surface of the water.

I waited respectfully till the aged chieftain should see fit to address me again, when another thought struck me, and with a chill not altogether accounted for by the cool of evening, I walked quickly over and laid my hand on his shoulder.

His arm slipped gently down from the gunwale to his side. He was dead.

I buried him the next day in his old canoe, with his muzzle-loading gun, his old-fashioned axe, and his beaded pouch of relics by his side, in the smooth ground beneath the birches near the lake-shore, where he may hear the singing birds trill in rippling melody their evensong, in the sad days of the Fall of the Leaf, and the North-West wind may bring a message from the Great Lone Land beyond.

And there he will always be, facing towards the West, so that the rays of the setting sun to which he turned so wistfully in his last moments, may, at the close of every summer day, bathe his resting-place, in the Glory of his Sunset Trail.

From *Men of the Last Frontier*.

EPILOGUE

At the brow of a high eminence stood two men, their figures etched sharply against the sky of a day now near its close. Beside them lay two bundles, rolled as though in readiness for a long and immediate journey.

To the South lay spread out a smiling valley of farm-lands, dotted thickly with the habitations of man; and at the foot of the declivity far below, were half-cleared fields, in which lay piles of burning roots and prostrate tree-trunks. And there came up faintly to the ears of the men the ring of axes and the crash of falling timber, as an antlike swarm hewed at the face of the forest, eating into it, as a rising flood eats into a wall of sand.

Beyond the valley, in the distance, stood a mighty city, its tall buildings rising in huge piles of masonry heaped up against the skyline, whilst from its bowels rose the dull roar and whirr of massed machinery, and a confused hum as of a myriad bees within a gigantic hive. Towering smokestacks belched forth heavy clouds of rolling black smoke, which hung over the city like a dark canopy, and spreading out over the farm lands, shadowed them.

On the other side the mountain descended in a gradual slope to the level of the dark waves of an endless forest, the tree-covered hills rolling into the north, row on row, rank on rank, sweeping on in ever-lessening undulation until they merged into the dimness of the horizon. The ocean of evergreens opened out as it neared the foot of the descent, to flank a long open meadow of beaver hay, down the full length of which there wound a long ribbon of a trail, winding and twisting its way amongst the yellow grasses towards the North, until, visible only as a thread where it entered the woods, the trees crowded down upon it, engulfed it, and swallowed it up, so that it would be no more seen.

The man nearest the edge of the cliff stood leaning on his rifle, gazing out over the tilled fields, towards the city beyond. His grey eyes were narrow, and stamped at the corners with crowsfeet, hallmark of one who has peered into the glare of a thousand suns, and faced the blizzards of many winters. His face, tanned to the colour of leather, was hollow-cheeked, ascetic almost. Once his glance strayed involuntarily to the panorama of forest that lay spread out behind him, but his eyes again sought the distant city, as though drawn by some powerful attraction.

The other, a tall spare man, his long black hair confined at the temples by a buckskin band, and with the vigorous features and calm bearing of an Indian, regarded not the city, but stood motionless, his gaze roaming over the sweep and swell of the wilderness; and at his feet were the charred sticks of a fire, now extinguished. He had the air of one who waits.

Presently he turned and touched the white man on the shoulder, and pointing to the West, spoke in his native language.

'The sun is setting, my ears are filled with the sound of falling trees; it is enough. See! the shadows lengthen; let us go.'

And as the slow wind of evening passed over the land, there seemed to come an answering murmur from the hosts of the forest, saying: 'Let us go: let us go.'

And the concerted waving movement of the myriad tree tops in the breeze likened them to an immense and restless concourse, gathered together for some great migration, awaiting but the signal for departure.

For a moment longer the frontiersman stood irresolute, and then with a gesture of finality, his face set in the stern lines of one who has made a sweeping and unalterable decision, he assumed his pack, and turning his back for ever on the haunts of man, followed the Indian, now already on his way.

And their moccasined feet left no track as they followed the winding trail, and as they marched steadily away, their figures grew smaller and smaller, diminished, dwindled, dwindled, until at last, no longer distinguishable in the gathering dusk, they vanished into the shadows amongst the trees.

And there nothing remained of their passing, save the empty trail, and the ashes of their long-dead fire.

In the darkness from over all the length and breadth of the wild lands there came a murmur, and the air was filled with the sound of a mighty rustling as of an innumerable multitude in motion. And the dark masses of the forest seemed to roll up behind those who had already gone before, to recede like the outgoing waves of an ebbing tide, as though, defeated at last, they retired before the juggernaut that was now upon them, fleeing in the face of the doom that had threatened them for now three hundred years.

And with them went all of the Wild that had life, following the last fading line of the Vanishing Frontier, Northward, Northward, ever Northward, back into the days that are long forgotten, slipping away over the hills into the purple distance, beyond the Land of Shadows, into the sunset.

From *Men of the Last Frontier*.